EVE MUIRHEAD

ICE QUEEN

EVE MUIRHEAD

ICE QUEEN

WITH ERIC NICOLSON

POLARIS
PUBLISHING

POLARIS PUBLISHING LTD
c/o Aberdein Considine
2nd Floor, Elder House
Multrees Walk
Edinburgh
EH1 3DX

www.polarispublishing.com

Text copyright © Eve Muirhead and Eric Nicolson, 2025

ISBN: 9781915359193
eBook ISBN: 9781915359209

The right of Eve Muirhead and Eric Nicolson to be identified as the authors of this work has been asserted by them in accordance with the Copyright, Designs and Patents Act 1988.

All rights reserved. No part of this publication may be reproduced, stored or transmitted in any form, or by any means electronic, mechanical, photocopying, recording or otherwise, without the express written permission of the publisher.

The views expressed in this book do not necessarily reflect the views, opinions or policies of Polaris Publishing Ltd (Company No. SC401508) (Polaris), nor those of any persons, organisations or commercial partners connected with the same (Connected Persons). Any opinions, advice, statements, services, offers, or other information or content expressed by third parties are not those of Polaris or any Connected Persons but those of the third parties. For the avoidance of doubt, neither Polaris nor any Connected Persons assume any responsibility or duty of care whether contractual, delictual or on any other basis towards any person in respect of any such matter and accept no liability for any loss or damage caused by any such matter in this book.

Every effort has been made to trace copyright holders and obtain their permission for the use of copyright material. The publisher apologises for any errors or omissions and would be grateful if notified of any corrections that should be incorporated in future reprints or editions of this book.

British Library Cataloguing-in-Publication Data
A catalogue record for this book is available on request from the British Library.

Designed and typeset by Polaris Publishing, Edinburgh
Printed and bound in Great Britain by Bell and Bain Ltd, Glasgow

CONTENTS

FOREWORD BY DAME KATHERINE GRAINGER ... ix

FOREWORD BY STEVE CRAM CBE ... xi

PROLOGUE ... 1

ONE: A farmer's daughter ... 3

TWO: Of Mice and Men ... 9

THREE: The pen and the piper ... 13

FOUR: Sport, sport and more sport ... 20

FIVE: Sanctuary ... 23

SIX: Monifieth magic ... 28

SEVEN: Curling in the blood ... 33

EIGHT: In the system ... 39

NINE: Pitlochry no more ... 45

TEN: Best in the country ... 48

ELEVEN: On the plane ... 54

TWELVE: Broken broom and broken dreams ... 59

THIRTEEN: 007 and Donald Trump ... 67

FOURTEEN: History on home ice ... 71

FIFTEEN: Growing up ... 76

SIXTEEN: Play hard, party hard ... 80

SEVENTEEN: Change for dad and daughter ... 85

EIGHTEEN: The penny drops ... 88

NINETEEN: Tennis, Turkey and a terrifying Russian ... 93

TWENTY: Curling Everest ... 98

TWENTY-ONE: The other side of Everest ... 106

TWENTY-TWO: Life is good ... 110

TWENTY-THREE: Picking up where we left off ... 113

TWENTY-FOUR: First Trump and now Putin ... 117

TWENTY-FIVE: A bronze earned not a gold lost	124
TWENTY-SIX: Hidden health scare	130
TWENTY-SEVEN: First one to leave	134
TWENTY-EIGHT: The last portion of meatballs	138
TWENTY-NINE: Brooks Koepka and Broomgate	143
THIRTY: The Ivan Lendl effect	151
THIRTY-ONE: Blast from the past	156
THIRTY-TWO: No place like home?	161
THIRTY-THREE: Summoned	166
THIRTY-FOUR: A wound that hadn't healed	171
THIRTY-FIVE: A broken body	181
THIRTY-SIX: Eve 2.0	186
THIRTY-SEVEN: Playing for the other side	191
THIRTY-EIGHT: Finding a curling geek	197
THIRTY-NINE: Piggy in the middle	202
FORTY: Bubble glum	207
FORTY-ONE: When silence is not golden	212
FORTY-TWO: A squad and a colour	216
FORTY-THREE: Inside the speed skating curtain	220
FORTY-FOUR: The Covid Games	228
FORTY-FIVE: Under the radar	233
FORTY-SIX: A game with a life of its own	240
FORTY-SEVEN: Am I fixed?	246
FORTY-EIGHT: The baubles of Beijing	252
FORTY-NINE: It's over	259
FIFTY: Happiness	265
ACKNOWLEDGEMENTS	271

To my family.

You were there long before the medals, the cameras, and the wins.

Mum and Dad, your constant love and belief in me laid the groundwork for everything I've achieved and taught me to keep my head up, no matter what.

To Thomas and Glen, thank you for the fun the fights and the memories we shared growing up. You were my first teammates and everything we did together helped shape the person and athlete I became.

This journey, every stone I threw and every lesson I learned, was never just mine. I couldn't have done it without you.

FOREWORD

DAME KATHERINE GRAINGER

Although I had a very happy childhood in Scotland, I was never gifted the opportunity to take to a curling rink and try my luck throwing that beautiful chunk of granite down the ice. So I was one of millions who, instead, were glued to their television when the big sporting moments came, gathering with family and friends to cheer on our teams at the Winter Olympics, shouting with confidence in a new exotic language of 'the house', 'the button', 'the hogline' and 'hurry hard'. One of the most memorable images of all is Eve Muirhead, the legendary skip of Team GB, knelt low on the ice, arm stretched out, steel blue eyes locked like lasers as she releases her final stone, a nation holding its collective breath.

Curling has always been a sport that demands incredible individual focus, skill, technique, stamina as well as an ability to work as a small team in extraordinary high-pressure situations. As the skip of that team the job is not only to support teammates and be a master strategist, but to take the ultimate responsibility of delivery of the last stone. That role is not for everyone, but it is a role Eve was born to play.

Eve is from a family of enormous curling renown and prowess. It is perhaps not a surprise, therefore, that she went on to be such a global success story in the sport. However, she could have easily ventured down other routes, being a very gifted bagpiper and hugely talented golfer in addition to her skills on the ice. But it is in curling where she found her true passion and where she flourished. When you look at her career highlights it would be fair to see only a past crowded with enormous success – an athlete who retired as a European, World and Olympic champion – but Eve would say herself that it was some of the low points, and those deep personal challenges that sport provides us with, that helped shape her into the champion we recognise now. Her ability to keep believing in the impossible dream, her discipline to continually search for self-improvement, her self-confessed stubborn resilience to overcome setbacks and come back stronger, is what lifted her to the heady heights of becoming a four-time Olympian, a Team GB flag-bearer, and the youngest ever skip to win an Olympic medal.

I have had the privilege over the years of cheering on Eve and her outstanding teams in person at the Winter Olympics and now have the pleasure of working alongside Eve at the British Olympic Association. The same attributes that saw her excel as an athlete made her the obvious choice as the Chef de Mission for the 2026 Winter Olympics. Her focus, discipline, attention to detail, ability to inspire others and to perform under pressure make her a natural leader, alongside the credibility she brings as an athlete who has experienced all the passion, pain and power that performance sport can bring.

Eve's standards are impressively high, her humour is beautifully dry and her story is special. This book is inspiring and uplifting, entertaining and honest, life-affirming and instructive and, most importantly, it is all about Eve.

FOREWORD

STEVE CRAM CBE

Vancouver Winter Olympics 2010 and I somehow find myself commentating on the sport of Curling and Team GB's quest to reclaim Olympic glory in this seemingly simple sport. I was a complete novice trying to fathom out the complexities and skills hidden on the ice, but Team GB were being led by a precocious teenage talent whose obvious abilities were matched by an equally evident desire to win. Eve Muirhead and her story were just beginning, and I would be lucky enough to follow her path to the ultimate prize in any sport, Olympic Gold!

Her story is not a straightforward glide across the ice coming to land in the place she had always dreamt about, rather it's a compelling account of near misses, injuries, doubts and frustrations which were conquered by the same determination and never-say-die attitude that saw Eve climb to the top of the podium when it seemed that her best chance had gone.

It takes unerring nerve to calmly send a 20kg lump of granite on its way with a slight push and turn of the wrist, knowing that your team, and at times a whole nation, is watching its precise trajectory towards success or failure. I watched Eve on countless occasions, play the big shot when it mattered, drive her team on, bounce back from defeat and find a way to win. As this book testifies Eve developed into one of our countries greatest female sportspersons with immense skill and resilience, but what also shines through is her engaging and inspiring character that draws people to her and fuels her passion to continually test and push herself whatever the context.

It's no surprise that when she asked me to help her train for the London Marathon, there was never a doubt about her dedication, it was just a question of how fast could she go? And the answer was very fast! Eve tackles everything she does with the same zeal and commitment that saw her become one of the greatest ever in her sport. Her story undoubtedly impresses and inspires but it also reminds us that even sporting greats suffer the same internal stresses and strains that daily life can bring. Of course, it's about what it takes to be the best, but it's also about what it takes to be Eve Muirhead.

She is a true Champion, on and off the ice.

PROLOGUE

Golf clubs and golf shoes tossed in the boot for a 10-minute drive that should have been the very definition of mundane. Out of my housing estate, on to the A905 and you're there – the ForthView Golf Range, near Airth Castle. My car knew its own way. The satnav was untouched.

It was May. Restrictions of the second national Covid-19 lockdown were easing and the golf season was beginning. Usually, departure to destination would be taken care of thinking about which swing issues would be sorted out (or made worse) in a walled booth with a bucket of 50 balls and a piece of artificial grass. Finding out a gentle draw had lasted the winter, and my backswing hadn't got any shorter, would be nice.

A humdrum journey like that should neither live with you nor provoke deep emotions. But there was nothing humdrum about late spring of 2021.

Just as I was turning off the main road, I took a telephone call. It had been a long time coming. Way too long. Weeks had passed since I had suffered my biggest career failure in Canada, crashing and burning at the World Championships. I was at my lowest ebb, unrecognisable from the athlete talked about as a generational talent, who had blossomed into a serial national champion and international medal winner at the very top of her sport for a decade and more. People who I had hoped would get in touch, hadn't.

There had been nothing. No calls. No emails. No texts. No WhatsApp messages. I knew what every man and his dog wanting a slice of reflected glory felt like. I had seen that on plenty of occasions. But there was no reflected glory to bask in on the back of an eighth-place finish at the worlds. A Winter Olympic Games was just over 30 weeks away and, for the first time ever, there was a realistic prospect that there wouldn't be a British women's team competing.

As I pulled up at the driving range, the stunning Ochil Hills as the backdrop, that silence was eventually broken by a doctor phoning me up. He had a list of questions. A long list. On a subject like this, mental health, my natural instinct was, deep down probably still is, to put my guard up and disengage. For once, though, I was candid with my answers.

That's what hitting rock bottom does to you. A person who hasn't and doesn't speak about her feelings, opens up. In a car. On speakerphone. At a driving range.

We got to the end of the conversation. The questions got more serious, and the last answer left no scope for misunderstanding.

'I don't want to be here.'

'Here' wasn't this picturesque corner of central Scotland. 'Here' wasn't a place where you hit yellow golf balls. 'Here' wasn't an ice rink, the British Curling elite athlete programme or the treadmill which should be culminating in a fourth Olympic Games. 'Here' was far more general. As general as it comes. 'I don't want to be here.' Full stop.

ONE

A FARMER'S DAUGHTER

Born to curl?

I suppose I probably was.

Not because I was one of those prodigies, the kicking a football with both feet before they can walk type; or wielding a plastic golf club like it's an extension of their arm, throwing a dart at a dartboard before they can throw a temper tantrum. There are no family tales or camcorder recordings of me skimming stones on a frozen pond while I was still in nappies or showing hand-eye coordination that was just waiting to be harnessed. Mum didn't have a knee-high kitchen helper, frenetically brushing the floor to shouts of 'hurry hard'.

The reason I was born to curl, or at least born to give it a try, was far simpler. A tale as old as time. A tale of a little girl wanting to be where her daddy was, and to do what her daddy did.

That would lead to curling, a sport which my dad, Gordon, was very good and successful at. But long before it was a shared passion, it would lead to hour after hour of wellies being pulled on for the muck and the mayhem of a working farm.

A farm was my first, most fundamental and longest-lasting happy place. It was Dad's too. He was actually in a lambing field when he got summoned to Perth Royal Infirmary as Mum, Lin, went into labour. We were the Kinross Muirheads then, had been through the 1980s and still were when I arrived into the world on 22 April 1990 (actually, I wasn't Eve until the May because it took Mum and Dad a couple of weeks to settle upon a name).

The 100-acre farm was at Hatchbank, through the town on the road to Edinburgh. Dad loved his Highland cattle and would show them. That was passed down from my grandad, Tom, who had pedigree cows where Dad grew up in the wonderfully named Corriemuckloch, between Dunkeld and Crieff. But for us, it was predominantly sheep that paid the bills. Sheep and a bed and breakfast guest house.

Mum and Dad were a great team, both hard workers. They had met after Mum moved from the south coast of England to Edinburgh and shared a flat with Dad's cousin, while she was training to be a nurse. Glen, my older big brother by a year, and I were always involved. B&B help could be described as a chore for both of us but not farm help. Sitting on the back of Dad's quad bike, darting through the fields, is my earliest memory in life. And my fondest. Even better when there was snow on the ground, and he attached a sledge to it.

The happiest year?

That would be the one when Glen had started primary school and I had Dad, and the farm, all to myself. We did have lots of fun as big brother and wee sister, though. As soon as we got home from Portmoak Primary School in Kinnesswood, it was a case of wellies on and find Dad. Glen and I would spend hours moving grain from one end of the barn to the other in our little tractors, pretending we were a big part of the whole operation. Marking lambs' tails was a fun task, even though there would be more paint on me, and everything in a two-metre radius, than on the actual sheep.

Santa Claus brought boiler suits and tractors. Then dirt bikes and quad bikes. I was only two when Mum and Dad nearly had a heart attack as I passed the kitchen window on a quad – too small to pull the gear lever while I was on it but smart enough to figure out that I could jump off, yank the lever, then jump back on. If Dad was baling hay, I'd have no problem entertaining myself for hours until I fell asleep beside a completed one.

Maybe for some farmers' children, getting used to the animals, the brutal realities of life and death, blood and guts is a step-by-step process. With me, Mum and Dad had nothing to worry about on that front. I was straight in the pens with the sheep and cattle. On one occasion, when the cows were moving fields, I was at the front of it all while Glen was breaking a world record for climbing up a tree.

When I came back from school in Primary 1, Mum and Dad had been dreading how to tell me that one of the lambs had died. I picked it up and said: 'Oh well, it'll just need to go into the dead hole.' That was that. You can't shelter kids from the life cycle if you're living on a farm. Animals dying is a constant. Being squeamish isn't an option. Lambing time is the prime example. They don't all make it. You might lose one in 10. There was no indoor lambing on our farm so a lot depended on the weather. I've seen Dad really struggling with calving a cow, when there would be a rope tied to its leg and a quad bike pulling it in a desperate attempt to save a calf. Everything that can happen on a farm, I was exposed to it.

And there were a couple of 'there but for the grace of God go I' incidents.

A bull getting electrocuted when it tried to jump a gate that was live was one. Straight to the ground, dead, while Dad screamed at me to get out of the shed without touching anything.

Life on the farm got even bigger – and better – when we swapped Kinross-shire for Perthshire. Say the word 'home' to me now and Blair Atholl is it. The title of being the gateway to the Highlands or the Cairngorms is a bit of a loose one, with room for many a town and village to claim to use it. But, for over 700 years, Blair Atholl has had a castle, complete with Britain's only private army, to back up its claim.

Little over a decade before we moved there, the main road north still took you through the heart of the village. The loss of trade that came with the A9 motorway by-passing it was counter-balanced by the new-found seclusion. Blair Atholl almost hides from sight, even on a clear day, with the gleaming, white exterior of Blair Castle teasing what can be discovered off the main road. The charm of the village centre, buildings uniformly created out of locally quarried stone to match the mill which dates back to the 1590s, ensured it would remain a tourist destination rather than somewhere you only drive through.

Born in a city, Perth, with the River Tay running through the heart of it, and then spending most of my childhood in a village which is flanked by the Tilt and bordered by the Garry, a career on water, albeit frozen, was appropriate. I got through all my swimming lessons (an Aberfeldy Shark every Tuesday and Thursday without fail) and enjoyed a bit of fishing in the summer months with my friend, Lorne Colthart, but it was the beauty and freedom of the hills and fields that captured my heart.

Our Uncle John's land was nearby and a place for me to get my farm fix, while for Mum and Dad, converting a former shooting lodge into a new B&B business was the task that consumed their time. It took a couple of years of hard work to get Ptarmigan House how they wanted it and for them to be in a position where they could get their own farm again and dedicate time to it. Dad took the lead at Ptarmigan while Mum balanced hosting duties with her work as a district nurse. Early wake-ups to wait on tables at breakfast (occasionally getting a tip) wasn't as fun as putting paint on a cute lamb, but it was part of the deal. Dad wasn't quite Basil Fawlty, but he wasn't a happy man when the guests sneaked yoghurts away for their lunch.

It took a lot of persuasion to get me to help changing the rooms. Give me animal mess over human mess any day of the week. Rolling wool was the dirtiest job in the world. Disgusting, but I loved it. The sheep is sheared, its fleece is thrown to the side, and your job is to pick the crap off it, roll it up and put it in a bag. Then repeat. There was nowhere to wash your hands, so I would eat my packed lunch while I was there. If nothing else, it would have strengthened my immune system, I suppose. School friends would jump on a train to Perth on a Saturday afternoon, but this was better than a Woolworths pic'n'mix for me. Sheep muck and unhygienic eating. Heaven.

Thomas completed our family in 1995. I had him to thank for racing off on his quad bike to get Dad after I went tumbling down the side of a hill on mine when I was helping to get the sheep in. The bike must have rolled about 10 times, with me on it. Nothing worse than a twisted ankle was a lucky escape. That, some bruised pride and a loss of fearlessness at the bottom of a steep slope was preferable to a day at school, though.

Well, maybe not primary school.

Primary 2 onwards at Blair Atholl, like Primary 1 at Portmoak before it, was fine. Fun even. We lived two minutes round the corner. There could only have been about 50 pupils in the entire school. I think it was eight for my year. Primaries 1 and 2 shared a classroom; 3, 4 and 5 were in another; and 6 and 7 in the third one. I was a tomboy on the farm and a tomboy at school, playing football at break and lunch. With two sons and a husband, Mum must have been gutted she didn't get a girly girl. There weren't many people to beat at sports day, but that didn't stop me being competitive, driven to win an egg and spoon race and claim the sticker for first prize.

It was a safe, carefree and happy environment. Just as primary school should be. The biggest thing in the day was who would get the honour of ringing the home-time bell, even though nobody was desperate to hear it.

Going to big school would soon change that. There, the bell would be music to my ears.

TWO

OF MICE AND MEN

There are much larger schools than Pitlochry High. But when your year group doesn't even reach double figures in primary, a modest-sized one is enormous by comparison. Little, jealously guarded friendship groups took form, and I wasn't part of them. I was neither used to, nor ready for this. Very quickly, it all felt very, very different – a big, bad world, even if it was still in picture postcard Highland Perthshire, and a short bus or car journey away from home. Who you hang about with, or are accepted by, becomes a big deal. With being perceived to be 'cool' suddenly a thing, it was time to keep those rolling wool stories to myself.

It might have carried less risk of carrying some sort of bacterial illness than sitting down for lunch among the sheep, but half a deep-fried pizza, a can of Irn-Bru or a couple of iced buns from the bakers wasn't exactly healthy eating. Fitting in was quickly becoming a more pressing concern than consuming my five a day, however. Some kids were fashionable from head to toe, in their school clothes and, even more so, at the weekend. I wasn't. There was no resentment towards Mum and Dad. Glen and I worked for any money we might get. We were driven to wherever in the country our hobbies took us. And I didn't expect £100 spent on me for trendy clothes.

Whether doing well academically would have made a difference for the better, or for the worse, who knows. That was never going to happen either.

As early as S1, I would gladly have left school if the option had been open to me. That's how quickly it became something to endure rather than enjoy. I wasn't lazy. I would have loved to learn. I just wasn't capable of absorbing what needed to be absorbed. Maths was bad. Scary teachers, no hiding from them or from the fact that, for me, the numbers didn't add up. But English was worse, much worse. I'm not sure if I've ever managed to read a whole novel from front to back. Homework of completing two chapters – and understanding them – was actually too much of a challenge at school. When the next lesson came and, after a night and morning of rising dread, the teacher putting me at the front of the class to talk about those two chapters or read a section out loud was a form of torture. The anxiety it would induce made me feel ill.

I'm sure *Of Mice and Men* is a very good book. But analysing Lennie and George's relationship was beyond me. Finishing it was beyond me. Whatever points I was able to make in an essay about a novel I couldn't come close to getting a grip of wouldn't have impressed any teacher.

The boxes I was ticking point to a form of undiagnosed dyslexia. Struggling to skim text, reading slowly, having to reread paragraphs to understand, finding it a challenge to listen and maintain focus, a short concentration span, being easily distracted, toiling to organise thoughts on paper. They are all familiar symptoms of dyslexia. It would explain a lot, just unfortunately not at the time.

Getting back what you put in is one of those mantras that sounds great and would be the fairest way to get through life. But it doesn't always pan out like that. And realising that a willingness to work hard might not get you to where you want to go isn't an easy concept for a child to grasp. Not giving up, a refusal to go under and thinking: 'OK, I might not be good at this, but I'll make sure I squeeze every last drop out of being good at something else' are sturdy pillars for life, however.

Before I was in any position to put that to the test in the real world, there were two more changes of school to negotiate.

The first lasted all of one week.

Four years was as much as you could do at Pitlochry High back then before you moved elsewhere to study for higher exams, Scotland's equivalent to A levels. A week was as much as I could take of Breadalbane Academy in Aberfeldy. The few friends I had made at Pitlochry already knew pupils at Breadalbane and migrated towards them. I was in classes with people I didn't know and on my own during breaks. Pitlochry was tough but this was loneliness on another level. Every night I came home in tears, not wanting to go back the following day. I was neither eating nor sleeping. There was no way I could have endured this for a year, so Mum and Dad took me out.

No offence to the good people of Aberfeldy – it's a lovely tourist town with a strong community – but my Breadalbane experience left me hating the place and vowing never to go back unless I really had to.

There was a brief prospect of finishing my education at Perth College but that didn't come to anything. Glen generally had a better schooling experience than me. He probably did less homework but was cleverer. Like Dad, he had gone to Morrison's Academy in Crieff, in his case after leaving Pitlochry. So, that's where I went next. It turned out to be my most enjoyable year of schooling. Granted, that wasn't a high bar. And two highers from four subjects – Cs in geography and business – wasn't much to show for it. That type of character-building is best avoided but that's exactly what it was.

THREE

THE PEN AND THE PIPER

A short concentration span in a classroom isn't a choice. It's an affliction. Thirty-five or 40-minute lessons felt like an eternity. Without focus, they're a pointless slog. I would have loved for the words of a teacher to engage and inspire. There wasn't fault on either side that they did neither. I wasn't looking for distraction, but distraction was at hand, figuratively and literally. With a pen or pencil, I could at least put my fingers to some meaningful purpose. Before a curling stone or golf club would become an extension of my arms, it was a bagpipes chanter.

Farming and curling were passed down from Muirhead to Muirhead. There was no such line of succession as far as the pipes were concerned. But I was in the right place to get hooked. Not long after we had moved north, watching the Atholl Highlanders' Parade, when the Atholl Highlanders march the day before the Blair Atholl Highland Games, was love at first sight. The raw sound, the pride that shone out of the band members, the theatre and the pageantry, the tartan and the patriotism. It was a powerful mix. By the time my birthday came round the following April, the desire to learn hadn't dimmed and my present from Mum and Dad was a programme of beginner lessons in Pitlochry. It was equal parts daunting and demanding at the start.

There has been nothing comparable, sporting or otherwise, to the feeling of being at the foothills of a seemingly insurmountable musical mountain.

Every Wednesday night at Pitlochry High School, the greenest of the green like me sat in a maths room, practising as best we could on our chanter, not much different from a recorder, until we were summoned for our half-hour one to one tutorial with the formidable teacher, Gillie McNab. Gillie was the first woman to join the Vale of Atholl Pipe Band in the 1960s and had an aura every bit as powerful as any curling coach I ever learned from. For two and a half years it was Gillie and my chanter – mostly at the school, sometimes at the house, or wherever else Gillie could fit me in. Eighteen months passed before I could get even a basic tune out of it. Seeing another pupil progress a bit quicker was frustrating but there were no shortcuts. Like all switched-on teachers, Gillie would know if you hadn't put the hours in between lessons. And, believe me, you didn't want that. She was strict.

Participation in Highland Nights on a Monday in Pitlochry was the first big goal. The tourists loved them. But when I was eventually allowed to join in, they wouldn't have actually heard me play. Until you had reached an acceptable standard, a bit of paper was put under your reed, so you weren't making any noise. The purpose it served was getting you into the rhythm of marching and playing at the same time. We would all meet at the car park behind the Fisher's Hotel, parade down the street to the Recreation Ground, where there would be Highland dancing and singing, and then the band would close the night.

I had given Highland dancing a go around the same time as I

started piping lessons but holding on to the back of a chair while doing a couple of steps was as far as that went. Not my thing or not any good? A bit of both, probably.

Music practice in the house would be an hour on the chanter before tea in the dining room. That routine lasted two years, before Mum and Dad bought my first set of bagpipes from Gordon Duncan, one of the best pipers in the world. After 12 months of squeezing and blowing with the drones blocked off, I had reached the three and a half years mark and was, at long last, able to produce a recognisable tune.

A life of band championships and individual competitions were my new horizons. The latter came first. And it was back to the Fisher's Hotel. Competition there was like a mini-Royal National Mod, Scotland's world-famous Gaelic festival. Waiting for the gallows would be the best description I could give that torturous time spent in a room with 20 or so other ashen-faced children for whom entering the under-14 chanter section had turned into a fate worse than death. On occasion, the nerves made me physically sick, but they instilled in me an 'it can't be worse than how you felt at the Fisher's' benchmark that served me well in the sporting arena.

Olympic hopefuls and psychologists could learn a lot in a chanter competition waiting room.

Your talent, temperament and composure are all exposed. Maybe not to a big audience but exposed, nonetheless. In sport, you can physically release nerves. Piping affords no such opportunity. Getting your breathing right is fundamental to being good – try mastering that when just breathing itself feels like a challenge. Blow too strongly or not strongly enough and the flat sound is painful on the ear, as I'm sure judges of my 15-minute pibroch would attest.

Solo piping was for yourself, your personal pride and the approval of your teacher.

Being part of a band in a Scottish, British, European or World Championship – that was about camaraderie, shared responsibility and determination to not let the group down, the like of which no team sport could match. By the time I was a fully functioning juvenile band member at the age of 14, the discipline, dedication and time management that had been ingrained into me through piping was greater than anything else I had pursued or would go on to pursue. And if you weren't in control of your nerves and your instrument, this was a brutal, unforgiving environment.

The World Championships were, as the title would suggest, the piping peak. They always took place on Glasgow Green. It was still dark when we got on the bus and the sun was barely up by the time we got off it. If you didn't sound good in the morning tune-up, forget the fact you had put in weeks of practice and made the trip, the band leaders would force you to sit the competition out.

Ruthless.

It never happened to me, mercifully. But I saw it a few times and it wasn't pleasant – travelling for hours to not even play so much as a note. For those who didn't get the dreaded tap on the shoulder, band by band you would inch your way closer to the start line, nerves and adrenaline building. Then the drums roll and that's you. Sweat on your brow, lips getting tighter, throat drier and breaths shorter.

'Just don't mess up, Eve. Don't let it be me.'

After you've marched out, you're in a circle. If there's a mistake made, everyone in the band knows who was responsible. And pipe majors hear everything. For learning how to control nerves, this is the stuff money can't buy.

We didn't become world champions in my time, didn't really have a near-miss, but we would have been contenders if there had been a world champion title for enjoying ourselves. Pipe hard, party hard.

If you were in a band, you travelled abroad. My first competitive excursion out of Scotland wasn't a sporting one. It wasn't a particularly enjoyable one either, mind you. A 14-year-old, not very confident piper who didn't speak a word of German being given lodgings with a family who barely spoke a word of English wasn't a recipe for a fun trip. It was a recipe for a homesick teenager who couldn't get back to Blair Atholl quickly enough.

France a couple of years later was a bit different. My friend, Katy Scott, and I were quite a combination over there. We were a piping, turned drinking, double act.

Katy took up the side drum about the same time as I started my lessons. She lived in Glen Tilt, and I would often head up to her house on my dirt bike over the spring and summer months. By the time we were reasonably proficient on our instruments we became a busking duo. Both of us kilted up, the customers at the Blair Atholl fish and chip shop, just off the Main Street, were the first to be treated to our set list. We couldn't have been too bad because the owner gave us £5 each so we must have been bringing in more custom than we were driving away. It was onwards and upwards to the grassy hill outside The House of Bruar – The Harrods of the North – where the tourists seemed to find us reasonably agreeable. Well, apart from one, whom my dad overheard in the shop saying: 'I hope the heat gets too much for those two.'

Peak earner was Princes Street in Edinburgh, at the corner of the famous department store, Jenners. A day's shopping for Mum and £100 or so each for Katy and me. Believe it or not, back then, there weren't actually a lot of buskers to beat us to a prime city centre pitch. Putting yourself in the spotlight, under a bit of pressure, is never a bad thing. Doing it in a pre-smartphone era was probably a blessing, though.

Our first taste of alcohol would have been on a bus back from a piping championship on the west coast. There was always a lot of drink bought for the return trip – beer, gin, vodka, Pimm's, cider. I started out on the latter. Brittany in the summer of 2006 was all about beer, though – its strength and its consequences. After one big night in Lorient, when the Grimbergen Challenge of downing pints of the stuff had taken its toll, Mum, who was one of the parent helpers, had to put me and Katy to bed. Unfortunately, she wasn't on the beach the following day to look after us. Katy's attempt to rub sun lotion on to my back left a lot to be desired and after we fell asleep, I woke up red raw, save for two white handprints. Agony. Putting the shirt and kilt jacket on to perform wasn't much fun that night.

Happy, happy memories.

It was fun in the sun on tour but, back in Perthshire, piping had all got a bit toxic and unsavoury on the back of a split that has endured as a community divider. There was a fallout amongst the pipe majors in the Vale and the upshot was a new band being formed, and me joining it. Christy and Sharon Kelly were my main teachers at the time – they had been since I moved from the chanter to the pipes. We got on very well and had a strong bond. My loyalties were always going to be with them, as was the case for all the pipers who were close friends. The Vale goes back centuries, so it was a big deal in a place like Pitlochry, steeped in piping tradition. There was awkwardness for some, bitterness for others, with a lot of people somewhere in between. Things would eventually settle down, with the two bands competing at the same events and both featuring in the local Highland Games, but it was bad for a while and friendships were irreparably broken.

Not for me, though. So many have lasted.

My regret was that spinning musical and sporting plates eventually became impossible to sustain. A piping life that instilled so many important attributes into me at a time when school life had settled into an unfulfilling, and at times painful, rut came to an end when the 'sorry, I can't make it this weekend' messages to Sharon and Christy became too frequent. By 17, I had competed in seven or eight World Championships, finished in the top three of the British with the band, picked up individual trophies and peaked as a grade 3B piper.

Without knowing it or planning it, though, I had been given an elite athlete grounding with a chanter in my hands and a set of pipes under my arm.

FOUR

SPORT, SPORT AND MORE SPORT

I tried them all and was pretty good at most sports. Football, definitely. Every break time at primary school, I would play with the boys. Same at a club on a Friday after the last bell. I could score goals and do keepy-ups for fun, certainly more than Glen, much to his frustration. Unfortunately, the absence of a girls' team in the area meant the end of that road was reached well before you could say my football talent was fulfilled. If it had been my one sport, and a pathway was in front of me, I might have been able to turn it into some sort of career.

Tennis was similar.

My story was one familiar to parents the length and breadth of the country – getting badgered to book a court (behind the caravan park in our case) during Wimbledon fortnight. Either that or we would tie string to a car outside the house to make our own Centre Court. I actually won a Pitlochry tennis championship at the Atholl Palace Hotel, coming up against and beating players who had taken proper lessons. Had I been a Dunblane, Perthshire girl rather than a Blair Atholl, Perthshire one, you never know, maybe Judy Murray could have sprinkled her coaching stardust on me.

Curling gets called 'bowls on ice' by some. How many transferable skills there are between the two sports, I'm not sure. But there wasn't a link in my case. I would have been happy to try bowls out, but when there was talk of a junior club getting formed in Blair Atholl, not enough children showed an interest to get it off the ground. Table tennis and pool tables bought for Glen and me at Christmas were well used. I would quite happily spend hours hitting against half of the table turned up if Glen didn't fancy a game.

There wasn't often an opportunity for me to shine at Pitlochry High School. School sports days were my time. Helping on the farm gave me core strength. Dad might have used the nickname Podge but that was more down to the amount of food I could put away rather than an inability to work it off! I wasn't a supple child and struggled to even do a cartwheel, so gymnastics was a non-starter. And, for whatever reason (whacking a poor girl on the head with a swing that was better suited to golf might have something to do with it), hockey didn't appeal. But I was built to be an athletics all-rounder – strength, decent stamina, coordination and a bit of speed.

In my year, Rhiann Macleod was more petite and quicker off the mark, so I never expected to beat her over 100 metres. But once the length of the race was doubled, my extra power and endurance would start to show, even more so at 800 metres, which was probably my best distance. I was also strong at field events. In becoming the senior school sports champion of 2005, I won the long jump, high jump and shot put. I don't want to take anything away from Hazel Forbes, who finished first in the discus, but I reckon I would have made it a full set if I had been able to make it to school that day. You couldn't circle a date in the diary. It was more a case of the PE teacher seeing a bit of sun and saying: 'OK, let's go and do the long jump today.'

Figuring things out for yourself is such a key tool for anybody with designs on a sporting career – even more important than being receptive to good coaching. Hone your own technique, find your own solutions and push your own boundaries. The high jump encapsulated that. PE teacher, Siobhan Penman, taught both the scissors and the Fosbury flop. I chose the flop but only after studying videos of them both and weighing up the pros and cons. If I had kept going with athletics, a running technique that certainly wasn't textbook would have required refining, but the building blocks for a heptathlete of some description were all there. There comes a point, though, when decisions have to be made. Sports have to be dropped, running spikes and football boots hung up, rackets, bats and cues put in the garage. You can't do it all, it's as simple as that.

If you're going to be good, the best you can hope for is two sports that dovetail well with each other, no competing skill sets or muscle memories, preferably a summer one and a winter one.

Golf and curling would be my ham and egg.

FIVE

SANCTUARY

I'm sure it wasn't Dad's primary motivation for buying the Blair Atholl guest house, but basing the family a crisply struck seven iron away from the first tee of the local golf club would certainly have enhanced the allure of the place. He was a very good golfer, got close to a scratch handicap and worked in the professional's shop at Crieff when he was a boy. Blair Atholl is an ideal nine-hole course to start out on – flat, parkland, elevated tees and greens, some open driving holes and an inviting mixture of short par fours and par threes, nothing over 500 yards.

It wasn't there I struck my first ball, however. Another nine-holer got that honour near Christmas one year when Dad allowed Glen and me to bring our plastic balls and clubs on to the fairways at Glenalmond College. I did my own thing with my own swing then and that seldom changed. A few fundamentals were established early but figuring things out as you go along was Dad's way, rather than booking lessons with a pro. A golf net in the garden and the opportunity to hit balls into the field below the house quickened the process of making me course-ready. You could call that practice, I suppose, but it didn't feel like it.

Blair Atholl was blessed with a strong junior section in the late 1990s. We would play about a dozen tournaments a year. Boys and girls. Making the next step or, more accurately, being prevented from making the next step, opened my eyes to the parochialism that you can too often encounter in golf. In my case, it wasn't a sexist thing. It was ageist. It was wrong. I was effectively barred from entering women's competitions. The reason? I wasn't 18. I wasn't even close to it. 'You can play but you won't be allowed to win' was pretty much the message sent down. A women's section, with an average age of about 75, couldn't bring themselves to open their arms to a golf-mad girl in her early teens who was already better than most of them. I entered a medal without even thinking it would be a problem, but it quickly became apparent this blissful naivety would be washed away by stuck-in-their-ways frostiness.

They just weren't keen on having me there and didn't want to risk a young girl winning their competitions. So, Dad took the next decision for me.

'Right, we're off to Pitlochry.'

There were plenty of people at Blair Atholl who could see that growing the game and growing their club's membership wasn't best served by blocking the progression of a talented and keen junior. And there were plenty of people at Pitlochry who accepted me for those exact reasons, without a trace of the pettiness and madness that had driven me down the road. Cathy Cant was my first competition playing partner. She couldn't have been nicer. Kathleen Duncan and Janette Kennedy were cut from the same cloth. Supportive, caring, delighted if I did well and on hand to help me learn the etiquette of the game, where to stand when someone was putting, how to repair a pitch mark – exactly how golfing generations should be bridged.

I kept my membership at Blair Atholl and would play three holes after dinner a lot of the time but never again with a card and pencil in my back pocket, unless it was an open competition that didn't have age restrictions.

Golf at Pitlochry – more than piping, more than curling, more than anything – was my escape from not thriving inside a classroom and not fitting in outside of it. Dad would drop off my clubs at the golf club during the day and myself and Laura Campbell, who was in my year at the high school, would walk up to the course together. Then, the routine was to phone Dad when I was coming down the 17th hole so he could time his drive to the course to pick me up in the car park.

Little over a mile separated the course from the school but it could just as easily have been a thousand. You couldn't wish for a more therapeutic environment to clear your head. I've played on some amazing golf courses in some amazing locations, often with eye-watering green fees, but none boast the views and the tranquillity of Pitlochry where the peace is only broken by the sound of club on ball and peacocks calling. The top of the course, on the fifth green and sixth tee, feels like the top of the world, with half of Perthshire stretching out beneath you on a fine day and the clouds settling around you on a bad one. Every round was an escape to look forward to and, more often than not, your world would feel brighter at the end of it, whether soaked or sunburnt, cutting your handicap or topping it up.

In the main, it did come down – from 20s to teens, then from single figures to a best handicap of one. Every golfer knows that satisfaction and sense of achievement. Beating yourself and bettering yourself. The big bonus for me was the time it gave me with Dad. County girls, Scottish girls, plenty of opportunities for a wee holiday for the two of us, booking into a bed and breakfast or hotel at places like Monifieth, Peterhead, Alyth. We were touring the country. Dad would go away and do his own thing, occasionally popping up on the course to check how I was getting on. By that stage he didn't need to keep me right. I knew the etiquette and behaviour boundaries that couldn't be crossed. I wouldn't dare smash a club into my bag or do something similar in temper.

Dad had also drilled into me a no-quit mindset.

I once shanked two tee shots into the garden of the house that sits beside the challenging par three fourth at Pitlochry, where the owner kindly leaves water out for golfers and hill walkers. I scored an eight or a nine. Mercifully, I didn't walk into the clubhouse. But even though I completed the 18 holes, I stopped marking my card and put it down as a 'no return', which was unacceptable in Dad's eyes. The message was to never do that again. You don't give up. Even if you're having your worst day ever and go into three figures, you keep counting score. The possibility of quitting becoming anything close to a habit was far worse than an embarrassing card being signed and handed over at the clubhouse. Every shot matters.

Dad didn't caddie for me very often. But he was carrying my bag in 2006 when I got to the semi-final of the Highland Open and didn't concede a tap-in putt for my opponent, Bobbi Waugh, to beat me on the 17th. I thought because it was for the win, I would see it in the hole. Dad thought different and the look let me know it. I lost the semi that year, but I won the tournament the year before and the two after. I loved that event.

How best to describe the Highland Open?

I'm biased but I don't think Pitlochry's description of it as one of Scotland's most iconic Open amateur weeks is an exaggeration. The men's competition has been going for over a century. It, like the women's, attracts top Scottish players and golfers from England who love the mix of the on-course competition and the social side, putting the week in their diary year after year. At 15, I became the youngest ever winner. The number of people who came out on to the course to watch the final was far greater than I had ever experienced. Hundreds, I would say. Mum and Dad were among them. To me, it felt like the last day of The Open or The Masters.

I was up against Robina Gilbertson, who would have been at least 25 years older than me and had won the Highland Open a few times by that point. Robina's husband caddied for her and, even though it wasn't gamesmanship, they were an intimidating duo – pretty stern, with not much chat between shots. Robina's golf was very consistent. She wouldn't beat herself. But Dad had made sure I remembered to not rush my shots, and I got the job done by winning the 17th and sparing myself the ordeal of the final hole. Walking down the steep hill to the clubhouse and the prize-giving ceremony was a great feeling. Winning the Highland Open at such a young age was my biggest sporting achievement by that point, no doubt about it.

Two more titles followed and a course record.

The second – and last – Highland Open win came in 2008. After the stroke play qualifying, I was 14 shots ahead of the next best. In round two I shot 69, three under par – five birdies and two bogeys. As every golfer knows only too well, though, even when you play brilliantly it's the chances you left out on the course that stick in the mind. I should have birdied 17 and 18 but missed short putts on both.

That year was my golfing peak, at the end of which the possibility of a career in the sport – or, at least, the beginnings of a career – would open up for me.

SIX

MONIFIETH MAGIC

I can always say I have represented Scotland at two sports.

I can only say I distinguished myself in one of them, sadly.

We lost the schools' international against England at the Westerwood Hotel in Cumbernauld. David Law, a future European Tour winner, turned out to be the star player in our team but it was a comprehensive defeat, and I didn't do myself justice. With just a white polo shirt to take home as a keepsake, all in all, playing for my country as a golfer was a bit of an anti-climax.

There was nothing anti-climactic about the British Girls at Monifieth. It was the only time I competed in one of the most prestigious under-18 amateur golf events in the world, certainly the most prestigious and historic in Europe. By 2008, overseas winners were out-numbering domestic ones, with Suzann Pettersen and Anna Nordqvist among the previous champions. The big names in my year were the likes of Carly Booth and Kelsey MacDonald from Scotland; English women's winner Hannah Barwood; the runner-up 12 months before, Kelly Tidy;

future Women's Open winner Sophia Popov from Germany; Belgium's Laura Gonzalez-Escallon and the girl with the most famous father, Daniela Lendl.

The top 64 after two rounds of stroke play progressed to the match play stages. I placed 27th following the first 18 (a two-over par 74) and had plenty of margin for error on day two when the heavens opened. A 78 got me comfortably into the knockouts, tied 31st. Only three other Scots joined me. Carly – who was the best player in the field on paper with a handicap of +3.1 and had already been selected to represent Britain and Ireland against America in the Curtis Cup later that season – wasn't one of them.

Scottish golf courses are built to absorb water but even the great, natural links can only take so much, and the second day downpour forced the organisers to shorten the course by two holes after the Ashludie Burn burst its banks to make the sixth and seventh unplayable. I birdied five of those 16 holes to beat the English amateur title holder, Hannah Barwood, another plus-handicap golfer like Carly, 2&1. My short game has never been my biggest strength – which isn't usually the case with Pitlochry members, used to playing off hanging and tight lies and putting across, down and over sloping greens. But it was on point that day, summed up by a pitch to concession range for my match-clinching birdie on 16.

It was undoubtedly the shock of the morning's matches. But from being the player getting talked about in the clubhouse at lunchtime, I would quite gladly have slipped back into 'Eve who?' golfing anonymity a couple of hours later.

Five down after five on a course shortened to 16 against Belgium's Chloe Leurquin should really have been an insurmountable challenge. But creeping embarrassment was married to 'it's not going to end this way' defiance. I could happily play a round of golf in my own company, me against me, beating a score of level fours in mind. But match play taps into competitive DNA that stroke play, with or without a card, can't get close to. Me against me becomes me against you. It's at the very core of what it takes to get to the top in sport. This was my one shot at competing at the top of European girls' amateur golf. I was 18. It wouldn't happen again. Deep down, I knew that.

I had Roseanne Niven, an international player, caddying for me, and by this stage, I was the last Scot standing. Roseanne was great. The long walk from the fifth green to the eighth tee around the unplayable holes gave her the chance to come up with the right words and for me to sort my head out and calm down. I got my game back but was still four down with seven left to play – far more respectable but heading home, all the same. Going down the last all-square was an achievement in itself. Chloe's touch on and around the greens started to desert her and after we both left our approach putts short on the par five 18th, I rolled my six-footer into the middle of the cup, and she missed hers from fractionally shorter.

Classic match play.

She didn't take it well. The bag took a battering from her putter. She had lost to a girl she wouldn't have heard of, and after she had won the first five holes. It was the stuff of nightmares. Chloe would go on to have a European Tour career and represent Belgium in the Olympics. In that moment, though, I was the one with a huddle of journalists gathered around me, looking to discover my backstory and future plans.

There was certainly no shame in losing to the eventual champion the next day. A bit of Belgian revenge was dished out. With Chloe on her bag, Laura Gonzalez-Escallon, who had qualified for the match play with the lowest stroke play two-round total, beat me 4&3. I knew my capabilities and my limitations. Laura played a different game to me and, even though I lasted longer than them at Monifieth that week, so too did Carly and Kelsey.

I was a good amateur golfer, very good at times. But you can't kid yourself – or you shouldn't. These girls were professionals in waiting. The sound when Carly and Kelsey struck a golf ball was different. Purer. The putts went in with more authority and the confidence was authentic. They were already career golfers. They had an aura.

I wasn't scruffy on a golf course. I would always wear a polo shirt with a collar, as was the done thing. But I wasn't kitted out in branded clothes. My bag wasn't a tour-type bag. My walk was a walk. It wasn't an 'I'm good and I know I'm good' swagger. Even after a bad round, in the car park or the clubhouse they would still have the air of someone who knew this was their natural habitat. I would be too inhibited to hit balls next to Carly and Kelsey on the practice ground before a round. I wouldn't put myself in that position. Nothing good would happen on the course by creating an inferiority complex off it. Sharing the practice putting green for five minutes was just about OK. You're not exposed there.

The balance I had in my golf life suited me perfectly. I wouldn't have wanted to swap places with Carly, who was very much in the prodigy mould from a young age. One junior county event stuck in my mind. While my dad was off enjoying some time by himself or with other golf parents, Carly's dad followed us around every hole of the course. At one point, I spotted him behind a bush, looking through his binoculars. That wasn't the sort of dad–daughter dynamic I wanted.

I would finish ahead of Carly and Kelsey on the odd occasion, but I never beat either of them in match play. And, on the one and only occasion I was in the last group on the last day with Kelsey (the Scottish Girls' Stroke Play at Auchterarder), the different levels were laid bare. I bogeyed the first, she birdied it. I missed putt after putt, she holed pretty much everything. I just about clung on to a place in the top 10, she won the competition by a distance. Both girls were nailed-on professionals. I achieved a lot, enjoyed fun times on the county scene with its barbecues and drinking games somewhere on a Scottish coast. I took plenty of competition-honing benefits out of the golf scene, while developing self-evaluation skills and an appreciation of the importance of the unquantifiable X factor the best carry. But when a couple of offers from American colleges arrived through the letter box on the back of my last-16 run at the British Girls, neither were given serious consideration. Not even the prospect of Florida sun turned my head.

I was done with education. And, even if an academic course would be the B-side to golf's A-side, as would have been the case at a college in the States, I was done with spinning sporting plates. Two would have to become one. If it was going to be a sporting future for me, curling was it. There wasn't anything else.

SEVEN

CURLING IN THE BLOOD

Piping was all me. Golf? I would likely have found a path to it even if a course wasn't on the doorstep. Curling may well have been different, though. Had there been no family history with the sport, it's possible, maybe even likely, it wouldn't have become the granite upon which my life has been built.

More than any other sport in Scotland, certainly at elite level, surnames have endured through generations. McMillan, Hay, Smith, Gray, Craik, Wood, Loudon, Brewster. And Muirhead. You can go back to my dad's two grandfathers for our lineage, possibly even further. It was with Dad's dad, Tom Muirhead, and Dad's uncle, Bill, that we started to make our mark. They played together for a while but a disagreement over a new third in their four-man team ended that. Thankfully, it was just a curling split and not a family one.

Both my grandad, Tom, and great-uncle, Bill, were among the best curlers in the country. Tom led (which means playing first) for the legendary Chuck Hay and competed in the Scottish finals. Bill was the more successful of the two brothers statistically, winning the Scottish on three occasions (1969, 1970 and 1976) and claiming two silver medals and a bronze at the World Championships. Thomas took Grandad's name, and he has told me that if there was one person he wished he could have got to know, it would have been him. Grandad passed away when I was seven. Unlike Thomas, I'm fortunate to have memories of him but they aren't curling ones.

It was Dad's storytelling about the sport, and the characters in it, that lit my fire. In early 1995, he left Scotland for the World Championships in Brandon, Manitoba a father of two. He came back from Canada with a silver medal as the Scottish team's skip and now a father of three. Thomas got Brandon as a middle name (a lucky escape from Manitoba), while Glen and I got a piece of shiny metal on the end of a red, white and blue ribbon to fight over.

There's a picture in the downstairs bathroom at home of Grandad in tartan trousers and beret at the Lake of Menteith for a grand match, when the north would play the south on outdoor ice. The last one of those was in 1979, thanks to a combination of warmer winter temperatures and health and safety regulations. The nearest I came to one was using a frozen puddle on the farm. The medals, the stories, the photographs, the old curling brushes and clothes in the house all helped build an appetite to curl. Most significantly, though, as with the lambs and the bales of hay, it was about me being Dad's little shadow.

He would test me.

'I'm going to be leaving the house at six in the morning. If you're not ready, I'll be going without you.'

I was always ready. If Dad said six, I would be there at half-five. So countless days were spent drinking gallons of Irn-Bru, amusing myself for hours and watching Dad curl. Then, if I was lucky, with the curlers heading to the bar after club games, Glen and I would be allowed to throw a few stones ourselves at the end of play, trying to copy what we had just been watching. Grandad didn't allow Dad on the ice until he had the strength to take a curling stone all the way back to make the lift delivery that was the playing style in those days. Smaller, children's stones, which are half the weight, quickened the process for me and got me started at nine years old.

When it was time to go home, Dad had to drag me off the ice, rather than me drag him out of the bar.

'I need my tea.'

'Oh please, just one more end.'

That was usually how it went.

Ice time, wherever and whenever I could grab some, was so important. Fifteen minutes here, half an hour there, Dad keeping an eye on us. 'Move your hand like this, turn the stone like that, put your back foot there.' I suppose you would call it coaching but it was a light touch. You need good fundamentals from the start, but curling is a sport that requires a lot of trial and error and figuring things out for yourself as you go along. As with the Fosbury flop in the run-up to school sports, that observe, process, imitate ability was in me. Before I could do something as basic as slide down the ice between shots, I had practised time and time again just balancing on one foot like Daniel LaRusso under the watchful eye of Mr Miyagi in *The Karate Kid*.

My determination to mirror Dad could be seen from the very start in how I delivered a stone. Glen must have decided to take his inspiration from further afield, and the video recordings we would watch of big games in Canada. Thomas would later be the same as him. Their style is known as the Manitoba tuck – basically sliding with the front foot toe of their shoe on the ice. Kerry Burtnyk is the curler Glen would have modelled himself on. He beat Dad in the '95 world final.

Like Dad, my front foot (the left) was flat on the ice and open at an angle of about 45 degrees. It's more of a textbook way of sliding, certainly in the modern game.

There are pluses and minuses. My base is more secure but, with less traction on the ice, Glen's way generates greater power and speed. As you would imagine, there are hybrid techniques somewhere in the middle. And, when it comes to what you do with the brush, mine would be tucked under my arm, others would have it on the ice, and a few would use one technique for shots with weight and the other technique for draws. Like a golf backswing, it's all about getting yourself into the best possible position at the point of releasing a stone. You want balance – an upper body that is neither too open, nor too shut, and a straight line in your back.

There was nothing textbook about my first set of curling shoes. I glued a cardboard milk carton on to the bottom of one trainer so it could slide. Granny, Dad's mum, had an old pair made by Bally in Switzerland, who were the best shoemakers of that time. They were my first 'real' ones – well worn, with white leather that was falling apart. Her feet were so tiny I could fit into them when I was about nine. They didn't get used for long, but I've never been able to bring myself to throw them out.

Pitlochry Golf Club was one happy place where whatever had happened in a classroom would get boxed away for a few hours. The Atholl Curling Rink in the town was another.

'You back again?' were the warm words that would greet me as I arrived. 'Still going?' a familiar comment as one hour of curling turned into two, three, four or five. In the early 1980s, the four-sheet rink was constructed in the town's old Festival Theatre, which moved to the premises it still calls home these days. Tartan carpets, low leather chairs, decor very much of its time, the long corridor to the ladies' changing room, a bar that would be opened if there was a big weekend event and an aroma that was a unique concoction of old women's perfume, Eau de Farmer, whisky and smoke. A lot of smoke.

I took for granted having a welcoming environment on my doorstep, which played its part in the development of several Scottish and international standard curlers. Without it, my own career foundations wouldn't have been put in place. It's that simple. Pitlochry was a centre of excellence, a curling academy in all but name. Yes, there was a development officer, or whatever the exact title Claire Milne was given for her work with a big group of juniors for a couple of hours on a Wednesday evening. But it was the volume of good curlers about the place who would happily give youngsters their time that was the most valuable – unofficial coaching you didn't even know you were getting.

I caught the tail end of a vibrant Perthshire curling scene that motivated then shaped me. At one point in time, there must have been at least 50 different clubs, most of which would have had well over 20 active members. For me it was the Dunkeld Curling Club, as it was for Dad and his dad before him. Playing for Dunkeld was a big deal. By the age of 12, I was taking part in a few club games with Dad. Squabbling over who would get to wear his world silver medal had been replaced by who would get to play with him. It would usually be a case of Glen one week, then me the next.

Those bits of advice you would get while practising with other kids were even more valuable when you were alongside experienced curlers, talking strategy and shot-making between ends, asking you why you played a certain shot, subtly turning you into a better strategist who would plot three shots ahead rather than one.

Not that I was anything special at that age or being spoken about as one to watch. I wasn't curling's answer to Carly Booth. There were hundreds of proficient young curlers taking part in the leagues and bonspiels across the country. And, if there were siblings being talked up as the next big thing, it was the Dick brothers from Edinburgh, as opposed to Glen and me. I had played a lot of games by the time I was 15 – juniors, women, club, pairs at school, even the Scottish Girls – but hadn't won anything big. There were quite a few better players than me.

It was as a 16-year-old that things changed. Talent had been spotted. Cate Brewster was about to turn a hobby into a job.

EIGHT

IN THE SYSTEM

I was on the farm when my pink Samsung flip mobile phone rang. It was the first time the word Olympics got linked to my name in any meaningful way. The Team GB medal-winning business was getting more serious. Rhona Martin's 2002 'Stone of Destiny' gold had been followed four years later by nothing for the women or men. That summer, a Futures Programme for curling was launched and Cate invited me to join it as the youngest of five potential Olympians. A future anything sounded pretty good to a teenager who was struggling to map one out for herself from high school into the real world. A future Olympian? Where do I sign?

I had been part of a regional coaching programme for a year so there had been recognition to some degree that there was raw curling ability worthy of attention and nurture. To dangle an Olympic carrot, however remote the possibility might be, was a real gear change, though. I knew it and Dad knew it as well. Even though all the established names of Scottish curling were still on the scene, the Scottish Institute of Sport were saying: 'Something needs to change.'

It was a foot in the door.

If nothing else, I was going to see a bit of the world without being on a family holiday or in a pipe band. The first big trip was to London, Ontario. There were two tournaments on the trip, and we were miles off where we needed to be in both. Any 'next big thing' talk wasn't coming in my direction, or another of the Scottish girls. Canada's Rachel Homan was getting the superstar-in-waiting treatment, and rightly so. It was an eye-opener. I was healthily self-aware. I hadn't even earned a Scottish title so the idea of being considered a curler of relevance in world terms wasn't in my head. The Futures Programme brought with it a bit of status, some structure to my life, good coaching, a strength and conditioning plan, and a hoodie that I loved. But it didn't give you a good team. You still had to rely on yourself and others to put one of those together.

Sarah Reid, also on the programme, was the best junior skip at that time. Getting asked by her to compete in the 2007 Scottish Junior Championships gave me the opportunity I needed. My own team wasn't good enough. Dad had always told me that it was better to be playing down the rink in a good team than skipping a bad one. Under Sarah, I played third, we won, and I was going to my first world juniors. So was Glen, who was part of the boys' team, and the full family flew out to Minneapolis.

The more people watching you, the greater the hurt and embarrassment when things don't go as you would hope.

For the first time as a curler – mercifully, it would be the last as well – I was benched mid-tournament. We were on the brink of not qualifying for the knockout rounds, none of us were playing well and I was dropped. I was upset that I took the brunt of the 'something needs to change' message. In a sport where, traditionally, an alternate only gets called into action when there's injury or illness, this was a battering to the ego. Missing two games in those circumstances – and at that age – causes big doubts to swirl through your mind. How will the team do without me? If they do well, what will it mean? If they don't do well, what will that mean? Do I even want them to do well? Is that me finished with this tournament? Is that me finished as a Scotland player, one and done?

In my small world, the best-case scenario played out – the girls got through to the semi-final, I was restored to the team, and we won the semi narrowly against the host nation, America, who had topped the round-robin table.

The biggest shock of the week, though, was the final.

It was no surprise that we faced Canada, but their end-of-game implosion was. As much as I would love to say it was us who produced our A game when it mattered most and earned our first world gold with superior shot-making, this was undoubtedly a case of our opponents throwing it away. Getting over the line when you are in front will forever be one of the biggest challenges in sport and this was probably the most startling occasion when that theory was proved in my career. We were on the back foot from the off. Stacie Devereaux's team took a 6-3 lead in the eighth of the 10 ends and their position was even stronger after the ninth, when we could only reduce that deficit by one. We should never have been allowed to steal two to level the scores and in the extra end, despite the fact Sarah played a superb shot to leave her stone covered and Stacie didn't have an easy one to win, the collapse was a Rory McIlroy US Open moment for Canada and a Bryson DeChambeau one for us.

The Canadian girls were as distraught as you would expect them to be. Stacie and her team would never get to world level again. Maybe they wouldn't have even if they had won. But I bet there aren't many days when they don't think about what happened in March 2007 in Minneapolis. I flew home a world champion, which was a giant leap given the gap that had been laid bare on our first trip across the Atlantic to Ontario the year before. There were bruises from the benching and, as thrilled as I was to have a gold medal round my neck, I wasn't kidding myself into thinking this was anything other than a small step to where I wanted to get to.

Firstly, I wanted to be a skip again.

Skipping has never been an ego thing for me.

Those first Scottish and world junior medals weren't diminished in any way because they were the only ones I got while playing third rather than fourth. Progressing as a player and winning competitions was far more important than carrying the responsibility and basking in the glory of being the player whose shots came with the greatest pressure. Dad had been right. I was progressing and winning as a quarter of Team Reid. But Sarah was four years older than me and had aged out of the juniors. That summer was my chance to resume the role that best suited my skill set and to put together a team that would give me a chance of staying on top.

After I took control, only one position stayed the same – Sarah Macintyre as lead. Kerry Barr replaced me as third, but the most important team signing was Vicki Chalmers as second. It wasn't a hard decision for me to get Vicki on board. Far from it. But it would have been an extremely hard decision for Vicki to accept my invitation because it meant leaving her sister, Kay. I'm sure that was an awkward conversation.

Before I settled into leadership duties again, though, I had one last tournament down a team line-up. And there was no debate about this one – Dad was the skip. Dad, Glen, Anna Sloan and I had won the Scottish Mixed in Aberdeen, with a September trip to Madrid for the European Championships (it's since been upgraded to the World Championships) the prize. Curling in Spain at any time wasn't normal, but at the back end of summer, it was particularly problematic. It was a very strange week, all told. I can safely say that dive-bombing into an outdoor pool isn't the usual routine on arrival for an international curling competition.

There's a good reason we don't go to warm countries to curl. The organisers really struggled to maintain the ice with it being so hot outside. On it, we struggled to play well. We beat France – just. And we beat England – again, just. Losing that one didn't bear thinking about. But it was all over at the quarter-final when Denmark beat us 5-3. Dad skipped but let Glen play last stones. Glen had a draw to the eight-foot ring to win, which nine times out of 10 he would make. This was the one out of 10 and he threw it through the house.

Anna and I fell out with our mums at the last night banquet because they wouldn't let their 17-year-old daughters go into Madrid with everyone else. Perhaps naively, I expected there to be other opportunities to compete with Dad, Glen or Thomas at an international competition, but it never happened for us again. Perth Super League was as big as it got for me with another Muirhead.

Back with my new junior team, and with the confidence of being a world champion, I took skipping in my stride. The benefits of being part of the Scottish Institute of Sport set-up were really starting to kick in. I was spending time with Olympians like Kelly Wood, Jackie Lockhart and Lynn Cameron, getting gym sessions at Strathallan School in Perthshire two nights a week and establishing a bit of an aura for my age group.

A second Scottish win brought with it the opportunity of a second World Championships. This time the gold medal game was emphatic, and I left Sweden without the caveat that our opponents in the final had rolled out a red carpet on the ice for us. Cecilia Östlund played an ultra-aggressive game, and it was she, not Anna Hasselborg, who was being talked about as the heir to the great Anette Norberg, an Olympic champion and one of my idols. That aggression certainly didn't pay off for her on this occasion. We jumped on their mistakes, stole six in one end and handshakes were being offered just as a hung-over Glen, who was in Östersund with the boys' team, was taking his seat in the arena. Winning back-to-back world junior titles was a statement, as was the fact I had done it more impressively as a skip than a third.

But there was a bigger picture.

Not only had I made a big leap forward in terms of my peers, with a couple of years still left as a junior, my development in the Futures Programme was being fast-forwarded. In my mind – and probably those of the selectors – participation at Sochi in the 2014 Winter Olympics was the realistic goal for any of the junior prospects. Vancouver, 2010? Given I wasn't even a Scottish junior champion at the point I was brought under the programme umbrella, it certainly hadn't been in my thinking. You need to walk before you run. Whether I had changed people's minds and progressed quicker than expected or was in fact on track with where they hoped I might be, I don't know. Either way, in the summer of 2008, the British Curling Olympic selectors decided to go early with their squad selection announcement, and I was one of the six women who would be competing for five places at the Games.

Good things were happening fast.

NINE

PITLOCHRY NO MORE

I can't say that I thought of myself as someone who had a media profile. But I was starting to get invited to awards ceremonies, and local journalists were deeming me worthy of a few paragraphs on their newspaper back pages for my two world junior titles. If anything, though, it was probably my golf that reporters were more interested in, particularly when I was beating proper players at Monifieth. Seeing my name in the daily newspaper for our part of the country, *The Courier*, was always nice. Even if it was a third place in a piping category at the Kenmore Highland Games, nothing was missed in the small print of the sporting round-up at the bottom of the broadsheet page.

Liz McColgan, Eilish McColgan, Eilidh Doyle, Carly Booth, Laura Muir and plenty of others from Perthshire, Fife and Dundee have had their names in *The Courier*, day after day, long before anybody beyond doting grandparents would have been paying attention. Who knows, maybe even a certain Andrew Murray (Dunblane) felt a similar buzz getting a mention for winning an under-12 tennis tournament in the back of beyond. At 18,

I certainly wasn't envisaging a future where I would become a columnist in my local newspaper for over a decade and would have to turn my notifications off on social media when hundreds of Novak Djokovic fans got extremely angry with me suggesting Roger Federer was the greatest tennis player of all time!

But I suppose I did have a public presence of sorts, even back then. And I was certainly willing to get behind a cause that was close to my heart. It didn't take a crystal ball or deep insight to predict that the closure of the Atholl Curling Rink in Pitlochry would have a devastating impact on the sport I loved in the area where I lived. The characters and camaraderie that would be lost to my life forever was one side of it and the conveyor belt of young talent that would be lost to curling was the other. Even a teenager who wasn't worldly-wise and didn't have a grasp of the social importance of a community sport staying rooted in that community could get upset and angry at the prospect of it being ripped away.

It all felt so cold and so clinical.

A developer from Aviemore wanted to knock it down and put flats in its place. I didn't need Dad to spell it out to me what the knock-on effect would be for curling in Highland Perthshire. Hardly anyone over the age of 60 would travel to Dewars Centre in Perth, a venue that had no familiarity to them. They would give up the sport. Friendships and a purpose to an afternoon or evening would be gone forever. That's exactly what happened. And talented young curlers with potential to be national standard players would also find another sport to pursue, or worse, not find another sport at all. That's also exactly what happened. Thomas was the last of the Pitlochry area curlers to make it to national level or higher.

Eight local business people had invested their time and money to build the facility in 1982 and countless others had contributed in other ways over the subsequent 26 years. I joined the campaign to see if an alternative solution could be found and financial support provided. The Atholl rink had been built on a sand floor. Finding the money from somewhere to put down a concrete one, that could be used 12 months a year, would have been the only hope. But it was a futile effort from all of us. Pitlochry became the latest in what was a worryingly long list of lost Scottish rinks to shut its doors.

When I had started out as a curler there were 31 across the country. Long before my career would peak, that total halved. This was a sport which, at one point, was statistically the most popular winter one in Scotland and the first to have a national governing body. The decline was (is) alarming. Unless lakes start freezing over again, it will be a postcode lottery if a youngster gets the chance to curl.

I was incredibly lucky. Even in the moment of Pitlochry's closure I knew that. I had won a world junior title in the same year that the environment that had shaped me was taken away. Also, I had been picked up by the Scottish curling programme in the nick of time. Glen was the same. Had Pitlochry been closed one or two years earlier, maybe the story would have been different. All career athletes have 'what if' points in their timeline before funding and a national umbrella insulates them. Those one or two years of daily ice time on my doorstep would have been lost at a crucial stage when my development accelerated.

It would have been handy to have been able to grab some ice in Pitlochry, but my roads for curling improvement now led to Perth and Stirling – maybe even Vancouver.

TEN

BEST IN THE COUNTRY

Although curling in Scotland had traditionally been about a team of four going through a season and the best one emerging to represent the country at a World Championships or an Olympic Games, a squad approach wasn't new. The Olympic selectors had done something similar ahead of Turin, 2006, but back then it was 10. The feedback was that such a big group didn't bring out the best in the curlers and was backed up by the fact that neither the men nor the women medalled. Whittling it down from six to five is very different from a cut of 10 to five. But even though the numbers game looked favourable for all of us (only one would miss out), by no means did I think my place was nailed down. Jackie Lockhart and Kelly Wood were both household names in the curling world and Lynn Cameron, Lorna Vevers and Karen Addison all had more than one Scottish title to their names.

I was still potential to their pedigree.

There was a changing of the guard mood but that had already happened with Rhona Martin retiring and others from her era, like Edith Loudon, overlooked. Nobody would have labelled

Jackie, Kelly, Lynn, Lorna and Karen as veterans if that was the route they decided to go down. They were in their prime. I had just turned 18.

It was getting closer to a life-changing opportunity. I wasn't in a position to give up my waitressing work at the Watermill cafe in Blair Atholl, but I was a paid athlete. That was all I cared about. And, after passing my driving test at the end of a fortnight of intensive lessons, my purple Corsa would clock up plenty of miles going to and from Stirling for three gym sessions a week. The days were even longer and the commitment even greater for Jackie, who lived in Stonehaven, just south of Aberdeen. Our routine was meeting up at Perth's Broxden Roundabout McDonalds, picking up a bacon roll and a coffee for the car and taking it turn about to drive the rest of the way down the A9.

As had been the case on the Futures Programme I had now left, Olympic squad commitments ran in parallel to competing with your own team. In my case, as I was now juggling juniors and women, that meant two teams. Not long after the squad was announced, I got a call from Karen asking if I wanted to play with her in the Scottish Women's. It was my lunch break at the Watermill, and I didn't even have Karen saved in my phone at that point. Lynn was in a Perth team and Kelly, Jackie and Lorna were joined by Kelly's sister, Lindsay. That was a well-established quartet, who had won the Scottish in 2007. My other option would have been to step up as a unit with my junior team, but I decided to try something different and our four was completed by Annie Laird and Rachael Simms.

When the championships came round at the start of 2009, it was our first tournament as a team and my first Team Muirhead out of the juniors. A couple of practice sessions and off we went. Not favourites, not even second favourites. This was a competitive time for curling in Scotland, with enough teams to fill silver and gold leagues. There were round robins in Kinross, Aberdeen and then the Dewars Centre in Perth. Kelly's team topped the Gold League, which got them straight through to the final, while we had to beat Claire Hamilton's rink in the semi-final with a two up the last end.

The night before the final, Kelly had the choice of whether she wanted the hammer (last stone in the first end) or wanted to choose the colour of stones they would play with. You log stones through the week, and some can be better to use than others, but give me 100 games and I would choose hammer 100 times, it's that simple. So, it was a real shock when Kelly chose colour and conceded last stone advantage. Only she will be able to say for sure, but we had heard that they had won a few games playing yellow and it was a bit of a superstitious call. I was delighted. It felt like going to the first tee for 18 holes of match play golf and being told you were one up before a ball was struck. I've seen plenty of superstitions through the years – from what people would wear when they were on a winning streak to the food they would eat before a game. But, despite the fact somebody once told me an opposition coach was reading things into whether my hair was up or down, I've never bought into them.

And I think it goes back to that decision by Kelly.

There was a slight problem for me, though. We were to play in dark tops for the first time that week and it dawned on me that we didn't have any. So, on my way back to the Holiday Inn hotel at about half-ten at night, Annie and I stopped off at the 24-hour Asda on Perth's Dunkeld Road and bought four ill-fitting men's T-shirts. Not the most professional build-up to my first Scottish women's final, maybe, but we all had a good laugh about it. In fact, that had been the way of things from the moment we got together in Kinross, and I was sick after consuming too much gin, trying desperately not to let the other girls see how drunk I was.

The final was nip and tuck until we stole a couple in the ninth end and saw the game out. Forget the Olympic connotations.

They could wait. Becoming a national champion at my home rink felt amazing. Alongside Pitlochry, this was where I learned the game; where I kept myself amused while Dad played; where I had my best geography lessons, putting country names to all the flags on the walls; where I had watched the greats from Canada like Kerry Burtnyk, Jeff Stoughton, Glenn Howard, Wayne Middaugh and the magnificently named Ferbey Four; where I had hunted autographs in the bar; where I would now be getting my name on the honours' board at the staircase I had climbed so often.

In the short term it meant one table at the Frankie and Benny's restaurant with four giddy curlers looking back on a great week and a great day and another with four others, contemplating the 'if onlys' and the implications. Then, it meant we were going to the World Championships the following month.

For me, before that, I had to put my juniors' hat back on as we had won the Scottish again, making me the first person to ever do the national double in one year and giving me a shot at making it a hat-trick of worlds. I was fortunate – this was a fun team to be a part of as well. Four teenagers enjoying themselves who, even when enjoying ourselves a bit too much, were still winning. There was one tournament in Inverness when I was so ill the morning after the night before that walking around the car park to try and sober up turned into an impossible task. Putting one foot in front of the other was too much for me. I tried to start our quarter-final but had to make a quick dash back to the toilets to be sick. I told our coach, Nancy Smith, that I had eaten a dodgy prawn sandwich but I'm sure she wouldn't have fallen for that one. While the other girls kept us in the tournament as a three, their broken skip slept, curled up in a ball on the changing room floor. I perked up sufficiently to join them later in the afternoon and, by the end of the day, we were raising another trophy.

It was a time when young curlers (and not so young curlers) were able to live a normal life, enjoy the social side of the sport and stay in the bar for what would often turn out to be one drink too many without drastic consequences. But Inverness taught me a lesson that a time and a place mattered.

The world juniors were held in Vancouver, with it doubling up as a test event for the Olympics the following year. For us, Anna Sloan had replaced Kerry Barr by this point. Sarah Macintyre and I were aiming for our third gold, Vicki Adams her second and Anna her first. Anna Hasselborg was now an opponent and Kaitlyn Lawes the Canadian skip – two players whose careers would run alongside mine. There weren't many inter-country friendships that developed in the juniors and the final against Canada, who had beaten us convincingly in the round robin and knocked out the pre-tournament favourites, Switzerland, in the semis, was a bit frosty. Black marks had been left on the ice from the grip on somebody's shoe and the Canadian girls were blaming us. At times like that I loved having Vicki beside me because she would happily take on anybody when it came to the feisty stuff – it even happened once with her own sister! She certainly didn't back down on this occasion in Vancouver.

It was a very tight game. I stayed calm throughout as Kaitlyn was getting increasingly animated. We were 7-6 up going into the last end but they had the hammer. Kaitlyn missed her final shot, which meant we stole a point and took gold. Beating Canada in Canada was then, and always will be, the biggest challenge a Scottish team can face in curling – and the biggest satisfaction when you do it. There was no extravagant celebration for me, though. I had another World Championships to get to – the women's.

It was my first visit to Asia. I flew straight from Canada and met the rest of the girls at the airport in South Korea for a five-hour bus journey to Gangneung. New countries and new tournaments meant a new adventure. I was lapping it all up, living off the only food on the menu in our hotel that I could face – cheese and ham toasties and spaghetti bolognese for the week. Some of the others were happy to choose a live fish out of a tank for their dinner but that wasn't for me.

Sewing badges on to our kit – big stitches – while sitting on the beach with some carry-out wine might not be everybody's vision of elite sport, but I loved it. The curling was OK. Jackie was our alternate and replaced Rachael halfway through the week, and we finished the tournament on five wins, six losses. Beating Mirjam Ott's Swiss team was significant for me because I had always struggled against them in the few times we had played. Mid-table, having lost to greats of the game like Anette Norberg and Jennifer Jones, was perfectly respectable. There was a gap between a world champion junior and a curler capable of contending for world medals with the women, as there should be. But it was closing. I was persuaded to play the pipes at the closing banquet and, as we all returned to the beach to watch a fireworks display, I could reflect on a couple of months that had yielded three big tournament wins and significantly enhanced my reputation.

Now the big question was – would it be enough for Olympic selection?

ELEVEN

ON THE PLANE

There were no big clues given during our time together as a squad of Olympic hopefuls. Either that or I wasn't picking up on them. I'm pretty sure it was the former. The coaches mixed things up anytime the six of us came together for a trip abroad, whether it was who roomed with whom, who played and in what order. They were thorough and fair in looking at every combination and every team dynamic. I think I found the whole squad experience – a full year of it before selection – the least mentally draining of all of us. That was because I was the youngest, with most to gain and least to lose. As the season progressed, particularly after winning the Scottish women's, I grew increasingly confident that I had put together a very strong body of work to get me selected. But even in a worst-case scenario, 2014 was looking good. I was 18, had left school behind me, had a purpose to life and was in with a shout of becoming an Olympian.

All six should be proud that, however challenging and however dog eat dog this process was set up to be, we looked after each other and kept the fun factor on tour.

On one trip to Canada, we got picked up by a driver in a stinking old car who took us to a motel that was in even worse condition. I was sharing with Lynn and as we opened the door to our room, we were greeted by the sight of a bloke lying on one of the beds. If the electricity stayed on for long enough to let us dry our hair with a hairdryer in the morning, that was a good day. Wherever we were in the world, it was gin for nightcaps. That sort of environment had the potential to produce rivalry, suspicion and bitterness, but my experience was one of no tantrums, no fallouts and no cliques.

It is just as well physical fitness wasn't the decisive factor. For somebody who would end up running marathons, learn to love the gym and make it such a core part of her everyday life, that side of being an athlete was a chore I would avoid if at all possible. Lynn's numbers would have been the best out of the six of us by a distance – she took it very seriously. Mine would have been bottom – I didn't. When Lynn and I did sessions in Perth together, I could barely manage a press-up or a chin-up. It was an embarrassing contrast. All the team members had to wear heart-rate monitors when we were doing fitness work wherever we were and then send data to our strength and conditioning coach. I discovered a way to cheat. Say, for example, I had to do a 30-minute even pace run, I would copy and paste one from the previous month and send that in. I can't believe I got away with it, and I can't believe I thought it was a good idea to cut corners like this.

It was an insight into my maturity and athleticism. Neither were where they needed to be.

I suppose the others could have been hard-nosed about it and seen my youthfulness and naivety as something they could exploit and use against me to help themselves but, instead, they were like big sisters.

I wasn't all-in as a professional athlete, but I was all-in with my commitment to curling. The pipe band had been given up and the golf clubs only came out if there were no clashes. And when the time came that we were told to expect a phone call, the phone call, I wanted this Olympic selection as desperately as the rest of them. I was with Kelly at her flat in Stirling when we were on tenterhooks, waiting to be informed if we would be Vancouver-bound. The fact we were both happy to be in a room with each other suggested a high degree of optimism. It wasn't misplaced. We had been selected, with our positions in the team still to be determined. Lynn had the chat we were all dreading. She had been cut. It hit her hard, as you would imagine. Maybe she had suffered because she was in Edith Loudon's Perth team that hadn't done well that season. Who knows? I sent her a text message but there was nothing I could say that will have made her feel any better about it.

I was more emotional than I thought I would be. The enormity of what it would have been like to miss out, and what it feels like to become an Olympian, only hits home in the moment you're told which one it is to be.

The next stage, a few weeks later, was a meeting for each of the Vancouver five with Nancy Smith, the women's coach for the Games, and Derek Brown, British Curling's performance director. They got straight to the point. Mine would probably be their easiest conversation. 'Congratulations, Eve, you're going to be skip.' Now this was a shock. The safe decision would have been to give it to Kelly. She'd been skipping her team with Jackie and Lorna, was a three-in-a-row Scottish champion, albeit not the most recent one, had the previous Olympics under her belt and was at the peak of her career. You need a relatable role model in sport and someone you strive to match and go past. For me, Kelly was both. The selectors would have studied all the data from our training camps and competitions but I'm sure the decisive factor was the Scottish Championships and that final head-to-head. Kelly would have been very disappointed. She had skipped all her days but never at an Olympics. This was the one she had been targeting, and a teenager had emerged from the juniors to deny her.

It was bold and was sure to be the talk of the curling world.

The real drama in the meeting room at the Dewars Centre occurred after I left it. Karen's nickname was Lady Add but I suspect the language after she was told they wanted her to be the alternate wasn't very Downton Abbey. I was still upstairs when she came storming out, having let Nancy and Derek know what she thought of their decision and given an unequivocal 'I'm out' verdict. Only three people will know just how heated it was, but I can guess. Karen had expected to be a starting player, and she was furious. She calls a spade a spade. When the dust had settled, Jackie spoke to her to say: 'Look, are you sure about this?' But there were no second thoughts. Bridges had been burned between Karen and Nancy and there was no prospect of a rebuild.

She had never been to an Olympics and never would.

This was August. We were the best part of a year away from Vancouver. So much could have happened in that time – loss of form for one of us, injury, illness. Alternates often get on the ice and, even if they don't, they can forever call themselves an Olympian. Karen had earned that honour. I've never asked her if she carries regrets. I never will. But, if it was me, I would have kept a lid on my disappointment and anger and gone to the Games. I had so much to be grateful to Karen for. She changed my curling life with the invitation to join her team for the Scottish. She had my back that week and for the time we were squad-mates. I piped at her wedding. But she wasn't going to Vancouver and a squad of six was now down to four. To the best of my knowledge, they didn't go back to Lynn to explore if she would be happy to be a reserve, so Annie Laird came from nowhere to get the fifth spot. Annie had won the worlds with Jackie in 2002 and played in my team in the Scottish. It made sense. She also had the perfect personality for an alternate – an incredibly laid-back person who was happy to be a fifth and wouldn't resent it. The team was set, I gave up my job in the Watermill to be a full-time curler and it was all beginning to feel very, very real.

TWELVE

BROKEN BROOM AND BROKEN DREAMS

An Olympic Games is all-consuming, months before it starts. There's always a milestone approaching. A year. Six months. A hundred days. Fifty days. You feel a curious mix of wanting time to quicken and slow down. Pre-Vancouver, I was leaning towards the latter. Not because I was lacking excitement. It was because we had a new team to bed in and there wasn't much time to do it. One pre-Olympics tournament stood out above the rest in terms of importance. The European Championships. I could have done without it being a home European Championships. They were my first Euros. And, in our circumstances, it would have been better to go about our business somewhere in Switzerland or Sweden, where the scrutiny would have been far less intense. And the curling conditions in Aberdeen were poor – awful ice and a lopsided floor.

We didn't play well. I didn't play well. Beating Anette Norberg was the highlight. The lowlight was a draw I had when Italy were sitting with five stones counting. The red light came on as I delivered my last stone of the end. I let it go a fraction beyond the hog line. The stone was taken off and I had cost my team a five. It had never happened to me before. You could compare it to a double-hit in golf, or a fresh-air swipe, but the penalty is much harsher. Your heart sinks and, in this case, the game was lost. Five wins and four defeats from our nine games wasn't enough to see us into the knockout rounds. But it was an accurate reflection of how we had performed and where we were as a team.

The pressure on me was starting to increase. This was very different from playing at the worlds in South Korea. I was now a 19-year-old Olympic skip in waiting, who had been chosen for the role ahead of two vastly experienced curlers. It was getting a bit suffocating in Aberdeen and after being knocked out, for the only time in my career, I left the venue and drove home for a couple of nights before returning for the banquet. Never mind the fact it was a near five-hour round trip, I just needed to get away, however long it took. Doubts were rising about myself and about the team.

Should I even be in this position? Have I just fluked it and got lucky? Those were the sorts of thoughts starting to creep in.

One of the good things about the Olympics taking place in February is that a family Christmas is perfectly timed to help you clear your mind and reset. That was certainly the case for me. Granny and Grandad's home village of Netley Abbey, near Southampton, was such an important place in my childhood. As soon as I arrived there, all the memories would flood back, like Glen and I getting taught to fish by Grandad and going to the park with him. In later years he used a mobility scooter to get about and once he had treated us to our snow cream and sat himself down on a bench, we would get turns to drive the scooter!

I only spent two Christmases at Granny and Grandad's house, and this was one of them. Nobody, other than our family, cared about curling down there. Right on the coast, it was the exact contrast to the intense, claustrophobic nature of our Stirling University base, which can be a bleak place in winter at the best of times. The sea air, longer days and walks were therapeutic. We had all received our 'everything in moderation' email from the team nutritionist with the dos and don'ts for the festive period. Opening up Granny's drinks cabinet with bottles that hadn't been touched for decades and showing her how to down a shot (Tia Maria, as I recall) wasn't on the list, though. On holidays to Lanzarote with Granny and Grandad when I was in my early teens, they had taught Glen and me so many important life lessons. A few years later, here I was, teaching Granny something altogether different!

After 2009 turned to 2010, I made my next trip to England for kitting out at Heathrow Airport's Terminal 5. I was in a much more positive frame of mind. The negativity and concerns of Aberdeen had been parked and there was a real sense of being made to feel special by a personal shopper and a big bag of Adidas kit. By the time we flew out to the Team GB holding camp in Calgary, Mum had just about recovered from the sight of my Olympic rings tattoo at the bottom of my back, which was a spur of the moment impulse when I was in Perth one day. That wasn't the only part of a new look. My hairdresser, Glenn, had given me a two-colour hairstyle that I read in one newspaper was being compared to Limahl of the 1980s band Kajagoogoo. I had to Google him.

A few practice sessions at Calgary's Glencoe Curling Club went well – Mark Shurek, one of the most renowned ice-makers in the world, was hired to prepare our ice – and there was a Team GB reception with Princess Anne before we moved into the Olympic village in Vancouver. Most of the advice to a wide-eyed rookie from support staff and people who had competed or worked at an Olympic Games before was well-meaning and useful. I could have done without being told 'I don't want to go home with just a bag of dirty washing' from a member of the British Curling team, mind you.

In general, I thought the media build-up regarding my own story was fair. There was a lot of attention on me because of my age but I didn't get a sense that we were being over-hyped. Team GB had a target of three medals. The men were one of them, but we weren't. Hope, as opposed to expectation, was the best way to sum it up. We wore red berets to the opening ceremony and, thankfully, there were no red faces after our first game. In fact, we couldn't have wished for a better start – beating the reigning world champions, China. I played well. If there had been overwhelming nerves they would have shown. The only time I felt them in the game was when I played my last shot, and I couldn't read Jackie's body language as the stone rolled slightly off to the right. The first thing I asked when I slid down for handshakes was 'did we win?'

There was no shame in losing to Anette Norberg and victories over Russia (when Kelly wasn't feeling well and had to be replaced by Annie in the middle of the game) and Germany, 10-3 and 7-4, put us in a strong position.

From there, though, it all unravelled. Five defeats in a row. The first of those was just a poor game, full stop. 11-4 to Japan, which included five for them in the ninth end. No complaints. The loss that defined our Olympics, however, was game number six against America. It was probably our best performance of the fortnight, controlling the scoreboard nicely to be 5-4 ahead going into the last end, with last stone advantage. But I made a bad tactical decision with the first of my two stones. I tried to win it there and then. I should have been more patient. I left it at the back of the button (the centre ring), Debbie McCormick played the perfect freeze on to it, and I missed with the game's last shot.

'USA, USA, USA.' The Americans in the crowd sensed before that final stone that this was the moment to find their voice and turn the heat up on me. It was like a Ryder Cup, and I had missed the three-foot par putt that had given America a win on the 18th green. They had stolen a game that should have been ours. And it was on me. There was no hiding from that. It was the first time my inexperience had been exposed.

I asked Pete Smith, an experienced member of the GB men's team whom I had a lot of respect for, what he would have done. But I knew deep down that I had made a terrible call, and I didn't need Pete to tell me. I should have cleared one of the stones at the front. It was the decision of a 19-year-old skip, and it was the reaction of a 19-year-old skip to let it weigh heavily on me, too heavily, as opposed to boxing it off and realising that qualification for the knockout rounds was still in our control. I didn't have the capacity to reset as I needed to. It doesn't matter how many people are giving you (the right) advice, it's the voice in your own head that speaks loudest.

Against Switzerland in our next game the following morning, I was short with a draw when they were lying four. Another big error. That was a 10-6 loss.

Then came the broken brush, an incident and an image that gave the newspapers the headline they had been waiting for. 'The ice queen has melted.' It was pure temper, a reaction to a terrible shot and the lid coming off emotions that had been building following the drip, drip, drip of bad play and things going wrong. The shot I missed against Denmark wasn't the worst of the tournament – a stone that went straight through the house. But I was getting so frustrated with myself that I smashed my brush into the hack that we push off for our slides. I lifted it up to have a quick inspection of the damage and the head came off in my hands. I would love to say it was unlucky and that it is the sort of thing that happens to angry curlers regularly but that would be a lie. I had smacked it off the hack with the sort of force you would expect to snap a brush with. Jackie was laughing. It might have been one of those awkward laughs. Who knows? I wasn't. I was holding back tears, embarrassment, frustration and still a bit of anger. So many emotions were in the mix.

I didn't even know what I had to do next. This was all new to me. They don't teach you the protocol at an Olympics after you've broken your brush in a fury. I slid all the way back up the other end of the rink to see if I could get a new brush. There were three other games on the ice and one of them was a very important contest – Canada against Sweden, which would end up being the final later in the week. But all eyes were on me and my slide of shame. It was an ice hockey crowd at Vancouver. In fact, it was an ice hockey crowd at every Olympic venue. Canadians put their name into a ballot, hoping they would be one of the 18,000 in the Rogers Arena to watch 'hockey', their country's biggest sport. There were between five and six thousand in our venue, most with a good drink in them by this point of the afternoon. And it felt like every one of them was slow clapping me.

A big box was opened up to get a new brush from. I would have gladly just climbed into it and shut the lid.

There was still time for a bit more controversy in the last end. We had no idea at the time, but the BBC footage showed that Madeleine Dupont, the Danish skip, had touched a stone with her foot, which she didn't acknowledge. Right or wrong, the game was done and so were our Olympics. We gave Cheryl Bernard's Canada a decent game but lost by one. Ranked seventh, finished seventh. Viewed as a whole, our efforts in Vancouver reflected our standing in the sport. Not far away from the top teams who competed for the medals (Canada should have won but blew big chances in the 10th and extra ends in the final), yet a significant distance away.

The squad system had been worth a gamble. None of the established Scottish teams were strong enough, even with minor tinkering. Perhaps, the final selected five should have been given a longer run and maybe the coaches should have picked the best player for every position rather than trying to smooth off some of the square edges to fill round holes. We were effectively a three skips team. We also had two leaders. Although I skipped and threw last stones, Jackie had been given captaincy duties so was, in many ways, the team leader. With my inexperience, I could understand the logic, but going all-in with one of us, or Kelly, would have made more sense. The other girls had been very supportive and, as was the case in the months leading into the Games, nobody fell out. But I did go into my shell a bit after results started to turn against us. That's not healthy. There is no hiding place at an Olympics. Small cracks in a team become big cracks.

As with the pre-tournament expectations, the post-tournament reflections were dominated by the men, not us.

I've never seen five more devastated people in my life than Dave Murdoch's team after they lost a tiebreak game against Sweden to decide who advanced to the semi-finals. They had been the favourites for gold and didn't medal. There wasn't much flak coming our way, but it was very different for the guys. It was an eye-opener. This is what broken dreams and broken athletes looked like. I was hopeful that my age and career trajectory meant I would give myself a shot at the next Games in four years, but I also knew it would be a different story for at least a couple of the other girls. As it turned out, three would never go to another Olympics and one would only make it as an alternate.

Using language like 'learning experiences', 'blessings in disguise' and 'Olympic journeys' would have been disrespectful. I was conscious not to speak like that in media interviews. And, with five days left to kill, there was next to no curling talk between us. I became a Budweiser drinker for one week only – it was free for anybody with Olympic accreditation at a place we found in

Downtown Vancouver. And there was plenty of gin smuggled into the Olympic Village. In many ways, my experience was everything you would expect of a raw newbie. I had made more good than bad memories, came away with plenty of kit to share around when I got home and had the obligatory five rings tattoo as a permanent reminder. But I wasn't the dedicated athlete I needed to be to take home the one thing more important than all of the above – a medal.

THIRTEEN

007 AND DONALD TRUMP

An Olympics is the peak of a four-year cycle but, for curlers at least, it isn't the end of a season. And a World Championships is no 'after the Lord Mayor's Show' event in any circumstances, certainly not when you've only competed in one of them, as was the case for me. Also, Dad's school of thought that the worlds were above the Olympics in the curling pecking order had been ingrained into my thinking. To put it into the context of my life, I hadn't even turned eight when the sport was officially added to the Olympic programme in Nagano. To be a great of the game, you needed to be a world champion. It was that simple. That's where the sport's heritage and folklore were rooted.

To get the chance to be a world champion, you first needed to win the Scottish. That task was laid out in front of us just days after flying home from Vancouver. It was a ridiculously quick turnaround from getting back into the country and getting on the ice at Dewars.

Outwith the actual Olympics, you would rarely see me in Team GB gear. I did turn up at Glenshee once in the red, white and blue, but that was because they were the only skiing clothes I could lay my hands on. If anybody had just caught a glimpse of this perfectly decked-out skier (in the loosest sense of the word) crawling and falling her way off a ski lift and down the slopes they would have wondered what on earth was going on with the British selection policy for the alpine sports. Practice at Dewars for the 2010 Scottish was another rare occasion when I was seen in full GB kit, head to toe, but again it was out of necessity. I hadn't had time to get back up the road to Blair Atholl for different clothes.

We were booked into a bed and breakfast for the week and managed to get ourselves into the final, despite the tiredness, the jet lag and the high standard of the opposition. It was all going well – until our half-hour practice before the final against Gail Munro, that is. Jackie fell badly on the ice and twisted her knee. Jackie is no drama queen. She was in agony and there was no chance of her playing. Annie had to play. While Jackie was getting examined in Perth Royal Infirmary, we were on the back foot for about six ends. But we did enough to win by a shot and I was a back-to-back Scottish champion with another chance to represent my country at the worlds.

I love Canada – as a country to visit and a place to compete. Curling is a national sport, with only ice hockey above it. The crowds are the biggest, the most knowledgeable and the most passionate in the world. You can walk into a bar and curling will be on the TVs, as football is in Britain. Normally, if you gave me the choice, I would prefer the big cities over the towns in the middle of nowhere. It's a nice contrast to home. But for these post-Olympic worlds, Swift Current felt like the ideal place to be. It was the most chilled I had ever been. I even had a few glasses of wine at the opening banquet, which I had never done at a big championship of that stature before and never did since. We weren't freewheeling, but we knew that our batteries were nearly spent and that staying as relaxed as possible was the best plan.

And it very nearly paid off.

Beating Jennifer Jones in the semi-final in front of a packed crowd and a huge live TV audience was my breakthrough moment in Canada, possibly also in women's curling. We should have won gold. Andrea Schöpp was a very good curler and had won this event back in 1988. And by beating us, she became the oldest world champion skip at the age of 45. But she wasn't Jennifer Jones. And Germany weren't Canada in their own backyard. Losing in an extra end was a case of one that got away.

Not that I was thinking along those lines.

I had gone from a distinctly mediocre performance at the Olympics and questioning whether I truly yet belonged at the elite level of the sport to beating the Canadian champions and being edged out in a nip and tuck final.

My glass was half-full. Kelly's was overflowing.

On the night of the semi-final, we were having a couple of drinks in the patch (curling's equivalent of an after-show party). The local mayor got up to make a speech and Kelly nudged me. It didn't take her long to get her introduction to Mayor Schafer. We had all earned ourselves a world silver medal that week and Kelly had bagged herself a future husband. I think she was on the first plane to Canada after we arrived back in Scotland.

World runner-up was great, and a bit of validation just when I needed it, but the summer after an Olympics doesn't throw too many perks your way without a medal round your neck. An appearance on the *Antiques Roadshow* in the gardens of Blair Castle to get an old silver trophy from Dunkeld Curling Club valued wasn't exactly A-list glamour.

Meeting Sir Sean Connery and Donald Trump was probably a bit more showbiz, though. I couldn't tell you how the invite to Dressed to Kilt in New York came about. It was probably through the British Olympic Association because I ended up walking down the catwalk in a GB tracksuit top, with a Lion Rampant kilt and a sweeper in a Union Jack kilt in front of me. I was just glad they had clothes for me because my suitcase hadn't turned up in time. Mercifully, it was a pretty understated outfit compared to some. The actor, Matthew Modine, had to carry a bike over his shoulder while swigging out of a bottle of whisky.

I must have been the lowest level 'celebrity' model by a distance. Mike Myers, Alan Cumming, Joan Jett, Kyle MacLachlan and Kellie Pickler were (are) properly famous. I was glad that I had got speaking to Colin and Justin, the TV renovation guys, on the flight over and the kilt designer, Joey D, who is from Edinburgh. Thom Evans was easy to talk to as well. You could still see his scars from recent neck surgery following a career-ending rugby injury. And I had Mum with me which, for someone who was feeling like a fish out of her Scottish water even on a night where there was tartan at every turn, made life a lot easier with the small talk at the cocktail party fundraiser. It also gave us a 'remember the night we spoke with an American president' story.

Scottish Curling had asked me to bring back a top signed by Sean Connery and Donald Trump, which I did. Sir Sean was very much the star attraction, but Mum had a friend back home whose gran was the sister of Trump's mother, so she wasn't going to miss the chance of a 'you'll never guess but' blether with him. There with his son, he was very polite, posed for a picture (making sure he got to check it was a good one) and talked fondly of Scotland because of his family connections. But he knew nothing about curling, nor Mum's pal from Blair Atholl. I don't know who got the signed top. Maybe it will appear on *Antiques Roadshow* one day.

FOURTEEN

HISTORY ON HOME ICE

Leadership, and everything that goes with it, had been thrust upon me in the build-up to the Olympics. Well, part-leadership. With Jackie sharing those responsibilities, I wasn't a full-blown skip, not as I was in my juniors' team, and certainly not in the mould of an Anette Norberg, Jennifer Jones or Cheryl Bernard. These were the leaders I aspired to emulate. Playing last stones is one thing but driving and shaping a team is something else entirely.

Swift Current was a timely bridge from one season to another and from partial leadership to full. I knew that a World Championships straight after an Olympic Games is the one where you see the biggest shocks. I wasn't going to get too carried away with my silver because for some of the top teams, their season, in terms of form and emotional commitment, had peaked in Vancouver. But it was certainly validation that I could play the big shots that won big games, beat the big teams and make the big calls. Now, to become a big leader, I had to make some big decisions.

The first of those was assembling a team for the 2010/11 season that didn't include Jackie. Jackie had everything you want in a top curler – experience, shot-making ability, calmness under pressure and a personality that made her great company during downtime. She was and always will be a Scottish curling legend. Everybody remembers Rhona Martin, now Howie, and her Stone of Destiny to win Britain's first gold. But it could just as easily have been Jackie's team in Salt Lake City in 2002. In terms of sporting achievement, their world gold a few weeks later in North Dakota was comparable, even though the publicity compared to Rhona's was night and day.

Jackie was a one-off. Only she could come up with her own curling terms and get away with it. Shouting 'boob weight' down the rink instead of 'barrier weight' was one Jackie-ism. 'Flobs' was another – not an acronym you're likely to find in any curling textbook – F***ing Little Outside Biters to describe stones around the house which have become a nuisance that you need to get rid of. But Jackie was 45, over twice my age, and would be nearly 50 by the time of the 2014 Olympics. And, more pertinently in the here and now, she was recovering from her third operation to an old skiing knee injury that had flared up in the week of the Scottish Championships. It certainly wasn't an easy decision to go with the four who won world silver, but I was in no doubt that it was the correct one. I felt myself, Kelly, Lorna and Annie made up a well-balanced team and that Kelly and I would be a very strong skip and third axis. Breaking the Swift Current group up would have been an unnecessary risk. In my mind, this quartet had the potential to last until the Sochi Olympics.

As so often happens in sport, though, we didn't get the chance to find out. For Kelly, the course of true love was taking her to Saskatchewan, not Sochi. At the end of the season she emigrated to Canada, married the mayor and started a new life and family.

My curling reset hadn't lasted long.

Before the season was over, getting back into the juniors' environment with three other girls of virtually the same age for one last hurrah was just what I needed.

Calendar clashes meant I didn't get the chance to make it four world golds in 2010. So, this was it in 2011. There would be no more straddling the junior and women's scene once I had competed in my last world juniors. If it was going to be four and history, it would have to be now.

There was actually a bit of a close scrape just qualifying. Quite rightly, the fact I was an Olympian and had won three worlds previously didn't get me a pass to represent Scotland. I had to earn my spot. As it should be. At the Scottish juniors in Aberdeen, we faced Hannah Fleming's team in the final. In the first end, Hannah was lying four when I played my last shot. It probably wasn't wise to make as aggressive a play as I did but that was my mindset at the time. I saw a two and I went for it. The gamble paid off, but it could easily have gone the other way.

The fact that the worlds were taking place in Perth added to the potential perfection of the storyline. But it also added to the pressure. It was a more serious vibe in general. That had a lot to do with what happened in Sweden two years previously. I had made a quick exit after our gold medal match because I had a flight to catch for the worlds in Korea. The banquet I left early had turned into quite an occasion, I was told. Plenty of drink was taken and all sorts had happened in the hotel, with fire alarms being set off. The World Curling Federation banned alcohol in 2010 on the back of it, and it hadn't been lifted in Perth.

There were plenty of curlers competing who would go on to become rivals for years. Anna Sidorova skipped for Russia; Sara McManus and Sofia Mabergs were in the Swedish team; and Alina Pätz played for Switzerland.

A sober week? Yes. A serene week? No.

We lost to Sweden and Canada in our last two games of the round-robin section – not enough to put our progression to the play-offs in jeopardy but enough to cast doubt on our chances of winning the whole thing. And the Sweden defeat topped up our motivation, if that was needed. I had a shot to win but was heavy with it. They were celebrating like they had won the tournament, beating the home-town girl on her own doorstep. The juniors were like that. At that age, everybody was less inclined (or less able) to mask their emotions, good and bad. Tears, accusations, brush banging and fist pumping were all common. Dad was our coach and turned out to be a great amateur psychologist that day, helping make sure that I didn't get too down about it. The stumble didn't derail us. If anything, it sharpened us up. Dad played a big part in making sure we were focused and ruthless. One of my abiding memories of the week is him smashing a table and stuff flying everywhere after I went for a six in one end of our round-robin game against Russia when I would have had an easy four and we only ended up with a two. Avoiding Dad's fury was powerful motivation to make sure there were no further slip-ups.

I wouldn't say there was one big rivalry in my junior days. Anna Hasselborg was on the scene, so too was Kaitlyn Lawes. For whatever reason, Rachel Homan never seemed to win the Canadian juniors to qualify. The one time she did was in 2010, when I wasn't able to compete. Anna Sidorova of Russia was maybe the closest thing to a regular rival, and she had the chance of a game-winning four in the ninth end of the semi-final, but her attempted take-out didn't have enough weight. We stole one and then edged them out in an extra end.

The final was one-sided. We dominated Canada's Trish Paulsen from start to finish, winning 10-3. It was the polar opposite of the round robin. They conceded with two ends still to play. It was a perfect afternoon. I had made history on home ice, in front of family, friends and people who had seen me grow from the young girl guessing the countries of the flags hanging from the metal rafters to a four-time world champion.

And the booze ban at the closing banquet?

Dad helped us out on that front as well. Let's just say it wasn't water he was bringing back to the table in the big jugs. Anyway, it was our junior farewell. What could they do? Ban us?

FIFTEEN

GROWING UP

Kelly's newly discovered domestic bliss three and a half thousand miles away not only set in motion the domino effect of me putting together a new team, it also made up my mind to move to Stirling. My training life was increasingly weighted more to there than Perth, so it made sense to cut down the miles my Corsa was clocking up and leave home. I bought Kelly's flat! This was a sporting changing of the guard and a bricks and mortar one.

The summer of 2011 was significant in so many ways. It was the final time I was semi-serious with golf. I played enough to earn selection for the Perth and Kinross Ladies team and when we competed in the North Division County Championship, I won six out of six in foursomes and singles at Inchmarlo Golf Club. It was a real throwback to the golfing trips I loved — barbecues and drinking games outside our lodges at night, playing through hangovers in the morning.

We got past Angus, Aberdeenshire and Northern Counties to qualify for the national finals in Dumfries. With no curling date clashes, I was able to play, but a wasp sting was a painful, symbolic reminder that no good would come out of juggling two sports any more. It happened while I was caddying for Laura Walker. I was holding the pin as Laura putted and the wasp got me on the forehead. Like a good caddie, I held in the scream because I didn't want to put her off her putt, and I was just about able to carry her bag for the rest of the round. But by the time we walked off the course my face was starting to swell up. I should have gone to hospital there and then. But it was a Saturday night, and I didn't want to miss out on the fun. Waking up on the Sunday morning, my eye was completely shut, and I spent a few hours at accident and emergency, looking like I had been fighting with the taxi queue drunks. Our curling team were due to fly to Oslo in a few days and I couldn't drive up the road. One of my Perth and Kinross team-mates got me from Dumfries to Stirling and Anna retrieved my car a couple of days later.

The antibiotics did their job just in time and, despite the fact I looked like the Elephant Man for a couple of days, the tabloid newspapers were exaggerating just a tad when they printed stories that I had nearly been blinded. It wasn't exactly Rory McIlroy injuring his ankle and missing out on his defence of The Open because he played football with his pals, but it was a reminder that curling was my day job. The golf clubs would be going back in the cupboard a lot earlier than late September from now on.

There was definitely some maturing going on. The new home quickened that process. In the early days I spent a lot of time travelling up and down the A9 with a big bag of washing for Mum to take care of, but after a few months, I was slowly but surely becoming self-sufficient, albeit the diet was a bit heavy on microwave lasagne and takeaways, not the best for a full-time athlete.

The flat was great. Kelly left a bit of a jungle for a garden, but it wasn't wild enough to jeopardise a friendship! And all the scrubbing I did when I moved in was more to do with my OCD than Kelly's cleanliness. There was a ready-made social scene of curlers in Stirling. Greg Drummond took my spare room as a flatmate and succeeded in being even less domesticated than me. Michael Goodfellow was another good friend on the British Curling programme who was happy to go out for food or a pub crawl at the drop of a hat. My old amateur golfing pal, Kelsey MacDonald, was based in the town as well. She would join us sometimes too.

I was never a student, so this was the nearest thing to it. And, after taking control of putting together a group of four curlers from scratch for the first time, I had what I would describe as the first true Team Muirhead. The choices all felt natural. I was clear in my mind that I didn't want to be the skip of a group of women from an older generation. I was looking for a different dynamic. Once I had arrived at that conclusion, the rest was straightforward. Anna, Vicki Adams and Claire Hamilton came as a ready-made package. I had played and won with them all in the juniors at various points. They had beaten us in the final of the Scottish, and being part of their set-up as an alternate at the worlds reaffirmed in my mind that we would gel as personalities and players.

The conversation between Anna and I was the key to it all. She had been skipping and if she wasn't happy to drop down to third, it would have been a non-starter. But Anna was on the same page, and we set out with clearly defined roles for the four of us, which was very different from the Vancouver team. Claire was very level-headed and calm. She was one of the best leads I ever played with and, even though she did most of her on-ice individual practice in Glasgow, which the coaches were fine with, she worked incredibly hard.

Every good curling team – probably every good team in any sport – needs a feisty character, who won't shirk confrontation. If there was a hint of it off the ice, Vicki would try and keep right out of it, but if it was on the ice with our opposition, she would be right in the middle. She had told her sister she wasn't going to be playing with her in the juniors, remember. And I once saw her coming up against Vicky Wright, one of her best friends, when Vicki was sledging her mate throughout a game after Vicky had played a lucky shot. Skip and third is the most important relationship in any curling team. Anna was a lefty to my right-handed technique, which was a bonus. We had similar thoughts on strategies and bounced off each other very well in the heat of battle.

It might seem strange that I chose my dad as coach at a time when I was making so many breaks with the past. But that felt like a natural step too. All the girls agreed. There wasn't a big conversation between us as a team, nor between Dad and me as father and daughter. There weren't many group training sessions anyway. One a week, maximum. The vast majority of practice was individual-based, which was a concept very much of its time. It just wouldn't happen these days. Dad was on board to share his experience and improve our technique and tactics. He would come with us on most of our trips to Canada and be at the other big events like the Scottish and hopefully the Europeans and worlds. I knew there was no chance he would go easy on me, that was a given. But he wouldn't be extra hard on me for the sake of appearances, as you sometimes see in some parent–child coaching relationships. Dad knew how to help us, whether that was chauffeuring us across Canada, holding a broom at the other end of the ice if any of us wanted practice, or giving us space when we needed it.

I had never been more confident that the team building blocks were in place to enable us to hit the ground running and that's exactly how it played out.

SIXTEEN

PLAY HARD, PARTY HARD

Dad enjoyed tour life. When we weren't playing or practising, he could do his own thing, stay in his hotel room and binge-watch *Storage Wars* on Canadian TV or head down to the bar and catch up with guys he had competed against down the years. That's the type of sport curling was, even at the top level. Think the 19th hole in golf – but even more sociable.

For the competitors, like us, it was a transitional period between that old world and what would become a new world, where gyms were more popular than gins. Although we were all ultra-serious about our curling, it wasn't frowned upon to be known as a party team. And that was our label in the first year. It wasn't just us. Niklas Edin and Kevin Koe are legends of our sport. They also knew how to have a good time.

Not only were the Grand Slams the biggest tournaments, they were also the most fun. The Players' Championship in Toronto was the prime example. Ben Hebert, who was in Kevin Martin's gold medal-winning team at Vancouver, led us astray. One minute we were throwing back the drinks in hospitality after our game on the Friday night and then the next we were in a strip club in Downtown Toronto. It's the bit in the middle that was a bit hazy! At the Players', everything was in walking distance from your hotel – the arena, a massive shopping centre, nice restaurants, busy bars. My suitcase always came back full after that tournament.

It was also the location for one of my most memorable birthdays ever. For the first and last time in my life I was relieved to be out of the tournament on the day of the final in 2012 because I turned 22 on 22 April and it felt like there were 22 shots lined up for me to down for breakfast.

The other big party birthdays were my 18th and 21st (neither of those in Canada). I turned 18 on a Tuesday and there's not a lot of choice in Blair Atholl in midweek to mark a milestone like that. Katy Scott took me to a local pub, the Roundhouse. It was my first and last brush with Aftershock. I fell asleep at the side of the road on the way home, Katy was up most of the night being sick and Mum put her nursing skills to good use by looking after her while I slept on the floor. It was like Grimbergen all over again, except this time I had to phone in sick for my shift at the Watermill, much to Mum and Dad's disappointment.

On the podium, alongside Toronto and the Roundhouse, would have to go my 21st. That was a proper party in the Atholl Arms Hotel, with family, curlers, school friends, old bandmates and golfers invited. One of the golf girls fell asleep in the toilets after we all moved on to there and it wasn't until a couple of hours later that we realised. Then it was bagpipes at four in the morning.

Toronto and its shenanigans weren't the norm when we were on the road in Canada. It was all very different when you were in the back end of nowhere rather than the big city. On those weeks, the routine was basically ice rink, restaurant and hotel room on a loop. They are not tiny places population-wise. You would be talking the equivalent of our big towns and small cities, like Perth. A lot of them felt very similar – one big street through the middle, a Walmart, a tractor garage, a car garage and a few restaurants. If there was a Starbucks, it was a big bonus.

I can't say I enjoyed being the designated driver when we were out in these places, especially in the sort of weather where you started the engine half an hour before you got into the hire car. There was one trip when I came out of the car park, hit a sheet of ice and smashed into the back of another car. We had a game that afternoon and I was still shaking during it. Taking on driving duties abroad isn't one of the skipping duties they tell you about when you're coming through the juniors.

We weren't the best tourists for getting out and about and going on sightseeing trips. There was a standing joke that even the Canadian teams did more of that than us. If we did venture off the beaten track, it was probably because Dad wanted to check out a farm.

Apart from being known as Canada's sunniest city (330 days per year apparently), Medicine Hat isn't the sort of place that has many claims to fame, certainly not in a sporting context. But it holds significance for me. A couple of months into the season we won there in the middle of a three-week trip. It was the first time a Scottish female team had won a World Curling Tour event in Canada. The only disappointment was when it came to the presentation of the trophy, the organisers had to break the news that the previous year's winners had 'misplaced' it. So, no big trophy to pose with for the photographs, but we had beaten good teams from Russia, China, Japan and a few top Canadian rinks to put down a marker early in the season.

We had momentum building for the European Championships in Moscow, which is all you can ask for.

You wouldn't have known it by watching me play in the first half of the week out there. I struggled. We were thrashed 12-2 by

Denmark in the second game. It was all over after six ends, one of the heaviest defeats I had ever suffered as a curler. Anna was probably exhausted trying to make up for my mistakes because by the time I sorted out my form, it was her turn to go off the boil. After an unconvincing victory over Latvia, who had long since been resigned to the fact they were going home before the play-offs, Dad called a team meeting in an effort to sort things out before it was too late. We had scraped through the round robin but didn't have the look of likely champions.

Apart from the odd exception, the Europeans, worlds and Olympics were the only tournaments when we had two coaches with us – team and head. Rhona, by now retired and the head coach for women's curling, wasn't too happy because it was just the players and Dad in the room when a few home truths were said. The team coach/head coach dynamic is a notoriously fraught one when things aren't going well. Who takes control out of the two of them if they have a different perspective? Who do we listen to? Any problems between Dad and Rhona weren't my concern, however. And Dad was right – we needed honesty and one voice of authority. There were a few tears, but it did the trick.

We completely reversed the roles in our semi-final against Denmark, thrashing them 10-2 this time. I hit 97 per cent for my shot accuracy. Sweden had beaten us in the round robin and hadn't lost a game all week. It had all gone so smoothly for Maria Prytz, who was playing last shots for them in her first season in their top team, having been a long-time alternate for Anette Norberg. But there's no dressing it up – the occasion overwhelmed her. She flashed her last stone through the house in the first end and then the same thing happened again in the second. It was six ends before she put a point on the scoreboard. Everything she tried went wrong. It was like watching somebody with a dose of the shanks in golf. The harder she tried, the worse it got. I could see Maria was fighting back tears during the game.

It would have taken a heart of stone not to feel for her, especially after my own brutal experiences in Vancouver. But sympathy only goes so far. We had to keep our foot to their throat and stick to a basic game plan, which forced Maria to play the types of shot she was struggling to execute. We did what we had to do and became European champions with two ends to spare.

The game had started at 10 in the morning and by the back of 11 it was all over. The Megasport Sport Palace, which can hold nearly 14,000 people for big ice hockey matches, barely had anyone in it to watch us claim our first international gold for our country in women's curling. There hadn't been a Scottish winner in the ladies since the very first European Championships in 1975. Since then, there had been 19 Swedish golds. They had been a powerhouse of curling in Europe for over a generation. Ours was an achievement worthy of proper celebration.

Even better that we were in the land of proper vodka for the party. We had been on our best behaviour through the week. The evening routine was guessing which prostitutes the rich Russian businessmen would choose, while we were having our dinner. We always made sure we had a table with a view to keep us entertained – spaghetti carbonara and a game of pick the prostitute. I had never seen anything as brazen.

By the time of the banquet, we were ready for a big night. Lots of straight vodka, with our Russian psychologist, Misha, making sure the good stuff kept coming and that we learned the proper technique to down our shots. It's all about when you inhale and exhale, apparently. I wish I had known that at Christmas when Granny had blown the dust off her bottle of Tia Maria.

We didn't need Dad to smuggle us alcohol in water jugs on this occasion.

SEVENTEEN

CHANGE FOR DAD AND DAUGHTER

The season was only half-complete at the point we were crowned European champions, but the next few months would prove that it had peaked.

We lost a couple of games in the round robin of the Scottish – one of those to Jackie, who was now back competing at national level after her knee operation. We got our own back in the semi-final and then beat Gail Munro's team convincingly in the final. Having been deposed as Scottish champion in 2011 and only been included in the worlds in Denmark as an alternate, albeit I did get on the ice, it was satisfying to earn my spot 12 months later. There was little to feel satisfied about at the competition that followed in Lethbridge, however. Aggressive tactics are good in theory, but you need to be at the top of your game to make them count. We weren't. Mid-tournament, Dad changed our strategy, stripping it right back. We became a hitting team, basically, which is what you would associate with a nation not expecting to challenge for medals.

We needed to win all our last four games to qualify for the play-offs and nearly managed to do it. I had a draw to the four-foot to beat Sweden and was short with it. The feeling when you do that is the same as a golfer not committing to a six-foot putt on the 18th green and leaving it on the lip of the hole. Maybe the other curlers saw me sobbing in the stand when the semi-finals were being contested and took pity because I was voted the winner of the Frances Brodie Award, presented to the curler who displayed 'the best sportsmanship, fair play, honesty and friendship'. Whether it was a sympathy vote or otherwise (for some reason the Asian girls seemed to find me hilarious, so they probably swayed it!), I certainly wasn't in a rush to make sportsmanship prizes a habit. Dad's face said it all when he heard the news.

Reflecting on a first full season out of the juniors, Scottish and European titles and a couple of tour wins added up to a respectable achievement. More than respectable, actually. It would have been greedy and unrealistic to expect more. I had transitioned from a young, raw skip to an established one who had earned the respect of the big names like Anette Norberg, Jennifer Jones and Sherry Middaugh. That was important to me, almost as important as medals. I had also transitioned into a young woman who was the same as millions of other 22-year-olds and had reached a point in their life when you don't want to have your dad with you all the time. From the daughter who was her dad's shadow, first amongst the bales of hay and then on the ice, to the daughter who decided that her dad was no longer the right coach for her, might appear incongruous. But it was because we are so alike in so many ways and view life and curling so similarly, that it neither felt awkward nor wrong to either of us.

It was my decision.

If the other girls had been speaking about Dad's situation, I certainly wasn't aware of it. And it would have been unfair to put them in the position of discussing it or putting it to the vote.

Firstly, I was the skip and captain. Secondly, he was my dad. It had to come from me. The time was right. There are plenty of occasions in elite sport when you don't get the chance to take control of important decisions, so you need to own them when governing bodies allow you a bit of autonomy. From a personal point of view, I was less reliant on Mum and Dad. I had left home and bought a flat. From a curling perspective, Dad had taught us everything he could. Both of us knew deep down that it had run its course. He had only been this team's coach for a season, but he had been my mentor for as long as I had been strong enough to pick up a curling stone. We knew that this last chapter of curler and coach wouldn't last forever. He would treat me the same as the other three girls and we would both be honest when the time came to end it.

Dad took on a coaching role with Glen's team and that was probably a more natural fit for him, if I'm honest. I knew he would be fine and that we would slip back into dad and daughter mode, Dad picking the right time and place to talk curling and me leaning on him emotionally above anything else. I've got so much love and respect for my dad. It wasn't a traumatic conversation for either of us but that doesn't minimise what I was doing. I was ditching Dad as a coach and replacing him with one of his mates.

We weren't looking to Canada or Europe for our next coach. We were looking to another Perthshire farm.

EIGHTEEN

THE PENNY DROPS

The Muirheads, the Smiths and the Hays are big family names in Perthshire and Scottish curling – literally, when you look up at the honours' boards at Dewars Centre. They are big family names in world curling as well.

You would struggle to find a more colourful character than Chuck Hay or one who better defined our sport in what many people will view as its golden age. He really was Mr Curling. Chuck was the first Scottish skip to win the World Championship, back in 1967. To do that, he was the pioneer in this country of adopting the great Canadian skip, Ernie Richardson's, open and attacking style of play that had changed the game. It felt like Chuck was a permanent fixture at Dewars and the visiting curlers loved to catch up with him and hear his stories when they were over for the Perth Masters. If they needed a tee time booked for golf at St Andrews, he was also the man to sort that. Chuck's love of curling was passed down to his four sons and, after his own successful playing career came to an end, Mike was Rhona's coach when she won gold in Salt Lake City and then he went on to become a Team GB chef de mission at Winter and Summer Olympic Games. It was Mike's brother, Dave, whom I had in mind to take over from Dad as our team coach.

I had watched them both compete on so many occasions and played with Dave, a former world champion, in the Perth Super League. He and Dad would alternate skipping duties as Dave's son, Finlay, Glen and I made up the rest of the team and we rose from the fourth division as 13- and 14-year-olds to winning the first division as 17- and 18-year-olds. That was all nostalgia, though. Bringing on board someone steeped in curling tradition and boasting an impressive playing CV wasn't relevant to taking my team to the next level in world curling. The things that caught my eye were much more recent. I had been really impressed with the manner that Dave had gone about coaching the GB men's team at Vancouver. There wasn't a more dedicated or invested coach at the Olympics, male or female. And there wasn't a more devastated coach when his team came up just short.

Dave was the epitome of all-in. And he was a World Championships-winning coach. He knew what it took to claim the title that was our next big goal, and he also knew how to navigate the last two years of an Olympic cycle. The only doubt I had was whether he would want to go back into a coaching environment after the crushing disappointment of Team Murdoch missing out on an Olympic medal. Would a year out be enough? Would life back on his Rhynd farm be more appealing than life on the road with a group of early-20s curlers? It was clear from the moment we met that I need not have worried. The competitive fire was still burning as brightly as I had remembered. He had learned so much from Vancouver and was confident that he and we could benefit from that near miss.

Dad wasn't a planner. Dave certainly was. He was more strategic – meticulous in mapping out our itinerary for the year with detailed thought and getting us switched on to the importance of the off-ice support teams that were available to us, whether that was for the mind or body. Nobody was more serious about his curling than Dad. Nobody was more serious about the process around it than Dave.

This was the next stage for us. We would increase the number of team sessions in Perth under Dave's watch from one to two or three a week, making individual practice the supplementary work rather than the core. When it came to championships, he would lay out what his and Rhona's roles were as team and head coaches so there were no blurred lines or room for misunderstanding and ambiguity. It was basically a mantra of 'everybody is here to support this team'. If we wanted to leave the hotel at half-eight in the morning, Dave would make sure the bus or taxi was ready for 25-past. I have always been the type of person who is almost never late and who hates when other people are. There was never any danger of that happening under Dave's watch. You can't exaggerate the importance of having nothing to stress about off the ice. Dave dealt with everything. In fact, he was probably responsible for me turning into a detail-driven, organised person. To be a more complete leader, I felt I needed that. Maybe I took it too far at times but in the grand scheme of things, for me and for my teams, it helped. Better to do too much than too little was my thought process.

It wasn't just my view of the team and who would be the best coach for us that changed in the summer of 2012.

Signing with a management company was a significant moment in the process of me asking big questions of myself and realising I was enjoying myself too often and too much and not fully grasping the concept that I had one shot at this career. Working with professional people who make their living out of supporting athletes tends to focus your mind. That's a given. But there was a bit more to the penny dropping than just that in my case.

It was recommended to me to get in touch with Red Sky Management. Back then, they were less than 10 years old and most of the athletes in their stable were rugby players. That made sense because the owner is Rowen Shepherd, a retired Scotland international. At one of our meetings, straight after the handshakes, Rowen said: 'Were you out last night?'

'No,' I replied, in a way I would have done to Mum or Dad if I had been caught doing something I shouldn't have. Rowen wasn't having a dig – he was from the old school era of rugby so would have enjoyed more than a few late ones, even on a school night. He was just having a joke. But, of course, I *had* been out. I didn't look the best and you could still smell the drink on me. I was mortified. Telling myself that there was no problem because I was young and had the capacity to bounce back quickly the next day after going out in Stirling wasn't good enough. I was committed to my practice and to my career, but I wasn't professional in every sense of the word. That meant going over and above what was prescribed for you.

That conversation, and being taken on by Red Sky in general, provided the life introspection I needed. 'Sort yourself out, Eve,' was the gist of it.

So, when Rowen invited me down to London for a weekend at the 2012 Olympics, I wanted to show to him – and myself – that I was serious about my dedication. I had a great time – lots of good meals and nights out, meeting inspirational people, but nothing over the top. We stayed in a flat owned by Scottish swimmer Hannah Miley's sponsor. Hannah was with Red Sky as well. It wasn't nice to see her just miss out on a podium place on day one in the 400 metres individual medley after being hyped up as our big hope to get Team GB on the medal table. I felt like I could really relate to Hannah. She is so down to earth, is from a remote part of Scotland and was trained by her dad. But, that disappointment for Hannah aside, the atmosphere inside the arena for her swimming final and at all the other events I was lucky enough to see was incomparable to anything I had ever experienced. We didn't have tickets for the athletics stadium on Super Saturday but did see Jessica Ennis-Hill compete in the heptathlon the day before.

If you failed to be inspired by a home Olympics when you were a young Olympian yourself, then it would have been time to look for another job. Anybody who saw live action in 2012 would have gone home wishing they had a shot at winning a medal. Well, I did have a shot. A switch had been flicked inside me. I knew my commitment had to be total from here on. Anything less would lead to a life of regrets.

NINETEEN

TENNIS, TURKEY AND A TERRIFYING RUSSIAN

Pre-London Games, gym work and getting my body in the best possible condition was something I knew I had to do but I wasn't invested in it. I wouldn't say it was a chore or that I was reluctant, but I certainly wasn't proactive. To get the full effect of any part of training – mind or body – you have to believe in its benefits rather than going along with someone who tells you about its benefits.

Maybe the change from Dad to Dave was part of my mindset switch. Dave, like Dad, was of the fag and a coffee for a game warm-up era, but the new world held a greater fascination. Also, without really noticing, the support staff available to me, all experts in their field, had mushroomed. The British Olympic curling programme for the cycle to Sochi 2014 was propped up by £5 million worth of investment. We had Dave as our team coach and Rhona as head coach. There was Malcolm Fairweather, a head of innovation and sports science; performance analyst, Kenny More; physiotherapist, Maggie Bush; sports psychologist, Misha Botting; logistics manager, Susie Elms; and strength and conditioning guru, Dave Leith.

Canada always had a lot of in-built advantages – chiefly, strength in depth of their talent pool. Every domestic tournament their top teams played was stacked with high-quality opponents, taking place in front of sold-out crowds. Sweden weren't at that level but they did produce top coaches and had long established a rhythm of knowing what to do to win major championships. The Asian nations were on the rise. And Russia were throwing money at it. But in terms of the curling scene as a whole, nobody had a more extensive support staff than us.

Kenny was a core part of our weekly routine, giving us all the nuts and bolts we needed from practice sessions and games. If technique needed improving, there was no hiding place. The same with Maggie and physio. Curlers habitually get shoulder, hip and knee pain and feel the benefit of a proper warm-up.

For me, Misha came into his own before and during a big competition. I became more interested in the psychology of leadership. I had never previously broken down what skipping a team fundamentally entailed. I had captained for a long time but hadn't thought about what my team-mates needed from me at a basic level. Because we were now four girls living in each other's pockets 24/7, little things can get magnified and end up being the difference at the end of a long tournament week, for good or bad. I wanted to know what the best things to say to them were in different scenarios and at different times. I also wanted to know more about when to leave them alone and when I should be left alone. Misha's advice made sense and probably the biggest thing was just speaking to someone who appreciated that leadership isn't easy. A burden shared is a burden halved, as they say.

I was increasingly tapping into the advice and experience others could share with me. Of all of them, though, Dave Leith had the biggest influence. The Stirling University gym would become as integral a part of my new life as any sheet of ice. I began to treat gym work as a different sport. Dave and I would set targets and work on technique. The beauty of it was, unlike the actual curling, you had a guarantee of seeing the results of your efforts – in what you could do at each individual station in the gym and in the transformation of your body. I was adding muscle in places that would be beneficial for my curling technique and my capacity to be as fit and strong for the last stone of an extra-end final as I would be for the first game of the round robin.

Core stability was the main aim. If my changing appearance helped create an aura that I was in better shape than my opponents, that was a bonus. I wasn't just pushing myself in the gym, though. Dave expanded my horizons as part of the pursuit of a new me. Stirling University was the base for the top Scottish tennis players. Andy Murray had long since outgrown it, but you would still see his mother, Judy, at the campus. Some of the best swimmers in Britain were familiar faces about the place as well. There was a collective energy and drive. On my part, I was increasing endurance, power and flexibility. And it didn't begin and end on the grounds of the university. That August, I ran my first half-marathon, in Glasgow. Claire joined me and Anna did the 10k.

We all came back from our summer break four weeks earlier than usual and shared the drive to take ourselves out of our comfort zone. We travelled to Sweden for a few days' practice and team bonding without our coaches and, even though we didn't get off to a fast start in the early tournaments, we were putting down foundations to make sure we lasted a nine-month season better than the year before.

My first two tournament wins weren't actually with the girls. They were as part of a mixed team at the Scottish and then Europeans.

The World Curling Federation tried to take mixed finals to places not synonymous with the sport. Spain with Dad and Glen was my previous experience of that, and this time it was Turkey. Ewan MacDonald, Euan Byers, Karen Barthelemy and I, having won the Scottish, made it a double. Keeping four players on the ice at one time was an achievement in itself. I'm all for expanding curling's reach and doing our best to help different countries emerge, but there should be basic standards for a host city and Erzurum didn't meet them. The arena, which was built for the World University Games, was fine inside but it was in a rough area, and it didn't make us feel much better when the locals told us it probably wouldn't last long because the ground underneath us was moving! Potential earthquakes turned out to be the least of our worries that week, though. Every day a curler picked up a bug and there were even a couple taken to hospital. We weren't immune. It was a case of hoping we didn't all get it at the same time. My turn was the day of the final, but I just about managed to fight my way through it, and we beat Sweden to add the European Mixed gold to my ladies' one. By the end, returning home without a stay in a Turkish hospital was the primary aim and it was mission accomplished.

Back with my regular team, there was curling relief when we came through the three-game head-to-head with Gail Munro to secure our place at the ladies' Europeans. We were the funded team, the full-time team and the reigning champions, so all the pressure was on us. Again, for different reasons, it was a case of job done and get out of town (Aberdeen). The only time we were behind was after the first end of the first game. From then on, it was routine.

Following my Turkey experience, it was nice to be back in a curling environment that was much more familiar for the women's Europeans – Karlstad in Sweden. Nobody could complain about the conditions, on and off the ice. We only lost two games in the round robin, beat Russia narrowly and all the rest were convincing victories. By finishing second in the table and then thrashing Sweden in the semi-final, we didn't need a second bite at the cherry to get to the final. My shot percentage in that first v second game was 96 per cent, so I was hitting form at just the right time.

We were the favourites to make it back-to-back golds. I had expected to be facing Sweden again in the final, but they let a lead slip against Russia and lost to Anna Sidorova. It was a very close final. We dropped our level a bit and they upped theirs. The shot percentages of the two teams were identical, so it was no surprise it went to an extra end. They had last stone advantage, but we had set things up well with two nicely placed front guards. Russia's second player, Margarita Fomina, produced the shot of the game to take out both, and another counting stone that we had in the four-foot. After that, Anna hit and stayed to secure their win. Three times we had made mistakes to allow them to steal earlier in the game, so we only had ourselves to blame for the loss. It was a third European medal in a row but a gold that got away.

Anna was typically Russian on the ice, and off it, actually – few words and a poker face. I think her team pretended they couldn't speak good English because it always sounded fluent anytime they were interviewed. They weren't what you would call an intimidating team. Their coach Olga, on the other hand – wow, now there was a scary woman! She was exactly how you would picture the caricature of an older Russian woman – slippers, a big woolly hat and a stare that went right through you. At that point, they were a team on the up and had the motivation of a home Olympics on the horizon. For us, although it was frustrating that we had saved one of our worst performances for the game that mattered most, I actually felt better about the trajectory of the team than after we had won gold the year before.

TWENTY

CURLING EVEREST

In the week of the Scottish Championships in Perth, we tried something different and stayed in the Landmark Hotel in Dundee all week. I had been roped into playing a snooker exhibition with Stephen Hendry and Shaun Murphy the last time I had been there, but thankfully, this time we were left to enjoy having great facilities to relax between games. I felt we were beginning to open a gap between ourselves and the other teams in Scotland and I wanted to make the fact that we were the only full-time athletes in the tournament show.

There were still a few experienced skips who would compete in the Scottish, but the landscape had changed over a short period. In just two years the standard at the top, as well as the overall depth, had dropped markedly. It wasn't that long ago you could have named half a dozen realistic, potential finalists and winners. Now, though, Kelly was settled in Canada, Jackie was a part-time curler and a lot of the other ladies whom I had competed alongside in the build-up to Vancouver had found other priorities in their life and were only social curlers. Lockerbie's

Hannah Fleming was the one to watch. She was the world junior champion and fought her way through to meet us in the final. At the start of the game, she and her team played like a rink with no pressure on their shoulders. We were two down at the half-time break. Far from ideal. But we took control after that. Hannah rolled out on an attempt for two and I drew for three. After that, we waited for their mistakes and capitalised on them every time.

Sometimes you have pre-tournament confidence that isn't necessarily born of results. That was undoubtedly the case for me as we flew out to Riga for the World Championships. It can be hard to explain. I wasn't daunted by our opponents or their form. Don't get me wrong, Rachel Homan was a superb curler back then and winning the Canadian nationals always means you're playing very, very well, but it was her first worlds. Canada hadn't won gold since 2008 and every year that drought piled more pressure on the next team to step up. They're like Brazil in football, Australia in cricket or the All Blacks in rugby union. Mirjam Ott would have been the defending champion, but she lost in the Swiss National Championships, so Silvana Tirinzoni was their skip. There would be big pressure on Silvana. I knew that Anna Sidorova was a big danger and Sweden were the favourites, but our practice had been on point, and this was the most confident I had ever been going into the worlds. It felt as if we were yet to hit our best form, as opposed to previous years when we were trying to hold on to form that had peaked.

I was happy to get Canada on the first day. Rachel and her coach, Earl Morris, admitted afterwards that nerves affected her performance. Rachel's shot percentage was way down at 73 per cent, while I reached 92 per cent. You don't win a game when there's that big a gap between the skips.

What happened next for us was the stuff of nightmares, though. It fell into the category of 'get your bad game out of the way early'. Losing 11-2 to Sweden and shaking hands after six ends was a horror show. The thrashing started off with a three for them in the first end and a five in the fourth. It was vital that we responded against Germany. We produced the fast start and early finish (9-2) that we needed. We were 4-2 down to China in the next game but a four in the seventh turned that contest on its head and I now felt that we had found our tournament rhythm. Not perfect, but the word I kept using in my post-game media interviews was 'solid'. After beating Japan and Latvia by four and Switzerland by seven, things were far better than just solid. A 9-2 win over Team Sidorova in our penultimate round-robin game summed up our form and our confidence. They were a different team from the one which won gold in the Europeans, and we were a different team from the one which had to settle for silver.

The page play-off system means the teams who finish top and second – Sweden and us – had two chances to make it to the final. The winner would go straight there, and the loser would have a safety net. Unfortunately, we needed the net. The 7-5 loss was a painful one. One ahead going into the last end, we had set things up nicely to make sure they didn't take advantage of having the hammer. I thought we had it sealed. But my second last stone picked up some debris on its way down the ice, leaving it out of position. Even after that bad luck, I was able to play a perfect freeze, but Maria Prytz tapped it out. Like a kick in snooker, you know that these things happen when you least expect it. But when it's at such an important stage of such an important game, it's a battle to quell the urge to feel that the world is against you. We were the better team and had deserved to win. That's the beauty of the page play-off system, though – in my eyes, the best of all the different formats the World Curling Federation has used to sort out which two teams get to the final after the round robin. There should be a reward for finishing in the top two after everybody has played each other.

Dave made sure we didn't wallow in self-pity. We had earned

our lifeline and now we had to use it. It was a do or die semi-final against Rachel Homan. Rachel was 23 at the time, and I was 22. We were both attacking players and it was a high-standard contest. The MC introduced all the players with his best Michael Buffer impersonation by stretching out our surnames. It was fitting because after the game, their coach compared the contest to a boxing match. They landed a blow, then we did and so it went on.

All the way to the seventh end, whatever I did, Rachel matched. I opened with a take-out to score a pair, Rachel answered with a draw to the button for a two of her own. I scored two more points in the third end, she scored two more in the fourth. Then it was alternating singles. Rachel finally broke the symmetry in the eighth for a 7-6 lead and we could only tie it in the ninth. The game was in her control rather than ours as Canada had last stone advantage, but we put the pressure on to sit two, albeit Rachel had a very makeable look at a double take-out. It was the type of shot she loved, and I must admit, I wasn't hopeful of her missing. It was a fraction straight, the stone jammed, and we had the one in the four-foot we needed to win.

I'm glad I didn't know the statistic Rachel had in her favour going into that last end. I found out afterwards that her team hadn't lost all season when they went into the 10th end or extra end of a game tied and had final stone advantage. Nineteen times in a row they had won, but the streak finished at the 20th. The match was worthy of a final. The 200 or so spectators got treated to a game to remember, making up for their ears being battered by blasts of 1980s dance music during the end breaks.

Having lost twice to Sweden in the tournament, if our mindset hadn't been right, we would have let ourselves believe they had our number that week. But we didn't actually need Dave (or Misha) to make sure our glass was half-full rather than half-empty. Winning a semi-final in that manner puts so much momentum behind you. It's better than going straight to the final and having a day's rest. Also, this wasn't Anette Norberg's Sweden, it was Margaretha Sigfridsson's Sweden. There had been three Swedish golds since 2005, all of them Anette's. Margaretha was yet to win one. And, as when things went so badly wrong in the final of the 2011 Europeans against us, Maria Prytz was throwing last stones. If I was in their position, I would be finding it hard to fight the feeling that after two wins earlier in the competition, this could be third time unlucky. Hearing their coach, Peja Lindholm, talk about us as a finals team rather than a round-robin team was another psychological boost.

There were no nerves, just anticipation.

We lost a two in the first end but got it back in the fourth, when they missed a chance of a four, followed by an exchange of singles all the way to the finish. It sounds simple but not when a first world title is on the line. That we stayed in control for those six ends was what made me most proud. When you want something so badly, you can push too hard and try to force things to get some clear blue water. It was the ultimate example of backing ourselves – trusting that we would be efficient and calm enough to manage the game for around an hour, shot by shot, end by end. In the final act, I had a clear route to take out one stone. It's what you would want in those circumstances, as opposed to a draw. I nearly played the shot too quickly but paused and slid down to the house to give myself a bit more time to collect my thoughts. The stone was delivered with a firm weight, and Claire and Vicki had my shouts of 'clean' ringing in their ears as they got to work on sweeping, and seeing it arrow to its target was an unforgettable feeling. I fell to the ice on my back and then quickly bounced up and punched the air with my broom before the four of us enjoyed the best group hug of our lives.

Queen's 'We are the Champions' played as we were paraded in front of our friends and family who had made the trip over,

Mum amongst them with her saltire face paint on each cheek, looking as if she was emotionally drained and Dad (without face paint, funnily enough) looking as proud as I had ever seen him.

Thomas had not long been crowned world junior champion – and phoned me for advice during their tournament, which he would hate to admit! It must have been an incredible couple of weeks for Mum and Dad. It was over 10 years since Scotland's women had won the worlds when Jackie was the skip, and I was just short of my 12th birthday. I knew my curling history. Becoming the youngest ever world champion skip, at 22 years and 336 days, was a big deal. That did feel like a weighty accomplishment, when you think about all the curling greats who had gone before me.

None of this was going through my mind on the podium. I mumbled 'Flower of Scotland' and couldn't wait to see Mum and Dad to properly take it all in. Standing in the middle of the podium usually opens the floodgates to a mixture of emotions, particularly later in your career. Relief would become a big one the older I got; sometimes I would even have a bit of 'I've showed you' defiance. But there was no blurring of the lines in this moment. I was too young to be overcome by anything other than sheer, undiluted exhilaration. I didn't have scars that needed to heal, not even from Vancouver.

It's a cliché but this was my sporting Everest.

I had been brought up on the stories of all the world champions and watched the old videos. I had subconsciously absorbed the mystique of the World Championships and the world champions. More legends were born from the worlds than the Olympics. I had always wanted to be world champion above all else. I had fought with Glen to be the one wearing Dad's silver medal from the moment he came through the door and more times than I care to remember after that. Every day, I would see the photo of us as a family and Thomas, born while Dad was in

Canada, balanced between Mum and Dad with that medal and the red, white and blue ribbon shining so brightly on top of his white baby clothes.

Jackie's claim to be the best on the planet was just as strong as Rhona's – and the sporting achievement also the equivalent – when they won their world and Olympic golds within weeks of each other. Who was the best team in the world (and Scotland) in 2002 is a fascinating debate. I couldn't tell you the answer. Both Rhona and Jackie have a powerful case. I could tell you, at that point in 2013, we absolutely were the best in the world. It might sound like I'm stating the obvious given we had just become world champions, but it hasn't always been the case. If we had won in Swift Current I wouldn't have felt like the best. I did now. And that does make a difference – in your own head and for your peers. The results hadn't necessarily shown it, but this had been building – during the week of the competition and since we all came back early from our summer break to start our preparations for the season in Sweden. Dave made us the best prepared team I had been part of and maybe the best prepared team in Riga. Repetition in practice was incredibly boring, but it was required. When we needed muscle memory to kick in during those last few ends of the semi-final and final, it did.

It wasn't the party to end all parties that night.

I was sharing with Anna and after the banquet we came back to our room with a pizza to share, more emotionally exhausted than drunk exhausted. In fact, my worst experience with alcohol was reaching to my bedside table first thing in the morning for a drink of water, downing it and then finding out it was vodka. That was what we did back then – poured drink into a Highland Spring bottle to save a bit of money. You would have thought that an unexpected mouthful of vodka would have woken me up properly, but it took Rhona bashing the door to do that. She shouted that if we weren't down in 15 minutes the bus would leave without us. 'I don't care, we're world champions,' came the response from Anna!

We did miss the bus but didn't miss our flight. And yes, we were indeed world champions.

TWENTY-ONE

THE OTHER SIDE OF EVEREST

There was a lot that was new to me after this gold. I knew what it was like to feel drained after a big event but not to this extent. I was utterly exhausted, and my body wasn't trying to hide it. Something had to give after keeping my emotions in check for a week and pushing myself to my limits. I looked awful – massive bags under my eyes and breaking out in ulcers. From that point on, it would always be the way after a major championship. Win, lose or something in between, I physically paid the price for a few weeks after.

The media attention was on a different scale as well. Winning my fourth world juniors brought attention, so too did the European title and there was obviously a bright spotlight on me in Vancouver. But this was the biggest level of interest after I had achieved something. As a group, we were happy to be as accommodating as we could be anytime broadcast or print journalists wanted to speak to us and 90 per cent of that side of things fell to me, which was fine. The ice queen melting and smashing her broom in 2010 was still fresh in people's minds so there was a bit of a redemption story. And this was the first time four Scottish girls in their early twenties had conquered the curling world.

It had been a very good year for Scottish curling as a whole and a big group of us were invited to put on our blue blazers for an evening reception to meet First Minister, Alex Salmond, at his official residence, Bute House in Edinburgh. When he read out all the achievements it did sound impressive. There could be no doubt that there wasn't another sport which could match curling for Scottish sporting success. Since 2002, our national teams had won 55 medals. Just before our gold, Kyle Smith's team, which included Thomas, became the first male world junior champions since 1996 by beating Russia 6-2 in their final; Hannah Fleming had to settle for silver after an extra end defeat to the same nation; and the men, skipped by Dave Murdoch, won bronze. With just a few canapés to keep us going, it felt like an eternity before the First Minister arrived, shook our hands, spoke for 10 minutes and said his goodbyes. Fair enough, I suppose, he did have a referendum to try and win.

A world curling gold doesn't open many doors, though. Mum and I headed to London in June for a day at Wimbledon for her birthday. There was no middle Saturday VIP treatment. It was my column in *The Courier* that helped get us a couple of media passes. Not a soul recognised me, which tells you all about the impact curling has on the British sporting consciousness outside of an Olympics. Mum was chuffed that we met Pat Cash. I had to tell him I wasn't even born when he won Wimbledon. I could remember Lleyton Hewitt's 2002 victory, and we saw him play doubles on one of the outside courts before we got into Centre Court late in the day when some All England Club members had handed back their day tickets.

As well as next to nobody south of Lockerbie, other than a small enclave of Hampshire, having the slightest clue who I was despite becoming a world champion, there was no life-changing pot of gold at the end of the Riga rainbow either. Curling, and the people who curl, know where they are in the sporting food chain – nowhere near the top. We had to go out and earn sponsors ourselves. Everything was gratefully received and those who supported us wouldn't be forgotten.

Our season wasn't over after canapés with the First Minister. Toronto beckoned for the Players' Championship. We got off to a bad start in our group, losing two of our first three games. Rowen had flown out and took the credit for the turnaround that followed. He gave us a rugby-style, call a spade a spade pep talk before heading for the airport. He hadn't even got on board his flight when a text message dropped from him saying 'that's more like it' after we beat Anna Sidorova to help us squeeze through. We were one of the eight teams to qualify for the quarters, where we beat Alberta's Renée Sonnenberg. Once again, a bullet was dodged in a semi-final. Stefanie Lawton would feel even more frustrated with herself than Rachel Homan had been a month earlier. They really should have put us away. Grand Slams are played over a shorter, eight ends format and Team Lawton, the reigning champions, who hadn't lost a match in their competition defence, were 5-2 up after six of those eight. Losing from that position is a collapse.

It was a Saturday night, the end sheet of the Maple Leaf Gardens, and thousands were packed in the arena. What an adrenaline rush it was to turn the game around and steal in the extra end. Echoes of Latvia continued in the identity of our opponents in the final, Margaretha Sigfridsson's team. I nailed a high tariff double take-out in the second end for a three and we never looked back from there. Anything they came up with when they had the hammer, we were able to match. It finished 8-5. We had another trophy and finished the Grand Slam season with the highest women's points total. Our best in the world status had been further enhanced.

There was more history as well. I was the youngest Grand Slam-winning skip – John Morris had held the record as a 25-year-old. And I was the first European. We were on a roll. Everything we touched was turning to gold.

TWENTY-TWO

LIFE IS GOOD

I couldn't have asked for more obvious proof that my commitment to physical improvement was worthwhile than the way the 2012/13 season had ended. Yes, I was ready for a few weeks off to get away from the gym and the ice but if there had been curling competitions in May, June and July, I would have been able to cope. I didn't feel like I had hit a wall, which had been the case in previous years. There was no other curler I looked at and thought, 'Maybe she's put in more hours than me.' Dave Leith could have told me anything and I would have believed him and followed his instructions to the letter. He had built a disciple.

But I was also inquisitive.

I wanted to take it to the next level by finding more out about the theory behind all the fitness work, so I enrolled on a personal training course that summer. It meant I could kill two birds with one stone. I got to earn my first qualification since leaving school and I got to spend three weeks with Granny and Grandad. Flying down brought back memories of the days when Glen and I were small and we would be seen on to the plane to Southampton by

Mum, looked after by the cabin crew during the flight and then met by Granny and Grandad at the other end. The course I had signed up for at Southampton was where they would take Glen and me swimming. At the end of it, I had the badges to become a personal trainer. But, more relevantly, instead of just following orders without knowing the reasoning, I had a deeper insight into what I was doing to my body in the gym and why.

Southampton was one trip during the curling off-season, New York another. Anna and I spent a few days there (I got myself another tattoo) before returning to Toronto, this time for a fundraiser for sick children and a first and last long night on whisky.

Life was good.

The only downside about being a newly crowned world champion was it meant you were automatically put on the ADAMS system, the database managed by WADA, the World Anti-Doping Agency. Every day you have to provide details of where you are staying and a drug tester can turn up at any time, from six in the morning until late in the evening. My flatmate, Greg Drummond, was on the programme too. Whenever the doorbell went at the crack of dawn, we knew one of us wouldn't be getting back to their bed. On average, I reckon I got tested once a month. It can be more than one sample per visit. If your urine is too dilute you have to go again, which usually means a long wait. It could take hours. The chaperone follows you everywhere until you're ready for your second try.

I nearly missed a flight because of it once. There were times when I was out for dinner with other athletes, and we had to ask for an extra place at the table to let the drug-tester join us. By some distance the most embarrassing moment was at the 2008 World Junior Championships in Östersund. I hadn't been educated about the ins and outs of testing. So, after winning the final, I didn't have a clue what happened next. I'm sure the testers have seen it all but that didn't make me feel any better when the tube wasn't big enough, let's just say! It was such a relief when the lady told me she had enough in the sample I had produced, and I could go and join the celebrations. I never resented it, though, whether it meant postponing a party after a big win or preventing a quick escape after a heartbreaking loss. I appreciated the bigger picture. Curling, which was becoming more and more about power, wasn't immune to drug cheating, as a couple of positive tests and bans have shown. I had no sympathy for the curlers who got caught.

I did have sympathy for Alain Baxter.

Alain winning his bronze medal in Salt Lake City made as big an impression on me as Rhona's gold at the same Olympics. Aviemore, where he comes from, is less than an hour up the road from Blair Atholl. He almost felt like a local. I've got such a vivid memory of the close-up picture in the papers of Alain with his medal, his saltire hair and his ear-to-ear smile. Brits just weren't supposed to win skiing medals and the guy who did it first lived 50 miles away from me. Then a couple of days later I was asking Dad why his bronze had been taken away from him. When you think of all the true drugs cheats and the drugs cheats who have got off on a technicality, a naïve skier taking a nasal inhaler that gave him absolutely no competitive advantage was so unfair.

Alain has sent me nice messages down the years, and there have been plenty of times he's popped into my head when I've had a bad cold or felt ill. Unless it's paracetamol or ibuprofen, I wouldn't take it. Not even a Lemsip, and certainly not a Vicks inhaler. Any supplements I ever bought would always be properly batch-tested, which usually meant they were three or four times the cost. It was a price worth paying, however. Certain memories never leave you. Alain Baxter making an innocent mistake and having his medal unjustly taken off him was one of them.

TWENTY-THREE

PICKING UP WHERE WE LEFT OFF

It was a summer break that we didn't really need, and it was nice to have one at last when there were no team line-up or coaching alterations to be made. That was a first for me since I had aged out of the juniors. When you have become a world champion and a Grand Slam winner at the back end of the previous season, the last thing you do is change things up or even tinker. If it ain't broke, don't fix it. We just wanted to pick up where we left off. This was an Olympics season and stability at the start of it was exactly what I would have wanted.

It was still summer when we received the honour of becoming the first Team GB athletes to be picked for Sochi. What a difference to my last Olympic selection. No meetings at the Dewars Centre this time. No anger or upset. No controversy. No drama. The selectors were still technically picking individuals rather than a whole team, but we were all the strongest curlers in our positions. The four of us were 99.9 per cent sure we would be safe. However, even that doesn't make you blasé about the phone call. The best bit about it becoming official so early was there would be no cause for panic if our season started slowly or if we lost a game to another Scottish team.

That didn't happen, though. We won another Grand Slam event in mid-October. There was a trend developing for our trips to Canada. More often than not we would go out there for two-week stints and we would perform better in the second of those. It made sense. The jet lag was gone, we had built up some competition ice time in the first week and because we were over there just for curling, it wasn't as if we were going home between tournaments like the Canadian teams would. Those few days offered up the opportunity of quality practice, particularly when Dave joined us, as he did in the middle weekend on this trip.

The Autumn Gold Curling Classic wasn't one of those slow burn-type weeks. We started well, finished well and there was no form drop at any point. We watched a Calgary Flames ice hockey match the night before the competition started which was apt, because for the next few days we were on fire. Over the four days, we won all seven games, two of those against Rachel Homan and one against Jennifer Jones. China's Bingyu Wang was our opponent in the final and it was a snapshot of the week as a whole – on top from start to finish. Put up two, give up one, put up two, give up one. On it went. I was now the first non-Canadian skip to win two Grand Slams and the first to win seven straight games in that event. In an Olympic year, we had thrown down a marker that the world champions were still the team to beat. The prize money would be very useful because the European Championships were in Norway the following month and you don't get anything cheap over there.

We certainly didn't give our opponents anything cheap in the Stavanger round robin. For the first time (it would be the only time) we won all nine of our games.

Some of the scorelines were very emphatic – 11-5 against Anna Sidorova's Russia and 13-3 against Mirjam Ott's Switzerland.

They were two of our main rivals for gold. We beat Italy and Denmark by 10 and nine, respectively. Even in the two or three tight games, I always felt in control. It didn't matter what our opponents tried, we were in that place all athletes talk about but can't really quantify how they've got there. The zone. If anybody tried a bit of gamesmanship to take us out of that zone, it didn't matter. Our game against Germany came down to the last stone of the last end. Mine. Andrea Schöpp had plenty of time left on their team's clock so before she played her final one, she made sure she took virtually every last second of it, which amounted to over five minutes. It was an obvious shot she was faced with but not as obvious as her delaying tactics.

They didn't work.

In the player percentages, three of us – me, Anna and Vicki – were all top for our positions. I was 7 per cent ahead, which is big at that level.

The first versus second game to get straight through to the final was just as convincing as the round robin. We beat Switzerland comfortably again and their misery was compounded by their second, Carmen Kueng, twice causing the red light to come on for releasing her stones after the hog line. We wouldn't have been human if the 'this is too good to be true' thoughts weren't going through our heads. But that wasn't a factor in our loss to Sweden in the final. And we certainly weren't guilty of letting complacency seep in.

I didn't play as well. The numbers told you that. Just 69 per cent for a final is poor. Completely missing in the first end to give them a steal was a bit unsettling. But by the sixth end we had levelled the scoreboard, and I fancied my chances of another big game win over Margaretha Sigfridsson. Something wasn't right with the clock, though. I'm convinced of that. From about the seventh end, we were running out of time, which is something that had never happened to me before. We were five or six minutes down on Sweden, and had virtually no time on our shots. We were rushing the last three ends and by the point I played my final shot in the 10th, I only had 12 seconds to spare.

I hate using excuses – we were chasing the game and that was our own fault after a slow start. But something had gone wrong with the clock. The game had passed far too quickly. The experience stayed with me. I'm convinced I became more of a worrier on the ice as a result. Before then the clock never really factored into my thinking because I was a decisive skip. After that, though, it would habitually come into my head during matches. I would have a split second of blind panic, frantically look at the clock and then relax again. My team-mates would get so used to it that they would start to roll their eyes at Eve the team worrier. If I woke up in the middle of the night with a stress-related nightmare, being denied an Olympic gold medal in the last end because I had run out of time was it. If that Norwegian clock was faulty, it had a lot to answer for.

Leaving for home, the defeat didn't dent our belief in what we expected to achieve in Sochi a few months later. Even the best can lose a game, and at times like that you shouldn't drill down too deeply for explanations and faults that weren't there. When I said 'it's all about the Olympics' to the journalists after we were presented with our silver medals, I meant it.

Glen and I are introduced to Thomas in 1995.

With a young calf on the farm.

Left: With my grandparents.

Below: Where it all began at Pitlochry Ice Rink.

Right: Playing the Perth and Kinross county championship.

Below: Part of Pitlochry and Blair Atholl pipe band.

Turning up to the Scotti
Junior Championships wi
red hair.

Shearing on the farm!

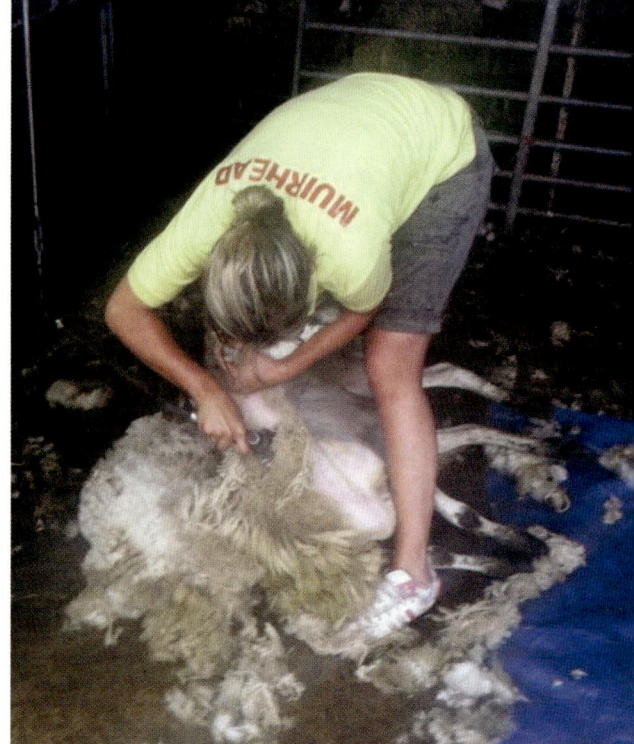

Playing against Switzerland at the 2010 World Curling Championships in Swift Current, Saskatchewan, March 2010. *PA Images*

Celebrating after the final shot to win the gold medal match at the 2013 World Women's Curling Championship at the Volvo Sports Centre in Riga, Latvia. *Dean Mouhtaropoulos/Getty Images*

Above: A world champion, 2013.

Left: Getting a world champion tattoo New York.

Above left: Hugging Vicki after we win bronze at Sochi. *Clive Mason/Getty Images*

Above right: Showing off my bronze medal during the ceremony at the Medals Plaza during the 2014 Olympic Games in Sochi. *Andrew Milligan/PA Images*

Below: The whole team with our medals. *Clive Mason/Getty Images*

Right: Dad caddying for me in the 2014 BMW PGA Championship Pro-Am at Wentworth.

Below: In action against Russia at the 2016 European Championships at the Braehead Arena. *Paul Devlin/ Getty Images*

Right: With Mum and Dad after gaining an Honorary Doctorate of Stirling University in 2018.

Below: My friend (professional golfer) Kelsey MacDonald caddying for me at the Celeb Cup event at Celtic Manor 2017.

Right: With my brothers (and a ewe lamb!) at the 2017 Royal Highland show after being amongst the first athletes selected to represent Great Britain at PyeongChang 2018. Ian MacNicol/Getty Images

Left: Me, Glen and Thomas at the opening cermony for 2018 Pyeonchang Olympics.

Below: Carrying the Team GB flag with Dave Ryding at the Opening Ceremony of the 2022 Winter Olympics at the Beijing National Stadium. *David Ramos/Getty Images*

In action during the gold medal game against Japan at the 2022 Beijing Olympics. *Lillian Suwanrumpha/Getty Images*

The moment you realise your dreams have come true. *Lillian Suwanrumpha/Getty Images*

Above: Olympic gold medalists! From left to right, me, Vicky Wright, Jennifer Dodds, Hailey Duff and Milli Smith. *Warren Little/Getty Images*

Right: At Windsor Castle with my mum and my OBE (on the day I received both my MBE and OBE).

Left: Coming in third place at the 2022 BBC Sports Personality of the Year Awards.

Below: Winning the World Mixed Doubles with Bobby Lammie in 2022.

Still chasing the buzz of competition. *Above:* Battling a hill during the 2023 Etape Caledonia. *Below left:* Taking part in the 2023 London Marathon. *Below right*: Pushing a sled during a Hyrox event in Glasgow in 2025.

Above and below: Things come full circle. Back in 2013 I share a joke with Team GB Chef de Mission Mike Hay during a press conference at Braehead Curling Rink to announce the Team GB Curling team for Sochi 2014. Now I have the role of Team GB Chef de Mission for Milan and Cortina d'Ampezzo 2026. *Mark Runnacles/Getty Images*

TWENTY-FOUR

FIRST TRUMP AND NOW PUTIN

British Curling was becoming more professional year after year and so were we as its funded athletes. But there were still times when the old-school side of the sport didn't fit hand in glove with the high-performance one.

Our gym sessions were pretty much set in stone – three a week, either in the afternoon or evening. For ice time at The Peak sports centre, though, there was no preferential treatment compared to the farmers or housewives of Stirling. You phoned up the day before to see if there was spare ice, the same as any keen curler would. Often it would be a case of: 'We've got club curling from nine until two but after that we can fit you in.'

The curling holding camp for the Olympics was in Stirling, which I was happy about. The longer I got in my own bed, the better. The only difference to our usual routine in the last few days before flying out to Russia was that we were now going to the Stirling University gym in full 2014 Adidas Team GB kit.

I didn't feel the need to seek Misha out for any psychological prep. I was happy with my game, my team-mates and my chances. We were the world champions and the world number ones. The favourites' tag sat comfortably with me. There was a body of evidence to prop up expectations and I felt confident that we would be able to follow through on them.

There was more media training before flying out to Russia compared to four years earlier. The last thing the Team GB bosses want is their athletes getting caught up in political side stories. There was no danger of that with Vancouver as the host city. Sochi, though, was a different matter. These were the first winter or summer Games to be held in the old Soviet Union since Moscow in 1980. Russia's attitude to gay rights and the 150th anniversary of a genocide in that area were high on the news agenda – as was the fact that this was the most expensive Games in history ($51 billion, compared to $8 billion in Vancouver and $15 billion for London). 'Find yourself a safe island,' was the advice I was given. Disengage, change the subject if you need to. Curling, curling, curling. It transpired that I wasn't asked a single question about any of the controversial topics. People wanted to speak about my four-year redemption curve, and I was more than happy to get on board with that.

The kit bag I had filled to the brim at the British Airways depot had almost as many items of summer clothes in it as winter. When we arrived at our apartment in the Olympic village, a couple of the guys from the men's curling team were sunbathing topless on their balcony. The organisers were stockpiling snow in case it melted, and I would have been concerned at a Games taking place on the Black Sea coast if I was a skier. But as an indoors athlete, it was a pleasant change to be able to wander about in a polo shirt. I was sharing a room with Anna; Vicki and Claire were in the other one; and Lauren Gray, our alternate, was on a sofa bed in the living room. Lauren would be coming back late most evenings, after she had matched stones for us (making sure we play with two that track as similarly as possible) so that would work out fine.

Opening ceremonies are always a long stand but I've never felt the urge to skip one. Hanging about for ages is the obvious downside and if we were on ice the next morning, it would be a different story. But there was a three-day gap for us and, even if you're there with a shot at gold like we were, you should never lose sight of the importance of soaking up as much of the experience as possible. Russia did a great job of telling the story of the country's history and culture and, even better, the athletes were paraded into the stadium at the start rather than the end, so we saw it all. One of the five big snowflakes didn't light up, but it was a spectacular occasion all the same. Plus, I could now say that I had got up close to Donald Trump and Vladimir Putin. I don't think Mum has any friends in Blair Atholl who are distant relatives of Putin's, mind you!

The main practical aspect about the geography of the Olympic Park, where we were based, was we could walk to the arena, the Ice Cube Center. We were marched on to the ice for our first game against Sweden by Russian bagpipers playing 'Scotland the Brave', but we weren't in tune as a team. We responded well to going 3-0 down but the middle part being on song isn't enough against one of the medal contenders if the beginning and the end are off key. Anna Sidorova's team competing on one of the other sheets didn't help us. Any time they played a good shot, or their Danish opponents didn't, the home crowd went wild. We had a few miscommunications in the early ends amidst all the noise. Working on our hand signals before the next game wasn't something we had foreseen.

For a bounce-back, though, claiming a bit of Olympic history wasn't too shabby. I would have taken a win however it was packaged. And defeating the United States 12-3 in six ends was just what we needed. I had scored a few sevens in my time as a curler – and seen it done by others – so I wasn't expecting our one in the fourth end to be such a big deal. But the media were quick to tell me that it had never happened at the Olympics before. The other girls deserved all the credit – they had peppered the house with red granite. My final shot was as routine as they come. All I had to do was take out one American stone, with nothing in the way. I felt a bit sorry for Erika Brown, the US skip. The end had got away from them, and she had set up the seven by trying to reduce us to a two. I would have done the same in her shoes. They only won one game in the tournament and finished bottom of the round robin. The attention Erika got for being on the wrong end of an Olympic record wouldn't have helped, that's for sure.

The attention we would have been getting had we lost didn't bear thinking about. That game, sandwiched by the reigning Olympic champions and Canada, was absolutely a must-win. Jennifer Jones's team had got off to the sort of start I would have loved. They were straight into their competition stride, having blitzed China and, even more impressively, Sweden. Nobody had taken them to 10 ends yet. At least we did that, but it was still a loss that left us on one victory and two defeats.

I always watch the Canadian trials and, as much as there was absolutely nothing I could do about who won to earn a spot at the Olympics, I wouldn't have chosen Jennifer. At that point, we had a better record against Rachel Homan and Sherry Middaugh, who were the other strongest teams. You can expect the winner to be in good form because the competition is so tough and because Canada leave their qualifier until the December before the Games, even later than our European Championships.

The first bit of flak came my way after this defeat.

Despite Jennifer hitting a 93 per cent shot rate, we had the hammer in the last end and were two down. A draw to the button would have tied the game up at 8-8 and sent it into an extra end. But there were three tightly bunched Canadian stones and I thought the shot was on to take them out and win the game with a three of my own. Weighed against the probability of Jennifer being able to control the extra end, I thought it was a chance worth taking. Unfortunately, I didn't strike the first stone at the right angle and that was that. There are plenty of shots I would take back, having reflected on the percentages, but that isn't one of them. Aggressive and high-risk? For sure. But it wasn't reckless.

The next game against China, tied 7-7, put the game-defining last stone in my control again, albeit with the odds stacked more in my favour this time. It was a good sign that I didn't feel under excessive pressure and even better that I pulled it off. We backed it up with a comprehensive win over Japan and now I was feeling far more positive about our chances. South Korea and Russia were then taken care of, with only one loss, to Switzerland, nestled among the victories. This was now the form of potential medallists at last.

Following the win over Russia, we were guaranteed a tiebreaker at worst to make it into the semi-finals, while Anna Sidorova's hopes of getting on the podium at her home Games were over. She looked crushed. That was a morning game and by the time we were back on the ice at night we knew that we had qualified for the semi-finals. Beat Denmark and it was Sweden we would meet. Lose and it was Canada.

Denmark had nothing tangible to play for. Not winning was incredibly sloppy on our part, even more so when you consider the way the game panned out. We were three up at the start of the last end. We had contrived to lose when nobody in the building would have given Denmark a chance. We had made a collective mess of it. Dave wasn't happy. He was interviewed afterwards and said we'd been 'careless' and 'took our foot off the gas'. I think it was just a case of poor shot-making and carelessness rather than complacency, but I can understand how it looked. Fog had forced the cancellation of the alpine events that day, and people were thinking we had been caught up in a fog of our own making at the curling arena. Of course, we wanted to be in the other semi-final. Canada had a 9-0 record and Sweden were 7-2. At that point, Jennifer's team were the stronger of the two. But the way I looked at it, if we were going to be champions, we would have to beat both. Gold was the only medal on my mind.

Canada had been missing nothing. This was Jennifer at her career peak. She was someone I really looked up to, not only for her ability and her fierce competitive streak, but for the way in which she wasn't afraid to make big decisions off the ice. When Jennifer ditched Cathy Overton-Clapham (somebody else I have a lot of time for) and broke up one of the most successful teams Canada had ever known, that was big, big news in our sport. But she wanted fresh blood and Kaitlyn Lawes, my old junior opponent, was a young, hungry player who certainly didn't weaken the team. We knew we were underdogs, but we also knew that we had a big game in us and hadn't yet brought it out in these Games. If we lost, it wouldn't be down to an inferiority complex. A pick-up on my stone in the first end (a hair off one of the brooms) wasn't a good omen. That happens once in a thousand shots. At least it wasn't the last end, I was telling myself. I had missed with my very first stone of the semi-final and we had given up a two.

We got ourselves into plenty of promising positions, but Jennifer was relentless. In the last end, she had to draw to the four-foot to win, which she did. That one-in-a-thousand pick-up of the smallest bit of debris on the ice was probably the minuscule dividing line between the teams. It was a brilliant game, with all eight curlers posting a shot percentage in the 80s and 90s. To put it into context, that was the only time it happened in the entire Games, men and women. For that game, in that moment, we couldn't have done much more. It was our best performance of the week. It was also the most devastating defeat I had ever had to absorb and the quickest turnaround to get it out of my system.

TWENTY-FIVE

A BRONZE EARNED NOT A GOLD LOST

Tears were allowed.

And, once we had got off the ice, there were lots of them shed. All our parents were in the Team GB home from home house. Anna and I decided to go and see ours. We found ourselves a couple of bikes, put our heads down and got ourselves there as quickly as we could. Maybe the security guards had been watching the semi-final because nobody asked to see our accreditation, which was unheard of in Russia. We spent a couple of hours there and, despite more tears, the family visit definitely helped me. There were no Churchillian speeches from Mum or Dad, but their positivity was what I needed in that moment. Sometimes when parents tell you everything will work out well in the end you roll your eyes and dismiss it. I believed them this time, though. And, by the time we pedalled our way back to our apartment, all four of us were in a much better place. There was no way we were going to come away from Sochi with nothing.

People had told me that a bronze medal game at an Olympics was the hardest in our sport and I was about to find out. It wasn't the best of sleeps and the nerves that kicked in from the moment I woke up were way beyond anything I had experienced. Our opponents, Switzerland, were world champions the year prior to us. We didn't have a great record against them and had lost in the round robin. They had the hammer and built a two-point lead after four ends. We weren't playing dreadfully but it wasn't a standard required to go out and seize an Olympic medal. Mirjam Ott doesn't give you anything. You know that whatever the occasion, her teams are always going to be seven out of 10, minimum.

From the fifth end, we stepped it up – taking twos and restricting them to ones. All square, one end to go, our hammer. It had come down to this. Claire played two perfect ticks to move their guards and then Vicki and Anna produced equally good shots to set me up for an open draw to the four-foot. Sounds easy when you say it quickly. Not so easy in that moment. Controlling my emotions was my biggest challenge. Do that and I would be in control of my arm. I did and I was. The stone never looked like drifting off target.

I knew what relief felt like now, all right.

Whether it's happy or sad tears, I can normally keep them at bay until I'm off the ice. This was different. I couldn't hold them back and neither could the other girls. We were a collective mess of red faces and smeared mascara.

There was no chance to celebrate with Mum and Dad in the arena because we were dragged here, there and everywhere for media duties. Winter Olympics don't get the same coverage as their summer equivalent. That's just the way it is. But we're a smaller unit and medals are much rarer. There were 56 British athletes in Russia and five medals won. So, a big fuss gets made of you if you do get on the podium. And we were the youngest curling team ever to do it. The next day we were able to spend time with our families and properly take it all in. There's no better place than the top of a mountain to do that – metaphorically and literally. Watching some skiing, while sipping a bottle of Corona, was a nice way to absorb the fact that this had been a steep, arduous climb and that it was a bronze earned rather than a gold or silver lost.

In the evening, I was on BBC commentary duty for the men's final. It was a superb achievement by Dave Murdoch and the boys to get that far. In contrast to Vancouver, expectations had been higher on us than the guys, but they produced big moments at the end of their tiebreak against Norway, and semi-final against Sweden, to win by one on both occasions. The final was a real anti-climax, though. Canada were 5-1 up after three ends and cruised to their win. Dave's team looked like their race was run. He was in the 60s for his shot percentage and the opposition skip, Brad Jacobs, was in the mid-90s. Those Games were Canadian curling at their best – two battle-hardened skips at the top of their game, without a weak link between them. Jennifer never played better and neither did Brad. No wonder there is such huge pressure on their curlers every four years when standards like that have been set. That's what the Canadian public expect and demand. We were the second-best women's team at the Olympics – and I would have fancied our chances against Sweden if we hadn't slipped up at the end of the Denmark game – but the best team won gold.

We all got our medals at one ceremony.

Everybody says the same thing – the weight of them really catches you by surprise. Vicki did some damage with hers when we were whisked off to do Clare Balding's BBC wrap-up show. She went to pick up a drink off the table and her medal swung across like a wrecking ball and smashed glasses everywhere. Olympic medals should come with a dos and don'ts instruction manual. It sounds a bit corny, but I went to bed that night with mine under my pillow. Team GB threw a party on the last day and there was an atmosphere of a job well done. UK Sport had set a target of three medals. At that point we had four and it would later become five when our men's bobsleigh team were upgraded to third from fifth after two Russian sleds failed doping tests.

It was Britain's most successful winter Games ever.

Much of that last night party is a bit hazy, but I do remember going on a midnight McDonald's run with Vicki that involved flagging down a golf buggy being driven by Kjetil Jansrud, who had won gold in the men's Super-G skiing. We had chosen a good driver.

An upgrade on the flight home helped deal with the hangover. That's what a medal gets you. It also gets you in the door at 10 Downing Street. All the medallists were taken there when we arrived back in London. Lizzy Yarnold was our golden girl. Anybody brave enough to lie on a tiny sled and fly around a track, face first at 80mph has my instant admiration. The fact that Lizzy was extremely good at it, and so humble and down to earth, made her status as the biggest story even more deserved. Watching Lizzy in Downing Street made me think: 'If I ever win gold, that's how I would want to carry myself.'

The irony was, of course, that the face of the Games for the British public wasn't posing for photographs, making small talk, eating nibbles and shaking hands with David Cameron at Number 10. Elise Christie's Sochi ordeal made her a household name way beyond Lizzy and the rest of the medallists combined.

Her experience was a harrowing one. Our Olympic journeys had run in parallel. We were the same age; like me, she had struggled at school; Vancouver was our first Games, where there was curiosity rather than expectation surrounding us; we won European and world medals over the next four years; and we arrived in Russia as athletes who now needed to deliver on their promise. With every disqualification in her short-track speed-skating events you felt more and more sorry for her. We all did in the GB camp. The mood change was palpable. The jeopardy of things going wrong in that sport is so high, unbearably high, but the same athlete crashing out on three occasions and then having to deal with the fallout, which included death threats, was heartbreaking to watch from within our team bubble. I had seen Elise around the village before her competitions started and had spoken for a bit longer with her mum. Scots always seem to find each other. I really don't know what I would have said if I had bumped into either of them after her last race.

One thing I did have to get sorted in my mind was what I would say about Scottish independence. Walking this tightrope would be much trickier than giving my thoughts on any of the pre-Olympics hot topics. We were only a few months away from the referendum and it was filtering into everybody's lives in Scotland. Anytime I was out in Canada, loads of people wanted to talk about it. From very early on, I took a straight bat to the subject. Feelers were put out from both sides, as I'm sure happened with anybody who was Scottish and semi-famous, but there was no way I was going to nail my colours to a mast. It sounds like a convenient get-out, but politics has never interested me. If I was going to get involved, it would have to be for a cause I was passionate about and was properly educated on. For Scottish independence, I was neither.

That didn't stop my post-bronze comments being spun. Apparently, because I had said that getting the chance to represent Britain once every four years was 'extra special' meant that I had 'sent a curved stone into the house of Alex Salmond', according to one newspaper. It was nothing of the sort. I would never take representing Scotland at Europeans and worlds for granted. But the Olympics is on another level, it's once every four years and yes, there is pride in being part of Team GB as well. Like a child caught in the middle of parents getting divorced, it's OK to love both. I had a mortgage, payments on a car and other bills to worry about. I was funded by UK Sport and part of a British Curling programme, so there was an inevitable question mark over the impact on my career if Scotland voted to go it alone. It was in the back of my mind that the future would be uncertain if the country voted yes, but that was the same for every Scottish Olympian or aspiring Scottish Olympian.

I was in Sweden when polling day arrived and content that I had kept out of the whole thing the best that I could.

TWENTY-SIX

HIDDEN HEALTH SCARE

There was a big change in my life that the public wouldn't have picked up on. The difference in the pictures of me when I returned home from Riga with my world gold compared to the ones when I came home with my bronze from Sochi was stark. People would have assumed it was a result of all the gym work I had been putting in. It was a factor but there was far more to it than that.

With all the layers we wear on the ice and when we're out and about at an Olympics – even one as mild as Sochi – it probably wasn't as noticeable on my body. But in my face, you could see the contrast. I had lost far too much weight. In the build-up to the Olympics, it came down to about 53 kilos, which is just over eight stone. For somebody 5ft 6in tall, that isn't healthy. I was 20 kilos lighter than I should have been. My appetite had plummeted, I was feeling painfully bloated, I was fatigued, I was suffering an upset stomach, and I wasn't sleeping well.

It was a real concern and people close to me were worried.

The stabbing sensation I would get in my lower stomach

after eating certain foods was incredibly intense. And having to take toilet breaks during games was far from ideal. Being part of an elite athlete programme, surrounded by specialists, helped quicken the process of diagnosing what was wrong with me. My strength and conditioning routines were closely monitored so it was obvious that I wasn't overdoing those. All manner of tests were conducted and within months of me starting to feel something wasn't right, I had been diagnosed. I had coeliac disease, an autoimmune condition.

I would now have to cut gluten out of my diet, which meant no more pasta, bread, cereals, cakes, biscuits and certain types of sauces. Up until that point I couldn't have told you what gluten was, let alone the foods it was found in. It took a while for it to be cleansed out of my system and for my energy levels to return to where they needed to be. That didn't happen until after Sochi. I never missed a training session before the Games – in the gym or on the ice – so it's impossible to quantify how much of an adverse impact, if any, the pre- and post-diagnosis spell had on my performance in Russia. All I can say for certain is – I couldn't have done any more, nor could the support team around me. Anything else is guesswork.

There were a few hiccups on the road to being completely gluten-free. Everybody who has coeliac disease will be able to relate to this. After a few drinks at the end of one tournament not long after my diagnosis, the pizzas looked too appealing to turn down. 'What would be the harm in eating a couple of bits?' I found out the hard way that the answer was 'quite a lot'. Once you have removed gluten from your body, it becomes much more sensitive to any that you do eat. The pain the next morning and the feeling that I was going to faint made sure that the temptation of a couple of slices of Margherita never got the better of me again.

The reason Vicki and I left the Team GB party and nearly

scared the life out of that poor Norwegian skier on his buggy was because the only choice to soak up the drink was pizza, pizza and more pizza. Having one of my team-mates and best friends as another gluten-intolerant curler was a big help for me. Vicki helped guide me through menus. When there were restaurants in Canada that had nothing apart from a bland salad that we could eat, at least we had each other to share the despair.

Once I was back to a healthy weight, my Team GB Sochi kit was redundant. It would be a struggle to get a T-shirt over my shoulders or pull a trouser leg on. And picking up a 20-kilo plate in the gym, which was roughly the amount of weight I had lost, was a regular reminder of how bad things had got.

There was a photoshoot I did in the wake of Sochi that was a different type of reminder – namely, that I should know when to politely decline.

Being more of a tomboy when I was growing up, there was never a burning desire to be a model. However, there has always been a girly girl side to me as well, which meant I enjoyed being pampered, having my picture taken by photographers from time to time or even doing a bit of catwalk modelling. Dress to Kilt was great fun once I had conquered my fear of falling flat on my face in front of James Bond. In 2011, Brad Askew did a brilliant job with the photos he took of me at Blair Castle for a curling calendar and I was happy with other charity photos taken in the gym or out on the farm. My take on these things was – I couldn't wait to get the make-up off once the cameras were put away, but it was usually fun at the time.

Golf Punk magazine asked me to do a photoshoot in St Andrews after the curling season had finished. The pictures were taken at the Hamilton Grand, an iconic old building, overlooking the most famous green in golf, the 18th at the Old Course. Unfortunately, my experience didn't match up to the surroundings. I hated the whole day and hated the pictures.

They were so not me – how I would want to come across or how I would want to be seen at the Home of Golf.

I was so far out of my comfort zone.

It's very hard to speak up when you're on your own and there's a stylist, a make-up artist, a photographer, a writer and somebody making sure the lighting is right all there for this one job. At that time in my life, in my early twenties, if the photographer had said: 'Walk into the sea, Eve, it'll be a great pic,' I would probably have done it. I had been naïve to agree to this, but I didn't feel strong enough to back out. My management team spelt it out to me afterwards that I needed to be better at saying: 'Thanks, but no thanks.' The Old Course is still one of my favourite places in the world – I've been lucky to play a round there, work for the BBC at the 150th Open Championship and enjoy hospitality at the Women's British Open. Standing on the roof of luxury apartments in high heels, wearing a leather waistcoat and pretending to hit a drive, or leaning up against the famous green fencing at the back of the 18th won't feature in my favourite memories, funnily enough.

It would be the first and last time I was a *Golf Punk* Swingin' Siren.

TWENTY-SEVEN

FIRST ONE TO LEAVE

Not many teams survive an Olympics intact. If you win the whole thing, there's a strong chance at least one of the four will think that life can't get any better and this is the perfect time to bow out. If your expectations exceed what you have just achieved, there is the temptation to tinker and see if fresh blood might be the missing ingredient. If you are somewhere in between, as we were, both scenarios are open.

Although, with a bit of reflection, I realised that the team had probably peaked when we won the worlds and then our first Grand Slam, but I wouldn't have pushed to break us up. However, Claire made her own mind up that she wanted out. At that point, we didn't know if it was out, out – as in quitting curling – or if it was just out of our team. She was the eldest of the quartet, had trained as a pharmacist and wanted to see what the big, wide world had to offer. Part of me envied the fact she had a back-up career. I wished I had one. I think it helps with your perspective on sport and, with none of us earning fortunes, it would have been nice to know there was a Plan B as a safety net. There was no bust-up or acrimony with Claire. It wasn't a great shock nor was it a slap in the face. After she told us over dinner one night at the Players' Championship, I didn't try to change her mind. Deep down, I realised this team had run its course.

Olympians are wired to think in four-year chunks. If you're not fully committed to another block, then the best time to get out is at the very start. A National Curling Academy was being built in Stirling and, even before then, we needed to be there for the vast majority of our practice. Claire hadn't moved through from Glasgow and the days of being able to do most of her on-ice work in her home city were gone. She was faced with three options – a five-day commute, a house move, or a new career. She chose the third. Anna, Vicki and I were all still tight, still singing from the same hymn sheet and still motivated. We were proud of our achievements thus far but hungry for more. Dave was the same. He was 100 per cent committed from the moment he signed up and nothing had changed. I don't think we even had a conversation. I just knew.

There was another decision taken that we had no control over. Rhona left the programme.

I had a lot of time for Rhona. She was always totally professional in her role as head coach and had an aura that only world champions and Olympic champions have. On top of that, she knew when to switch off and have a laugh. Rhona was part of a different curling era, but she was certainly no dinosaur. She knew the game inside out. Her opposition analysis was spot on. She was a crucial part of our team and our success. And she had been a permanent fixture on the Scottish curling scene for as long as I could remember. Both Dad and Dave liked and respected Rhona. They weren't ego-driven, any of them. They all wanted the best for us, not themselves. That was their cornerstone as head and team coaches.

Rhona's replacement was Tony Zummack. I didn't know much about Tony beyond the fact he was Canadian and had coached the British wheelchair team. He had a lot of different ideas about the technical side of curling – some I agreed with, some I didn't. Tony's big thing was keeping your weight on your driving leg as you slid out of the hack, which was the opposite to other coaches I had worked with. He had this drill with eight stones tied together to build up strength in your driving position. The theory was that if you were training with weight eight times heavier than you would be throwing in a game, you would have more power and control when it mattered. I understood the theory, and went with it, but you click with some coaches more than others; that's one of the realities of a long sporting career.

I clicked with Sören Grahn.

He was one of the best coaches I never officially had. Sören, who had been a good player but not an outstanding one, was a career coach. I first encountered him when he was with the Swedish men's team at Vancouver, and I was very jealous of the work he then went on to do with Dave Murdoch as part of the British programme. I would catch myself looking across the ice and listening to what he was doing with the guys. I subtly tested the water about getting Sören more involved with us, but I quickly realised that idea wasn't a goer. Dave Hay wouldn't have minded at all – he wasn't territorial and knew the benefits of tapping into expertise from different areas. But the big bosses wouldn't have liked it. Noses would have been put out of joint.

So, I had to make things happen on the quiet. I would never have had the courage to do that in the build-up to Vancouver. There were a few days when I would sneak on to the ice with Sören at The Peak first thing in the morning before the rest of the curlers arrived. It would be a case of: 'Any chance you can come and have a look at this for half an hour?' There was nobody better on the technical side of the sport. Sören was totally in synch with my game and what I wanted to tweak. Stroke placement, alignment, body position, weight transfer – a curling coach can break down the delivery of a stone into as many components as a golf coach does with a ball being hit. Sören had my total trust.

If it wasn't a seven in the morning shift on the ice, we would play rounds of golf together and talk curling. Some of his big fundamentals stayed with me for the rest of my career. For example, I always tried to keep the stone tight to me but get my body as wide as possible so I would get crossover stability. A guy who worked with me fewer than 10 times had such a profound effect. That is the definition of good coaching.

TWENTY-EIGHT

THE LAST PORTION OF MEATBALLS

For the 2014 European Championships, we had a new team member, one I knew well. Sarah Reid was our lead.

The three of us, and Dave, had talked about all the potential replacements for Claire. A few names were mentioned but there was a basic problem – there wasn't another ready-made player out there who was as good as Claire in her position. Not a Scottish one, anyway. Claire was among the best in the world at what she did and her numbers in Sochi backed that up. So, rather than head-hunting someone who played first stones to a standard we didn't think was high enough, we decided to bring someone in who we hoped could transition into a lead. Sarah was the unanimous choice. I had played under her in the juniors and now it was going to be the other way around. Sarah was a trained nurse by that stage, but we knew she would give this shot at becoming a full-time athlete her all. British Curling could see our logic and backed us.

There was a new performance director as well, Graeme Thompson. Graeme had a rugby league background, had played for Scotland in that sport and been an administrator. For tournaments like the Europeans, the number of seats at the dinner table in the evenings was getting close to double figures, a far cry from when I had started out. One night before the championships started, the waitress handed the menus out and said: 'Just to let you know, we've only got two portions of the meatballs left.' One of the people at the table piped up, quick as a flash: 'I'll have one of them.' Dave came back just as swiftly. 'No, the athletes get first choice.' He was right, of course. I loved that about Dave. He would do anything for you. The size and make-up of the support team didn't matter, the curlers did. Mind you, it was a bit of a tumbleweed moment and I'm not sure who got the meatballs!

That awkward incident aside, it was all going relatively well over the first couple of days. The draw was quite kind, giving us the opportunity to pick up a couple of early wins over nations we would expect to beat every time, Latvia and the Czech Republic, while losing to Denmark was balanced out by getting the better of Switzerland. But we then suffered a couple of defeats that put us on the back foot for different reasons.

Losing 8-2 to Anna Sidorova wasn't good. We offered handshakes with four ends left to play. But losing by any scoreline to Estonia is a result on another level, the type that shakes your confidence and really catches people's attention. There were similarities to our fateful defeat to Denmark in the last game of the Olympics round robin. We were three ahead again going into the final end, and I had to accept the blame because I made a mess of my last stone. I wasn't much better in the extra end. It was the first time Estonia had competed in the European Championships, and I was the first skip to lose to them.

We (me, in particular) needed to step it up and we did. Frustration and a bit of anger was channelled in the right way, and we were 7-0 up on Germany after just three ends before going on to beat them 10-2. If ever there was a case of it being a good thing to play two games in one day, this was it. I wouldn't have enjoyed facing the media if the Estonia result was the only topic of conversation. It did get a mention, naturally, but I had a positive 'kick up the backside we needed' spin to put on it.

Next, we narrowly beat Sweden. It was a crucial win in the context of that tournament because without it we wouldn't have made the play-offs. But, widening the focus, it turned out to be the first game of a rivalry that would dominate the rest of my career. Margaretha Sigfridsson had taken some time away from the sport after Sochi and Anna Hasselborg was selected in her place. We had faced each other a couple of times in the juniors. I wouldn't say Anna's talent stood out from other curlers back then, but her mentality did. She had a temper and loved a brush slam, but you knew that she would mature into a curler able to control her emotions without losing a ferocious desire to win. They were knocked out after the round robin, but you still saw them in the arena after that, watching and learning. That wasn't as common as it should be and marked Anna and her team-mates out as ones to be wary of.

For that competition, we didn't deserve to be in the final. We were far too inconsistent over the course of the week and were well beaten by Denmark in the semi. That we were able to pick ourselves up to gain revenge in the bronze medal play-off encapsulated how yo-yo the whole week had been. Over the last couple of years, that really wasn't like us.

I was pleased that we had kept our run of medalling at the Europeans going. That was four in a row. But I was even more pleased that Sarah had her first one. We all played well in that game, but Sarah's numbers were outstanding – just 3 per cent short of perfection. People would have been looking for a reason a medal-winning machine had suddenly returned home without one and they would have put two and two together to get five because Sarah was the new team member.

The Europeans were sandwiched by a couple of big wins in Canada.

First was the Colonial Square Ladies Classic in Saskatoon. They told us the wind chill temperature was minus 23 degrees. Curlers are used to being cold, but this was something else. We were going on to the ice to heat up! Winning all six games, the last one a final against Sherry Middaugh, who was a local to that part of the country and had all the support, made the conditions a bit more bearable. We didn't manage perfection at the Canadian Open in Saskatchewan but winning our third career Grand Slam was even more satisfying. Rachel Homan was the opponent in the final and it was a typically tight contest between the two of us. I had a tricky shot that needed to curl quite a bit to win it. A win is a win, and you would always rather have it easy as a skip, but it's a bit sweeter if you do produce a high-quality shot to seal a big victory.

Back-to-back triumphs over Jennifer Jones – the last qualifying game and then the quarter-final – had made this tournament one to remember. Not many curlers can claim that accolade, particularly in the year she demolished the field at the Olympics. I thought about Granny after those wins. In fact, I always thought about Granny when I beat Jennifer. She was my biggest fan. There were nine grandchildren, two of whom, my cousins Sophie and William, did very well in the sailing world, but there would always be newspaper cuttings of me everywhere when we went down to Netley Abbey. It certainly didn't escape Glen and Thomas's attention! Granny was a disciple spreading the curling gospel around a small corner of the south coast of England. I had surprised her and Grandad by popping in with my Sochi bronze medal after I had been in London to film *Question of Sport*. She was obviously over the moon about my achievement but threw in a caveat as only she could.

'Oh, but that Jennifer Jones is very good, isn't she?'

'Thanks, Granny. I know she is.'

So, yes, being able to phone Granny, wish her Merry Christmas and tell her that I had beaten Jennifer Jones twice in a row was something to look forward to when I got home.

TWENTY-NINE

BROOKS KOEPKA AND BROOMGATE

We didn't lack motivation to become Scottish champions in February 2015.

A decision had been made the year before that the Olympic teams wouldn't get the chance to compete in either the nationals or the worlds. Not only did that mean we couldn't go for five Scottish titles in a row, it also denied us of the opportunity to defend our world crown. Even though I could see both sides of the argument, that hurt. Particularly the second bit. So, we wanted to be officially the best in the country again and we wanted to be back at the World Championships.

I had a feeling this was going to be our toughest one to win in a few years. There were six teams competing in a double round-robin format and we lost a game to Gina Aitken's rink quite early. It didn't surprise me that it was Hannah Fleming who got through to the final, though. And the law of averages factor was a nagging doubt after we had beaten them three times. Hannah's team produced their best form in the final, but we made a big jump in the eighth end and seized our title back thanks to a 6-5 win. The only slight disappointment was the BBC putting their highlights out at twenty past midnight. Almost a year to the day that we had won bronze in Sochi, it showed that the dial hadn't moved as far as the exposure of our sport outside the Olympics was concerned.

Unfortunately, when it came to the worlds in Japan, motivation didn't equate to achievement this time. It just didn't happen for us. There were a few high points over the course of the week – notably, beating Russia, Sweden and then China in the tiebreaker to get to the play-offs. But our good play never felt sustainable.

Losing 13-4 to Anna Sidorova in the bronze medal match left us no room for feeling we were unlucky.

If there was a flaw in my game at that stage of my career, it was being too aggressive too quickly. This was another example of it. We went overly hard in the first end, kept a lot of stones in play and it was a strategy that effectively finished the match there and then. I had never conceded five at that stage of a medal match before. It would never happen again. The opening end is not the time to be that bold. You need to have a surer grasp of how the ice is playing. Statistics don't tell you everything in sport and curling is no different. But finishing the Sapporo tournament with low numbers across the board as a team painted an accurate picture on this occasion.

The positive to take was that we fought our way to the play-offs despite that poor form so there was no big inquest. And those battling qualities saw us end the season with a flourish. Naturally, it was in Toronto, my curling home from home. Holding off a Rachel Homan comeback in the semi-final of the Players', then holding our nerve in a low-scoring affair to edge out Anna Sidorova in the final, showed that although we had lost consistency, our good spells were still a match for anyone. To make it an even more satisfying season's end, we had one last tournament in St Gallen, Switzerland where we beat the home team and new world champions for another title.

A first season after an Olympics is notoriously unpredictable. We had come through it with a new team-mate and some tournament wins, underpinned by a collective determination that Olympic bronze shouldn't be the height of our ambitions.

Unfortunately, after the curling shoes were put away for a couple of months, I discovered that my golf game was a bit unpredictable as well. Of all the competition pro-ams I was invited to play in, Wentworth's PGA Championship brought on the biggest nerves. Dad was on the bag and the draw had been kind (or unkind, depending on your perspective) by partnering me with Brooks Koepka. I had played with Jonas Blixt the year before but, even though he was yet to win a major in 2015, Brooks had a much bigger profile in the sport and hundreds of spectators wanted to see this emerging American player showcase his incredible power off the tee.

They certainly weren't lining the fairways to check out my golf game.

Despite Dad moaning that he was doing more sweeping in the bunkers after I had been in them than he would in a game of curling, I thought I played pretty well considering the size of the galleries and the fact I had barely finished the curling season. But I hit a spectator hard on the wrist with a drive I blocked on the dog-leg 17th. I did shout 'fore', but I felt dreadful about it, nonetheless. There was nothing that I could say or do to make the poor woman feel better, but Brooks came to the rescue by giving her a signed glove. Brooks and his Irish caddie, Ricky Elliott, were brilliant company for Dad and me. Brooks seemed to have a genuine interest in curling. I found out that wasn't just polite fairway chat when I got a WhatsApp message from him a couple of years later as he sat and watched us playing against an American team.

'Focused. Love it,' it said, alongside a picture of me with a steely look after delivering a stone out of the hack.

Whether it was playing in pro-ams with the likes of Brooks, Victor Perez and Brooke Henderson, sharing the fairways with Phil Mickelson on BBC on-course commentary duty as he won the Scottish Open, watching Andy Murray drag Britain to Davis Cup glory in front of an adoring Glasgow crowd, or even being part of the biggest party in the world at the Ally Pally darts extravaganza, the common denominator that links every sport at the highest level is that word 'focused' Brooks used. It's what all athletes strive for and when you witness it close up, it leaves a mark.

Dad got Wentworth and Mum got to join us in Paris. A great summer of sport took us to Roland Garros and the final of the French Open. We were gutted that Andy Murray was knocked out in the semi-final, but we saw a real underdog story play out after Stan Wawrinka was able to overcome the odds and the loss of the first set to beat Novak Djokovic. For once, the great Djokovic lost his focus.

Back on Perthshire turf, I followed in esteemed footsteps when I was chosen to be the chieftain at the Crieff Highland Games. My fellow (and somewhat more distinguished) former Morrison's Academy student, Ewan McGregor, had performed the role back in 2001 – and enjoyed the hospitality, I was told! I certainly didn't make a schoolgirl error of driving there. We got a taxi back to Blair Atholl after a great day, where my old school friend, Lorne, was tossing the caber with the rest of the heavyweights. I didn't bring my pipes, so there was no temptation to roll back the years and make a late entry into the Piobaireachd competition.

Fine margins get talked about a lot in sport, particularly in curling, which can often become a game of millimetres. My first big final of the new season, the European Championships in Esbjerg, Denmark, gave me a bitter reminder of just that. We had secured our spot with one of our best-ever comebacks – 5-0 down after three ends to Oona Kauste's Finnish rink, turned around into a 9-7 win. It was a knife-edge gold medal contest against Anna Sidorova. They were 4-3 up after we blanked the seventh end, and I sensed my opportunity in the eighth. A double takeout was on and, if I had pulled it off, would almost certainly have won us the game. It missed the target by the smallest of margins, however, meaning a steal for them and a one-point defeat. The normally stoic Anna couldn't keep her emotions in check this time, which was fair enough, even if kissing the ice in the middle of the house was a bit out of character and over the top.

We were back on the podium but, again, not at the top of it, where we wanted to be.

That season wasn't a vintage one by any stretch of the imagination. But we still ended up third in the world rankings, which shows how high our standards were. Yet again, we delivered in Toronto, completing a hat-trick of Players' Championship titles. And there was real adversity to overcome on this occasion. Anna had fallen at her home in Lockerbie and was diagnosed with a torn ACL that would need surgery, ruling her out for the last few weeks of this season and the next few months of the following one. We had next to no time to get someone in for a new event in the calendar, the Perth City Ladies Championship, which had attracted a strong international field.

After Dave and I had had a chat about who would be available, we got in touch with Mairi Milne. Mairi had a couple of world silvers on her CV, but they weren't recent, that's for sure. The first of the two was won in the year I was born! But, despite the fact she was getting close to seniors' curling age, Mairi was great that week and played her part in a tournament win on home ice, beating Switzerland's Team Tirinzoni in the final.

Then, for Toronto, we were on the hunt for another gun for hire. This was an easy choice. Cathy Overton-Clapham had the nickname Super Spare in the Canadian media. Since her acrimonious split with Jennifer in the pre-Sochi cycle, Cathy had stayed at the top of the sport and played a key role with a few teams. She had won three Players' titles with Jennifer and the 2014 Masters, filling in on Val Sweeting's team. Cathy and I gelled very well together. Chatting to the greats of the game off the ice is one thing but having the opportunity to pick up little nuggets when you are in the same team is priceless. Cathy still didn't talk to Jennifer, all these years after they parted ways, and nobody was more motivated than her when it came to winning this final.

I made a big shot in the first end, drawing to the button for one when they were sitting with four counting stones and a couple of guards at the front of the house. My weight was spot on throughout, and I produced another draw for three in the sixth. To win a Slam in those circumstances made it one of the most satisfying achievements of my career.

There were some special family memories that season as well.

Thomas, who had graduated with his farming qualifications in the summer, was starting to make his mark in the men's game. He was part of Kyle Smith's rink that played in the Europeans in Denmark, and we were also on a couple of trips to Canada at the same time.

There was a Muirhead World Championships family hat-trick in 2016. We retained our Scottish title, Glen played third in Tom Brewster's team that won the men's and Dad finished first in the seniors. Three national champions coming from one family was something to be proud of.

We were up first. Sadly, for the curling community, the 2016 World Championships will be remembered as a dark time for our sport. Broomgate had become a thing and had the potential to wreck curling.

The scandal fostered bitterness and suspicion and jeopardised friendships. It had been building since the end of the previous season. There was talk that one of the manufacturers of the broom heads had come up with a development that would transform the game. And not in a good way. Sweeping had always been a crucial part of curling, but it was about making a stone travel further and curl less. These new brooms were flipping that long-established principle on its head and enabling a totally different form of sweeping – namely, scratching the ice and altering a stone's direction. The governing body hadn't seen this coming and, despite the fact that top players on the traditionalist side of the debate had tried to force gentlemen's agreements to ensure the art of shot-making wouldn't be eroded, our World Championships in Swift Current got under way with it being a brush free-for-all.

Would it be a curling winner or a carving winner?

Up until that point, we had competed at every tournament with our normal brooms. British Curling hadn't been testing with different fabrics. There was a game against Japan when it dawned on us all that, to paraphrase one of Sean Connery's great lines in *The Untouchables*, we had brought a knife to a gunfight. In the first end we had built what would have been a strong situation in the old world, with one stone behind a second guard, a foot and a half from the rings. It was an ideal set-up for a steal. Satsuki Fujisawa came round this guard and her sweepers moved the stone so hard, virtually sideways, that it nosed my stone.

I had never seen anything like it.

We were all looking at each other thinking: 'How on earth is that even possible?' It was defying curling physics. The brushes, or hard inserts in the brushes, used by certain teams had created a new game-defining technique – directional sweeping. The ice was getting chewed up. Tracks were being dug. It was a totally different sport. Technically, no rules were broken, and you could tell that some of the curlers had been working on the angles and mechanics of it all since the summer. A 10-4 defeat to Japan and then a loss in our final game to Canada's Chelsea Carey saw us miss out on the medal play-offs. I thought we did well to win seven games in the round robin, given the circumstances. Nobody missed a shot in the final between Switzerland and Japan – but for all the wrong reasons. It was a horrible atmosphere in Swift Current that week and it wasn't any better in Switzerland a couple of weeks later for the men.

You couldn't find a curler more respected for his sportsmanship than Norwegian skip, Thomas Ulsrud, who brought attention to the sport with his skill and his colourful harlequin trousers. Thomas spoke for a lot of us when he said: 'We're off to the World Carving Championships.' Thomas was putting his head above the parapet for the good of the game. He knew this was serious. I went out to watch Glen play and in one game when a skip couldn't see any part of the stone he was aiming to move, I heard him shout down the ice: 'It's fine, we can carve it. This is a fresh pad.'

Just hearing that sent a shiver down the spine. It was unashamed.

The World Curling Federation needed to act. Better late than never, they did. The rules regarding what fabrics could be used were tightened up at the end of that season. No swapping of brushes between team members was permitted and you weren't allowed to change a pad during a game. Curling stepped back from the edge of a cliff but there are tournaments and tournament winners from that year who should have asterisks alongside them.

THIRTY

THE IVAN LENDL EFFECT

If I take a step back and reflect on all the personnel changes we made, coaching and playing, it does look like a lot in a short period of time for a team that was dominating domestically, regularly winning championship medals and Grand Slams abroad and never dropping out of the top 10 in the world rankings – rarely out of the top five in fact. The coaching changes, in particular.

We had switched from Dad to Dave, with, for me, a bit of Sören's input on the quiet, and now I had made up my mind that the time was right for another roll of the dice. I felt that Dave, like Dad before him, had taught us as much as he could. The pair were different personalities, with different strengths and weaknesses, but they were both what I would describe as tactical coaches. The technicalities of the game weren't their thing, I had always known that. My mind was open to exploring that aspect of curling. Sören had really opened my horizons in that regard. Perhaps if I had been more receptive to Tony Zummack's ideas, this yearning wouldn't have developed. But, on many fundamental aspects of the nuts and bolts of throwing a stone, Tony and I weren't on the same page.

I wanted to meet Dave in person. I was absolutely dreading it – more so than my conversation with Dad even. Dave had done so much for us, and I knew that his desire to see this story end with gold medals in PyeongChang in 2018 was as all-consuming as mine. But it was part of my job as skip and captain to come to these decisions and then see them through in the right manner. Vicki and I drove through to a hotel in Perth. It instantly became apparent that Dave had no idea of the type of awkward conversation we were about to have. We sat down with our coffees and, before I had the chance to say anything, Dave produced his proposal for the next season's itinerary, making a few tweaks and showing us which foreign trips he would be able to commit to. This was getting even tougher, and I hadn't opened my mouth yet. I cut Dave short and cut to the chase. After I had explained my reasoning, he totally understood. There were no hard feelings nor lost friendships, which meant a lot to me.

It was every bit as difficult telling Sarah that her race with us was over. I had Vicki and Anna for moral support on this trip to the Hamilton motorway services. I picked Anna up because she was still recovering from her ACL surgery and couldn't drive. It might seem brutal but the three of us had talked things through and had arrived at the conclusion that we needed a new lead. With Anna still a few months away from returning – and none of us knowing whether it would be a smooth comeback or one with bumps in the road – the easiest thing to do would have been to give Sarah another season to limit the scale of the change. New coach, new lead and a stand-in third is a lot in one go. But we were less than two years away from the next Olympics and, even if there was going to be some short-term pain, this couldn't be put off. Plus, it wouldn't have been fair on Sarah now that we had made our minds up.

Sarah didn't do a Dave and open up with a preamble about team-building camps and trips to Switzerland. I did all the talking. I can only imagine how horrible that experience was for her. This was the end of her Olympic dream. She would have been hurt and angry, probably in equal measure. There was no way of sugaring this pill, however. Again, I just had to be honest. Sarah is a good person, a good friend and was a good team-mate, but the numbers were black and white. Anybody who would be qualified to provide input, I spoke to, because I wanted to be 100 per cent sure we weren't getting this wrong.

But we weren't.

I was upset as well. However, I was now capable of making hard decisions. I wouldn't have had the strength to see those two big changes through a few years ago.

Those types of judgements aren't usually made by team captains in other sports. They are made by coaches and managers. Football captains don't sack people. And it wasn't as if I had been on a course to learn this sort of stuff. But living with a 'what if' was far less palatable than being decisive, whether letting Sarah and Dave go turned out well or not. Having gone through all this, we had to get it right in picking their replacements. Sören was out of reach. He had a job with the Russian men's team. And there was nobody in Scotland who appealed. I was fixed on the idea of working with a coach who hadn't been in our system.

There was one name at the top of my wish list. Glenn Howard. Glenn is a true curling great. He had won four World Championship golds – in four different decades. Nobody in the sport comes close to that sort of longevity at the very top. A shot he played at the Canadian nationals in 2009 is regarded as one of the best of all time, defying angles and logic when he needed two with his last stone. His last world title was in 2012, and he was still a highly competitive curler so I wasn't sure if he would be ready to coach. But if you don't ask, you don't get. It was a bit of a shock to him when I planted the seed, and I was pleasantly surprised that he said he would have a good think about it. Once that thinking turned into an agreement between the two of us, I left it to British Curling to handle the negotiations.

I did fear the worst given he was such a big figure in our sport, and he wouldn't be able to commit full-time, however, to my delight, a deal was struck.

Our first training session with Glenn was that summer. We managed to get ice at the Green Hotel in Kinross and it was the one and only time my arm was shaking with nerves as I threw a practice stone down the ice. Here was Glenn Howard, one of the best of all time, holding his brush in the house for me to aim at. It was surreal. That night, we had a big meeting with all the support staff. Strength and conditioning coach, psychologist, lifestyle adviser, video analyst, head coach – it was a cast of thousands. There must have been about 15 people round the table. Glenn whispered to me: 'How can you work with this many people?' It was so different from what he was used to in Canada. For Glenn, less is more.

The plan was for him to be at all our big events – Scottish, Europeans, worlds, Grand Slams and a few other competitions in Canada. When he wasn't with us in person, he would get access to all the game and practice footage, and we would debrief and discuss technical stuff on Skype or FaceTime. This was the time when Andy Murray's game had been taken to its Wimbledon and US Open-winning peak by Ivan Lendl. I was hoping for my own Lendl effect and had someone with that type of aura in my corner. Glenn knew my game inside out already and I knew he was right with his fundamental opinion. He wanted to curb my aggression, to get me to pick my front-foot moments more judiciously.

I knew there would be times when Glenn, a typically social and laid-back Canadian, would sleep in and maybe miss the start of an odd game because he had been catching up with friends in the bar the night before. I also knew there would be even more times when he would despair at the overkill of us practising twice a day, five times a week compared to a routine of meeting up once a month with team-mates who lived a four-hour drive from each other that had served him so well – and continued to serve him well.

But we would be a point ahead of our opponents merely by having him in our corner. Aura combined with one of the sharpest minds in curling made me confident we had found ourselves the full coaching package.

THIRTY-ONE

BLAST FROM THE PAST

We only had half a team after letting Sarah go. A new lead and a quality stand-in for Anna, who was targeting a couple of events before the European Championships for her comeback, were urgently required.

We took the risk of choosing a skip again. We had gone down that road before with Sarah, trying to convert a player used to shot-making and leading into a player with more restricted duties, laying foundations for the end and sweeping. The technical and mental adjustment is one thing. But the physical aspect of a huge increase in the amount of sweeping a front-end position entails is just as significant. I also still had Vancouver in my mind and the potential pitfalls of a team with too many players who had been brought up as skips. The harsh truth was, though, there really weren't many other serious candidates out there in Scottish curling. That's when you see the advantages Canada have over us. Their strength in depth is the envy of the rest of the world. Jennifer Jones swapping Cathy Overton-Clapham for Kaitlyn Lawes – one world-class curler for another – was a case in point. In Scotland, we were victims of our own dominance. We had opened such a big gap to the rest of the teams that it was becoming harder and harder for anybody we cherry-picked to make the jump. There's no hiding place.

Lauren was worth the gamble because she was a very good curler, and she had the confidence in her own ability that was an absolute must for joining our team.

We had been spoiled at the conclusion to the previous season by the standard of short-term replacements for Anna we managed to find. Mairi and Cathy got to be part of trophy wins and it was no reflection on Swiss curler Nadine Lehmann that the best we managed was a quarter-final in the two competitions she played. So, it was a high bar. And we went back to the future. Kelly Wood (now Kelly Schafer, happily married to the mayor and mum to son, Darby) wanted to dip her toe back in the competitive curling waters and our situation suited her perfectly.

Kelly and I had stayed in touch, and she had kept her hand in by playing club games. The fact she wasn't a Canadian citizen put a ceiling to her ambitions over there. Kelly was 27 when we won our world silver in Swift Current and she had her sliding doors moment in life, meeting Jerrod. I was now 26. Mid to late twenties and then early thirties is when you should be hitting your best curling years in the modern-day game. I'm sure Kelly had no regrets about how the last six years had gone – her career had effectively ended – but we were different people. To make it black and white – there was no way I would have allowed myself to put a partner before my curling. That was a conscious decision. A contract with myself, if you like. Post-Vancouver, I had a deep appreciation of the dedication, sacrifice and selfishness I would need to get to where I aspired to be, which was the very top of my sport. I was completely devoted to curling and that's the way I chose it to be. I didn't want anything, or anyone, to divert me from this journey.

It was tunnel vision.

These are the sorts of big life decisions you need to make or, at least, I felt I needed to make.

Yes, curlers can enjoy longer careers than athletes in some other sports, but I knew I had a window to operate at the very top. The more physically demanding the sport was becoming, the smaller that window.

Nobody knows the answer to hypothetical situations. Would I have carved out a career in golf if I had accepted one of the American university offers, for example? Would we have won gold in Sochi if we had seen out that game against Denmark? Would we have defended our world title if we had been allowed to take our place at the start line? Could I have squeezed every last drop out of my career and sustained a long-term relationship like other curlers have managed to?

The last of those is such a personal but fundamental decision when you are an elite athlete, particularly a female one, and, for me, the answer was a hard 'no'.

I knew how I felt, and I embraced the focus and drive that was within me. I was happy with the job I was doing, the family I had around me and my tight friendship group. Of course, there was the odd on-off relationship. But you have to be open to the concept of a change in work–life priorities, and I just wasn't. You do become self-centred in my circumstances. I was consumed by my sport. It's not the most rounded life. It was monotonous, routine-driven and dull in a lot of ways. But there was nobody in curling who I looked at and thought: 'You've got this cracked better than me.' Nobody I looked at and thought: 'I'd love to swap places with you.'

So, Kelly's return to the Scottish curling scene didn't fill me with pangs of regret and envy. I was all-in when we took different forks in the road, and I was still all-in now.

Ironically, I had only just sold the flat I bought off Kelly. A house with a garden and patio doors were all I had on my wish list. Thankfully, Mum and Dad were a bit more discerning and sensible on my behalf and talked me out of quite a few 'this is the one' properties. The woman who owned the house I ended up buying made me put those blue bags you wear to view show homes on my feet. For someone like me, who is afflicted by a bit of OCD, this was a very good sign. The OCDs aren't so bad that I'm on edge if I see cushions not lined up at the same angle. I don't have to fight an urge to make sure crisps packets are colour-coordinated in a cupboard. But it does go a bit beyond not being able to live with clutter or mess. I was brought up on a farm so I can't say this was inherited. Go round to Thomas's and Glen's and you'll find the lid off the butter, milk sitting out and no clean mugs.

I genuinely wouldn't be surprised if the percentage of elite athletes, and even more so, captains, who are like me is much higher than the rest of the population. Leaders do crave control and can be a bit obsessive – not always for the better.

I watched a documentary about David Beckham, ticking off OCD traits that he admitted to. 'That's me. Yeah, that as well.' Like him, I couldn't sleep at night if there were dirty dishes in the kitchen. In fact, I couldn't eat my dinner if there were other plates needing to be washed. I'm not far off having to hoover once a day and when I leave the house for a trip to Canada, or even just an overnight stay in Scotland, I have a compulsion to make sure the house is spotless. It wouldn't matter what time of day I return at, or how long I've been away for – a weekend at Mum and Dad's or a fortnight at an Olympic Games – I'll unpack there and then. There is no way I could leave it until after I woke up.

It's a small miracle that I managed to survive with a flatmate.

When Greg first moved in, he couldn't even turn the oven on. It was baby steps. Once he figured out how to do that, the next hurdle was realising that he shouldn't be putting a pizza inside it, still in its cardboard box. He once cooked a chicken and the fact that it was still pink in the middle didn't put him off. He just cut round it!

At least he was tidy, though.

THIRTY-TWO

NO PLACE LIKE HOME?

We had always opened our season in Europe before but, now that Glenn and Kelly were on board, it made sense to change things up and head out to Canada.

It was my fault that we didn't start the new chapter with a tournament win. We were 5-1 up on Casey Scheidegger's team in the final of a World Curling Tour event in Edmonton. From being in total control, we let our lead get whittled away end by end, one by one. Even so, I had an open draw to the four-foot with my last shot. The ice was getting softer, and I knew as soon as the stone left my hand that it wasn't getting there. However, having gone unbeaten to that stage, we left feeling good about ourselves and reached another final before returning to Europe. Glenn came with us. Going out early in Stockholm proved to be a blessing in disguise as we put quality practice time to good use by beating Margaretha Sigfridsson in the final of the Women's Masters in Basel, the first Scottish team to lift that trophy.

We were top of the tour money list and ready for the play-downs against Hannah Fleming's team to represent Scotland in the European Championships. So were our opponents, mind you. I expected this to be our toughest Euro qualifier to date. Hannah's team had two future Olympians in their four – Vicky Wright and Jen Dods. They were runners-up in Stockholm, semi-finalists in Basel and were seventh on the money list, ahead of some big names like Rachel Homan. They were talking up their chances. The stakes were even higher than usual because the Euros were on home ice – Braehead, near Glasgow.

We needed to play well, and we did. In a best of five format, we settled things in three, with a day to spare.

Pressure to stay ahead of the pack in Scotland was intense. I felt it more – and was driven by it more – than getting the better of Jennifer Jones, Rachel Homan or whoever was at the top of the sport internationally. Everything flowed from being the number one team in the country – funding, Grand Slam participation and places at the Europeans and worlds. If it started to go wrong domestically, a steady career decline was inevitable. I was proud that week – and most weeks, whether it was a European qualifier or a national championship – of being able to channel that pressure into focus.

Anna was now ready to return and joined us for a couple of tournaments abroad in the build-up to Braehead, while Kelly accepted the reserve's spot. Kelly had brought everything to the group I had hoped – professionalism, high standards and positivity. With Glen having earned his spot as part of Team Brewster, I was more excited about this tournament than I had been in a while. I could remember going to the worlds when they were held at Braehead in 2000. Dad was an alternate for Bob Kelly's team. I was 10 and had started to get into the sport in a big way. That event made a lasting impression, and I came away with a deeper passion for curling as well as plenty of autographs – legendary broadcaster, Dougie Donnelly, among them! Sixteen years later it shocked me how few youngsters came to watch this championship. There would have been more at Dewars when I won my last world juniors. Something had either gone badly wrong with the marketing or the closure of ice rinks and a downturn in curling participation was kicking in. A bit of both, probably.

A game of count the spectators under the age of 50 wouldn't have passed much time.

Even if there were loads of up-and-coming curlers watching on their phones and tablets in the comfort of their homes – which I very much doubt – it's not the same thing. Back in 2000, I was like a sponge, fascinated by the interaction between the players, the body language and the nuances of how a game played out, as much as the shot-making. With my growing the game hat on, it was a bit depressing. Dougie Donnelly wasn't there this time. Even if he had been, there was nobody I could see with the same sort of enthusiasm for curling that I had in me as a 10-year-old, who would have been hunting his autograph.

We got ourselves into a nice routine for the week. Lauren was the local, keeping us right on where to go for dinner at night. It's a slick operation at Braehead, turning the arena around quickly from one sport to another. They didn't manage to erase all the traces of the big darts competition that had taken place before the curlers moved in, though. If you looked up at the rafters, you could still see some of the ticker tape that hadn't found its way on to Michael van Gerwen and his shiny trophy. When a men's game in the round robin got halted because the air blowers that control the temperature blew some down on the ice, the guys playing saw the funny side!

Unfortunately, there was no ticker tape falling on us at the end of the week, literally or metaphorically.

It had all been going so well. Too well. For the first time at a Europeans, worlds or Olympics, I had negotiated a round robin with a 100 per cent record. And out of the nine games there were far more emphatic wins than narrow ones. I had mixed emotions. I was delighted we were in form, but I knew my curling history and how rare it was for teams to have no losses to their name all the way from beginning to end. The organisers had changed the format the year before to straight semi-finals, meaning there wasn't a second chance for the team which finished top of the round robin. If you polled curlers, certainly from the top nations, I'm pretty sure the vast majority would favour the old page play-off system. There should be a greater advantage to being the best team over the course of the round robin stage than just having the hammer in their semi-final.

To lose 11-6 to Russia (Victoria Moiseeva now, not Anna Sidorova) was a tough one to take. We knew we were a better team, but a slack start meant we were chasing the game, and the error count rose. Braehead arena is in the middle of a shopping centre, and this was a two-game day so there wasn't long between the semi and the bronze medal match. We didn't have time to go back to our hotel so, after doing my best not to be rude to all the Christmas shoppers telling me 'bad luck', I found a quiet corner of Starbucks to get myself in a good frame of mind to bounce back.

The semi turned out to be the blip we thought it was, and we beat the Czech Republic convincingly. Russia beat Sweden in the final, which we watched at the hotel, and seemed a bit incredulous about it. Not as incredulous as Anna Hasselborg. She had an out-turn draw to win. It ran too straight, and she caught the edge of a guard. Anna just couldn't comprehend how this stone had dared not to curl. It was like Tiger Woods when a six-foot putt to win a major hadn't taken the break he had read.

It stuck in my mind.

I had already marked Anna down as the likeliest of the other European teams to emerge as a big rival at the big events and this confirmed it. She had built a team around her that shared her curling dedication, talent and temperament and I knew that once her rage had died down, she would leave Glasgow emboldened by another big career step. Out of all the skips on the world scene, Anna was the one who reminded me most of myself – from her mindset to her intensity, the way she led her team-mates and her calmness in the big moments. The Swedish curling succession was in safe hands.

We had set a record of seven medals at successive European Championships. That was a badge of honour in terms of consistency, but I only had one gold and that was an irritation. Improving on that wasn't going to get any easier.

THIRTY-THREE

SUMMONED

Between Braehead and Beijing a decline set in. Not a falling off a cliff decline – we won the Scottish Championships without dropping a game and the Glynhill Ladies International – but we dropped to eighth in the rankings going into the World Championships in China.

The few days before the worlds were fun off the ice. We visited the Great Wall of China and the Forbidden City, and watched a spectacular acrobatics show. But the most important bit, practice, was a shambles. After driving round in circles for ages trying to find the rink that had been chosen, somebody eventually noticed a tiny sign for a curling club. No wonder they didn't want it up in big, bright lights. The place was disgusting. It would be a disservice to old snooker halls back home to compare it to one of those but that was the general theme – run down, poorly lit and in a rough part of the city.

Slumming it for a couple of hours a day would have been OK if the ice was of an acceptable standard. It wasn't. I turned a stone over to clean it and the handle fell off. As I stood at the hack with a handle in my hand and the stone at my feet, the girls were looking up the ice in disbelief. I suppose I was lucky not to break a foot. Curlers don't expect luxury, but this was the worst place I had ever seen by some distance. After an argument about how much we were due to pay, we cut short our practice and cut our losses. With ice that wasn't level and stones falling apart, there wasn't much choice.

The hotel accommodation was fine, the hotel food less so. One of us ordered chicken and it arrived yellow in colour, with the skin and feet still on.

The curling? We had no rhythm, no consistency. We were losing games we should have won and winning games we should have lost.

My state of mind was at the core of our problems.

Three years of striving to be better as an individual curler had brought me to a place of intolerance of any failures in a game, no matter how small. Not only was I seeking perfection in myself, I was demanding it and was intolerant of anything less. It was utterly unrealistic, and it was undermining the team. Every shot had to be inch-perfect. If it wasn't, which was obviously a lot of the time, I was furious and beat myself up. I hadn't noticed the change in me. It had crept up. Young and fearless had been replaced by inhibited and unforgiving. In Beijing, an issue that I hadn't even identified in my game and psyche had come to a head.

Our third contest against Russia captured it perfectly. We had just taken a four in the fourth end to go 8-1 in front. We were cruising. It was effectively game over. They got a couple back. Nothing to unduly worry us, or it shouldn't have been. But I was already getting edgy. Then they got one. And another one. It was now 8-7. I had an open draw to stop the rot – bread and butter stuff. Anywhere in the house would do. The stone ended up in the back of the four-foot, which wasn't a problem. It was like a drive, iron to the middle of the green, two putts, hole won in par in match play golf. Standard stuff. Move on. It was absolutely fine. Even if it had just nibbled the 12-foot and still counted, it would have been absolutely fine.

One of the girls shouted 'good shot' down the ice, but I wasn't having any of it. 'No, it wasn't. It was heavy.' This was me at my pernickety peak.

We won that game (as we were always likely to) and just scraped into the play-offs with a seven and four record. Anna Hasselborg had beaten us in the round robin, and she beat us again in the page play-off. That left us with a bronze medal match – against Anna again, after she was surprisingly beaten heavily by Russia.

Nobody gave us a chance. If we were being honest with ourselves, we and our coaches didn't either. After two full games and eight further ends, we had never been in front of Sweden all week. They looked nicely set for a two or three in the ninth end, but my draw to the back of the four-foot got us a steal. With the hammer in the last end, Anna had a tough angle for her final shot, but it was very makeable, possibly for a two and a win, but definitely a one and an extra end. She feathered the target stone and despite that now familiar look of disbelief as she surveyed the house, we were lying shot.

How we got a bronze at the end of that week, I'll never know. I would put it into my top five career games for that very reason. The odds were never more stacked against us.

Sadly, though, what was to follow would go down in my bottom five life experiences.

The four of us went to a Japanese restaurant next to the hotel after we had been presented with our medals. We even had a glass of champagne. Getting on to the podium at the World Championships should be toasted, however it has happened. It was Lauren's first world medal; Anna and Vicki's second and only my third. For most curlers it would be a career high point. The happiness and sense of accomplishing something worthwhile didn't last long. I got a text message from Glenn Howard, asking me to come to his hotel room. That brought an end to the sushi and the celebrations. I was expecting to read one along the lines of: 'Where are you girls? I'm coming out for a drink.' There were no pleasantries or emojis on this message, though. It was one of those that leaves you in no doubt that there's a serious reason he wants to see you. I also got the impression that the other girls knew more about the subject matter – and what was waiting for me – than I did.

When I walked into Glenn's room, it was a four v one of officials and me. To put it bluntly, they sat me down and went through me. I wasn't leading the team well. I wasn't giving the girls the support they needed. Other members of the team had raised issues with them about me. If we were to have any hope at the Olympics the following year – or even go to the Olympics – things had to change. I had to change. There were probably other themes touched upon, but I was quickly becoming overwhelmed by a wave of criticism. A million and one things were racing through my mind. Which team-mate or team-mates would it have been? When had she or they spoken up? What was said? How long have they been feeling this way?

Glenn was doing most of the talking. He was calm but, knowing him as I do, I can imagine how hard this would have been for him. I did understand that something needed to be said. And something needed to be done. I recognised a lot of the flaws that were highlighted. I hadn't been a good captain that week and I was putting myself under far too much pressure. It's impossible that wouldn't affect the other girls. And, as a team, we had flatlined at best. We were probably going backwards, but we definitely were not progressing, which is a big concern less than a year from the Olympics.

A lot of this stuff needed to be aired.

But there is a time and a place. A hotel room, a couple of hours after we had won a World Championship bronze medal, with four of them and one of me just wasn't the right way to go about this. My guess is that they thought there was no hope for us in the Sweden game and had planned the meeting before it had even started. They had teed it up with the expectation we were going to finish fourth and had then decided a surprise bronze didn't alter the big picture. It was near the end of the season, so this was the obvious opportunity to convene everybody that needed to be in the meeting.

The timing was horrendous and the experience awful.

There was one line delivered that impacted deeper than anything else that was said and would stay with me, no matter how hard I tried to erase it.

'How would you feel if those three girls didn't want to play with you again?'

I was in floods of tears by this point. I wanted the girls to come into the room.

They were a bit less to the point with their choice of words, but they weren't disagreeing with the thrust of the argument. They didn't feel supported; my leadership had disappeared; if things weren't going well, I would take it out on myself and them; there was no fun factor any more; and none of them were enjoying being part of the environment. Somebody tried to end the meeting on a positive, saying this could be the moment we all look back on for the right reasons – a turning point that might change the team for the better, and me as an individual, in particular. It was a message I wasn't ready for.

We still had the end-of-tournament banquet to endure. Unsurprisingly, I didn't stay long.

Who could have predicted that the day I won a world bronze would be the day I was at my lowest ebb as a curler and a person?

I would gladly have thrown the medal off the Great Wall of China.

THIRTY-FOUR

A WOUND THAT HADN'T HEALED

I had lost plenty of games of curling, but I had never felt lost.

This was a horrible kind of new.

I wanted to get on a flight out of China as soon as I had left that hotel room but there were no home comforts on my return. Anxiety had kicked in as soon as I was back in Scotland. Real anxiety. It doesn't care about geography.

I didn't want to see anybody – friends or family. It was a struggle to cross the doorstep and do something as mundane as put the bins out. The mere thought of being around other people brought on bouts of paranoia. It was ridiculous. The bin man didn't have a clue what was said in a Beijing hotel and, even if he did, he couldn't care less. But, even at the best of times, I was the type of person who would worry about what other people might be thinking or saying about me, so a situation this bad was guaranteed to heighten those emotions.

I didn't trust my team-mates and I didn't like myself. I was scarred by what had happened. It was depression.

I knew I had to see a doctor.

I didn't have the life experience to appreciate what depression felt like and, even if I could identify it and articulate it, I certainly would not have wanted to admit it. I did know that crying at the drop of a hat and not being able to face going out wasn't my normal.

The girls were good with me. They could see I was struggling. But, when I saw two of them chatting, that didn't stop me thinking: 'Are they talking about me?' That's not a criticism. How could they possibly fathom what was going on inside my head? Of course, I didn't see myself as somebody who would find themselves suffering from depression. Who does? But I did know that I had never been the super-confident and super-tough person that fitted the 'ice queen' image.

The doctor put me on anti-depressants straight away and they helped.

It was just as well because I still had a couple of Grand Slam events in Canada to get through. It was no great surprise that we were knocked out in the quarter-finals of the Players' Championship and then didn't get out of the group in the Champions' Cup. This was a season that needed to end. The good thing to come out of that trip was a few days' holiday we had in Mexico as a group of four girls. We didn't pick at the scab of the Beijing wounds, but we did make a conscious decision to be much more open and honest with each other moving forward.

Despite the talk in China about 'if' we were selected for the Olympics, we all knew it was a case of 'when'. And it was another early announcement. For the Muirheads, PyeongChang was going to be a family Games. Thomas was a member of Kyle Smith's Perth rink, who had earned their spot in a competitive men's field. You could have made a case for Dave Murdoch's team but, on form over the previous year, Kyle and the boys deserved it. Glen was later confirmed as their alternate.

Three Muirheads. The BOA weren't going to let a good photo opportunity like this pass them by. We had all been to the Highland Show in Ingliston plenty of times before but never in Team GB gear. The pictures taken of us amongst the hay and sheep were great. It kind of summed the whole thing up for me – family, farming, curling and the Olympics. Thomas was actually working at the show that day, would you believe. He had done a brilliant job to get this far with two jobs. Both my brothers had. When I won my bronze in Sochi, Thomas was in the middle of a farming lecture at college, while Glen was selling sheep at a market.

Everything seems to speed up in an Olympic year.

The time away from curling always feels shorter for starters. You never truly switch off from it. There isn't a day when you don't think about or do something Games-related. Then when you come back to work, which by now meant a newly built National Curling Academy in Stirling, life becomes a series of staging posts and boxes ticked.

For our team, I wanted to see signs that cuts were healing. Or, if they weren't healing, that at least the sticking plasters covering them up were holding firm. A gold medal in the European Championships certainly stopped the bleeding.

It was Sweden's turn to feel the pain of a flawless round robin not being converted into the big prize.

The two teams we lost to in the group were the two teams we beat in the knockout rounds to claim our second Euro gold – Switzerland in the semi and then Anna Hasselborg in the final. As usual, there wasn't much between Sweden and us. Anna letting her percentage drop to 70 per cent, compared to my 86 per cent, was the most significant individual statistic out of the eight curlers.

Unfortunately, Sweden got their own back in the men's final so there was no double Muirhead gold. 'You always have to go one better, don't you,' Thomas joked. The 10-5 scoreline didn't tell an accurate story of that game. Kyle Smith's team were actually a point ahead going into the last two ends and only conceded a four in the 10th because they had to gamble.

Sharing this Olympic build-up with my two brothers gave us all special memories. We didn't talk about my problems, but just having the two of them around a lot of the time was a help for me.

Media attention wasn't as intense as it had been four or eight years earlier, which was another bonus.

Elise Christie was the main story. She was a world champion by now and PyeongChang was trailed as her opportunity to banish the demons of Sochi. Lizzy Yarnold having a realistic shot at making history with back-to-back golds was the other big narrative going into the Games. There was also a lot of talk about Britain perhaps being on the cusp of becoming a major snow sports nation for the first time. James Woods, Izzy Atkin and Katie Summerhayes were all established ski slopestyle world-level performers, while snowboarder Katie Ormerod also had a strong medal chance. They were 'prospects' while I had quietly slipped into the 'experienced' bracket.

Don't get me wrong, there was still expectation. We were the reigning European champions and were one of the five medals that Team GB had set as their pre-Games target.

The last time we had flown out to Asia for a camp before a big tournament, it had been a disaster. But the facilities at Karuizawa in Japan were excellent. All handles were securely fixed to their stones. And we even managed to squeeze in a trip to Tokyo Disneyland. All told, given everything that had happened in Beijing and my subsequent mental health struggles, we were actually in a far stronger position than I thought would have been possible. I wasn't deluding myself that we were better placed than four years earlier but if you had offered me another bronze before a stone was thrown, I wouldn't have entertained it for a second. Probably not even a silver. It was all about gold.

State-sponsored doping at their own Games in Sochi had caught up with Russia. They were banned from these Olympics, albeit there were plenty of people who felt the IOC hadn't gone far enough by allowing around 200 Russian athletes who had no previous drug violations and a consistent history of drug testing to compete as an Olympic Athlete from Russia.

They might not have had the flag, the kit and the anthem, but it was still Russia, and they were our first opponents. The fact that it was Victoria Moiseeva's team and not Anna Sidorova's was a bit controversial in itself. Team Sidorova were originally selected but, after they had a poor European Championships, the Russian curling federation changed their minds and held a play-off, which Anna lost. Talk about moving the goalposts. They should have stuck with Anna. A lone Russian fan in the crowd dressed as Santa Claus couldn't help her. We thrashed Victoria's team 10-3 and they ended up finishing second bottom of the round robin with a 2-7 record.

It was a double game day next – lost one (USA), won one (China).

We had to grind it out to narrowly beat China and there was only one point in it when we got the better of Denmark as well. However, back-to-back defeats (South Korea and Sweden) in the middle of the round robin changed the picture significantly and piled the pressure on. Comfort had changed to no margin for error.

We only had ourselves to blame for letting things get away from us in the last three ends of the loss to South Korea, but the Sweden game was a tough one to take. Whichever sport it may be, you will never hear me criticise the use of video technology after my experience that afternoon. We had taken Anna's team to an extra end and there was one stone left for each of the skips. I was first to go and just after I delivered it, the red light flashed on my handle to indicate a foul had been committed. I had either released it after the hog line or touched it twice. My stone was kicked away before it came to rest, and Anna had a free shot to win the match.

I had been playing an out-turn draw and had the chance to put real pressure on her. We'll never know if she would have risen to it. There were no rules in place for TV replays to be checked. All you can do is get the umpire to test the stone, which I did. But, to compound my frustration, he tested it at the opposite line to the one I threw from, said the stone was fine and it was a case of 'shake hands, girls'. Later in the competition another team got penalised on the same sheet and at the same end as me. Their umpire tested at the correct line and a fault in the stone was found. TV evidence backed up my gut instinct that there had been no infringement. I had released the stone a few inches before the line and hadn't touched it again. I got a message from the skip of the Swedish men's team, Niklas Edin, later that night to tell me it wasn't a foul. There was annoyance at what might have been and a sense of injustice, but another factor was the impact it would have for the rest of the tournament. The last thing you want mid-competition is for doubts to creep in, like a sprinter who has been penalised for a false start in the 100 metres or a long jumper who has put a toe over the board.

Shot-making in curling is rooted in muscle memory and repetition. If I throw 100 stones, 99 of them will be released within an inch of each other. I didn't want to tinker with my technique or even have cause to contemplate it. In our next game, Kelly saw me throw a stone for an open hit then whip my hand back off the stone as if I had been electrocuted.

We had three games left after Sweden and, in our heads, we needed to win them all.

In the first of those, against Switzerland, I had about an inch of stone to aim for to turn an 8-7 last end deficit into a 9-8 triumph. I was proud of myself for that one. It was now a 4-3 record and beating Japan then assured us we would have a play-off, at worst, to get into the semi-finals. Our last round-robin game was against the pre-tournament favourites, Canada. The pressure was even greater on Rachel Homan's team than us. Lose and they were out. In the penultimate end my raised double take-out – like a plant in snooker – removed two of their stones – to swing the match in our favour. It restricted them to one and then, after we loaded the house with stones in the last end, we got our two without me needing to use my final stone.

Glenn described the last four ends as our best of the Games, and I wouldn't argue with that. He was a quadruple world champion for Canada and, at one point, actually had a shot at earning selection to compete in the Olympics with a maple leaf on his back rather than wear GB colours as an important part of our team. Within minutes of our win, somebody had changed Glenn's Wikipedia page to say 'traitor curler', which was terrible. There is nobody more patriotic about his country than Glenn, but he was in our corner and had no divided loyalties for those two and a bit hours. I did feel sorry for Rachel, the rest of the Canadian girls and the men's team. None of them came home with a medal, which prompted the sort of national outcry that you would only see over here if there was a footballing calamity. Even Rachel's husband, Shawn Germain, a former ice hockey player, was caught up in the post-mortem for being spotted with a pint in each hand during one of her morning games. Being a Canadian curler when you win at the Olympics is great. Being a Canadian curler when you don't win is a world away from great.

From our point of view, we had eliminated Switzerland by beating them and had now done the same to Canada. If we could complete the hat-trick against Sweden, we would be the favourites for gold against Japan or South Korea, who met in the other semi.

We didn't.

There was no controversy about this loss. Anna raised her level. You could see in her body language that she knew her game was in great shape. It wasn't even close. Their team outplayed us in every position, from the leads through to the skips. I knew it was game over in the seventh end when I failed to pull off two difficult but makeable shots. A potential 5-5 became an irretrievable 8-3. This was a different kind of disappointment to losing to Jennifer Jones in the semi four years ago, when we had traded punch for punch. We weren't good enough this time. I can't speak for the other girls, but I found that easier to process.

The day before, I had watched Thomas and the guys miss out on getting to the semi-finals. It would turn out to be their one and only shot at an Olympic medal. Their tournament exit had intensified the focus on us, with Britain still one short of its pre-Games target of five medals. The media talk about curling underperforming and not justifying its £5 million funding allocation had already begun before our bronze medal match.

From my perspective, we did a good job of not being distracted and of not dwelling on the Sweden defeat. For Anna, Vicki and myself, the prospect of winning a second bronze wasn't dismissed as unworthy in any way. You're in a small club as a British Winter Olympic medal winner and a very small club if you earn two. And Lauren and Kelly didn't have one yet. Emotions weren't as raw as in Sochi – we were four years older – but motivation was just as intense.

Glenn changed our tactics for the game against Japan.

They loved to see stones all over the place so they could create a bit of chaos. Glenn felt the best way to beat them was to keep things simple, be defensive and keep as few targets in play as possible. It wouldn't make for entertaining TV viewing – there wasn't more than a single point scored in any of the ends – but he was right. And the game plan put us in a position of being one down with the hammer in the final end. We always thought this contest would come down to the last shot and I couldn't ask for more than that last shot being in my hands. It was one I would make nine times out of 10 in practice and expect the same of myself in tournament play. We were lying one but knowing this would be the last opportunity to be in control of our own destiny – forcing an extra end would hand over the hammer for the extra end – there wasn't a decision to be made about going for two.

No skip should turn that down.

But the difference in how I felt as I prepared to deliver this stone was night and day in comparison to when a bronze medal was on the line in Sochi. I can't explain why. Both shots carried enormous pressure. If anything, it was even greater the first time. My right leg was shaking – not just a tremor. It felt as if it wasn't attached to my foot. The right arm wasn't much steadier. This was new. I'd never been physically gripped by nerves in such a way. I could now understand what people meant by an out-of-body experience. The house looked double the distance away it would normally be, time dragged, and the stone slid down the ice in slow motion. Whether it was a simple case of nerves getting the better of me in a way they hadn't before and would never again, or it was the culmination of a chapter in my life that had taken me into depression without being fully healed, nobody will be able to answer. All that mattered in that moment was I got a fraction high on my release, popped the stone a bit wide and it knocked a Japanese stone into a scoring position. The game was lost.

As a team of five, we were equally devastated but, as skip, I carried the responsibility. In that moment, the opportunity to win us an Olympic medal was mine alone. Curling, more than any other sport, is built for it to routinely be this way.

It had been a night game and by the time we got back to the food hall, I couldn't face anything. I walked back to our apartment on my own and phoned Mum on the way. That's when the tears came. In floods. 'Don't do anything stupid,' said Mum, who knew what I had been through over the last few months. Lying on my bed, phone switched off and the tears still coming down, I couldn't tell you how long it was before the rest of the girls got back. If Mum hadn't been able to make me feel any better, my team-mates had no chance. I couldn't tell you how many days we had to spend in South Korea before we flew home. Too long, that much I did know.

The shot that defined four years of my life was as clear in my mind as the moment I played it – and would remain that way – but everything else was almost instantly a blur.

THIRTY-FIVE

A BROKEN BODY

An athlete needs to be equipped to cope with the emotional demands of elite sport. That was clearly becoming more of a challenge. The physical demands were now taking their toll as well. I was broken. More specifically, my hip was.

Genetics and the mechanics of curling were conspiring against me.

Dad had suffered from bad arthritis for a while. Glen had a hip problem and Thomas had knee issues. The most common injuries in curling are shoulders (from sweeping) and knees (from sliding). Hips are far less common, but I was at the forefront of a new era of professionalism in the sport when repetition was far higher than it used to be.

My generation was the first of full-time, professional curling so it stands to reason that new injuries would be the consequence. There was no rulebook on how many stones you should throw a day. For me, it would be 60 or 70, putting my body in a position that is far removed from natural. I did a rough calculation that it would be over 4,000 per year. And it's not as if you can switch sides to address the imbalance. There has never been a curling equivalent to Ronnie O'Sullivan being able to play a World Championship snooker final right- and left-handed. Oskar Eriksson, a member of Niklas Edin's Swedish team, is the only one I've seen who would get pass marks on his wrong hand. If I delivered a stone with my left, it would be embarrassing.

My body had grown accustomed to the punishment that was being inflicted upon it and, as hard as it is to gauge where you are on a pain threshold scale, I suspect I'm very high up it. Coping with physical discomfort didn't faze me. In fact, I actually got myself to the stage that I performed better in tournaments when I was overexerting myself. There was a correlation between pushing my body and success. In a long format championship like the Europeans, the worlds or the Olympics, it wasn't enough that I would be out on the ice for three hours during a game. I needed to go into it on the back of a good gym session.

It sounds crazy but a session of lifting heavy weights, which left me sore and fatigued with DOMS (Delayed Onset Muscle Soreness), meant I was more focused on my body being in the optimum position for throwing a stone. My concentration would be where it needed to be. It certainly wasn't common for pain to be looked upon as a good thing in curling. Switching off and relaxing was the norm and would work for most, but it didn't work for me.

I knew what the post-tournament payback would be.

As soon as the last stone was played, overwhelming tiredness would hit me. Increasingly, I would go to closing banquets only out of duty and be the first to leave, whether I had won a gold medal or come away with nothing. Then back home, the ulcers would start to show, and the next level of fatigue would take hold. What I didn't know was that for a long time I had been destroying my left hip. Pain specific to that area, above anywhere else in the body, first became a problem not long after Sochi.

For a couple of years, I didn't speak about it, which was stupid. Basically, every time I got myself into the flexed, sliding position I was sore. It was a sharp, stabbing sensation deep in the hip joint as if someone was jabbing a needle in. Then I would wake up in the middle of the night, sweat pouring off me, with the same pain. Sometimes when I got out of bed to try and walk it off, the hip would collapse on me. It was bad.

We were halfway through the four-year cycle to PyeongChang before I eventually had the good sense to speak to the British Curling physios. They knew there was no way I would contemplate an operation that would jeopardise my Olympic chances so we needed to manage it the best we could. Activating everything around the troublesome area – my quad and glute muscles – did make a difference. If my game was due to start at nine in the morning, for example, I would get up at five and do work on those muscles. If there was a gym, great. If not, the hotel room would have to do.

I was worried but didn't think it was career-threatening.

Unfortunately, one of the worst things for this type of injury is the cold. Standing around for a long time isn't great either. I really was in the wrong sport. That meant getting heated trousers and shorts made, with a wetsuit-type material that kept things stabilised. I got my last scan not long before PyeongChang. It showed that, even though I was getting better at dealing with it, the hip was in fact getting worse and it would need to be opened up to see the full extent of the damage.

A date was put in the diary – 2 May. And I went into the Games knowing there would be surgery on the other side. The beginning of a new four-year cycle was an acceptable time for something big like this. It was a relief to have it on the horizon. I could tell myself there was the prospect of a life without feeling light-headed as a result of all-consuming pain and a life without increasingly strong medication that wasn't doing anything apart from helping me sleep.

Devastated after the Olympics and closing in on my surgery, the Scottish Championships had never felt like more of an ordeal. For the first time, I lost a final. Hannah Fleming had her moment. And I really wasn't surprised. We told ourselves that the fight was still in us, but we were burnt out. We were just ticking boxes to see out the season. The only date that mattered was the one with Paul Gaston, the orthopaedic surgeon who would have my future career as an athlete in his hands.

After a roast dinner at Mum and Dad's the night before, Mum and I were up at the crack of dawn to drive down to Murrayfield Hospital in Edinburgh. I wasn't allowed breakfast and was gowned up by eight in the morning, not knowing whether I would be first on the list for the day or last. The most worrying thing was the needle. I would love to give blood, but I just can't bring myself to do it. I hate needles. They gave me an epidural in my lower back to relax everything. There was no chance of relaxing after I caught a glimpse of the needle that would be going into me. The surgeon chatted about curling as the anaesthetist put it in, and the last thing I can remember was telling him about starting out in Pitlochry as a nine-year-old. My next memory was a nurse asking me to wiggle my toes.

There were three or four patients in the post-operation room, and I could hear her saying the same thing to someone else. The drugs were still doing their thing because I shouted out, 'He's not OK,' when I couldn't see a guy moving his toes. I had been out for nearly four hours. Mum came back in and I phoned Vicki. She was kicking herself that she didn't record the conversation we had because, apparently, I was still talking absolute gibberish.

Then the surgeon arrived, my blood all over his gown.

The whole world knew how bad Andy Murray's hip was – he had been operated on a couple of months before me and the expectation was his career was probably over. My surgeon had spoken to Andy's surgeon before the operation and there wasn't much difference in terms of the severity of the damage between the two of us.

'The bottom line is, your hip isn't in a good state,' he said. 'You've got bad arthritis and even if you never do any sport again and lie on your sofa for the rest of your life, it will still deteriorate. We'll be seeing you again for a hip replacement at some point.'

I had a bone spur, which had caused a massive tear in my labrum, the ring of cartilage on the socket part of the hip joint. Every time I moved, it was rubbing and extending the tear, bit by bit. He had given the area a good clean, had shaved the bone spur down and micro-fractured the labrum to stimulate more cartilage growth.

There was no sweetening the pill. I might never be a professional athlete again. My career could be over.

He didn't put a percentage chance on it, and I didn't even ask. In my mind it was 50/50 and, surprisingly, I was at peace with that.

THIRTY-SIX

EVE 2.0

Big picture stuff could wait. The thought of my career being over at the age of 28, and everything entwined with that possibility, didn't consume me after Mum drove me back to Blair Atholl. Excruciating pain is a powerful distractor from 'why me?' And that excruciating pain lasted a while. For three weeks the medication was as strong as you can get, and I took it several times a day. The feeling in my left leg was very strange. It was as if it wasn't attached properly to the rest of my body. Lying on the couch for hour upon hour was torture. I only had the most basic of exercises to do that broke up the monotony. The weather was lovely, and I managed to pick out a few weeds with my crutches when I got out into the garden for a bit of fresh air.

I was grateful to Mum and Dad for driving me down to Loch Lomond for Vicki's hen party, albeit I missed the best bit and only got to catch everybody for breakfast. I had felt so sick on the journey over but not as ill as they all looked on the back of the night before.

Getting home to Stirling was the first big milestone and then walking without crutches the one after that. With every physio appointment that passed, I was growing steadily confident that, at worst, I would be in a position to give curling a go again and, at best, I would be able to manage the hip and be good at it.

Big decisions by others didn't stop, even though my own career had been put on hold. Within a few days of my operation, Anna Sloan texted. She was leaving the team.

I had a fear this might happen. Anna and Glen had been dating for a couple of years. The pluses were obvious – Anna was one of my best friends and in the time she and my big brother were an item we had lots of fun – Christmases together, that sort of thing. But it was always going to go one of two ways – they would last the distance, and our friendship would remain the same, or they would split and there would be the potential for awkwardness. I stayed out of it when their relationship ended so I didn't know how much of a factor, if at all, the break-up was in Anna deciding she wanted out of the team.

Aside from that, the foundations of Team Muirhead weren't as strong any more. We had done the best we could to keep everything together in the wake of Beijing and had done a pretty good job of that. But I can absolutely understand that there were fewer reasons for Anna to keep going than there were to quit. She was ready to close this chapter.

I understood her decision and there was nothing I could do about it – even if I had a good hip and career certainty. But I did struggle with this one, more so than previous team line-up changes. With so much time on my hands to think about things – too much – Anna's abrupt departure from the team gave the missed shot in PyeongChang a run for its money in terms of brooding. Change can be good. It had been good at times. But it can also be overwhelming.

I had no option but to think of it as a curling and life reset.

That new beginning came close to involving a new house. In the summer, mine nearly burned down. I hosted a barbecue and put the dishwasher on before we all headed out to the pub, 10 minutes' walk down the road. Thank goodness it was only a couple of drinks because by the time we wandered back there was a fire in the kitchen, started by the dishwasher. It took about a year for all the damage to be sorted.

Eve, the curler 2.0, began again on 4 September, four months after I had been operated on. My first slide.

Every member of the support team came to the National Curling Academy that day. Dave Leith recorded it for posterity. It certainly wasn't to marvel at the technique. Like a kid, tentatively cycling a bike with stabilisers on, I picked up one stone in each hand and sent them down the ice. It was a huge moment. So was standing up and discovering everything in my left leg was still where it should be. Dave Murdoch had replaced Tony Zummack as head coach over the summer, and he loved the fact that he had a blank canvas to work with. We could take my slide apart and put it back together differently – to protect my hip and improve my technique. I was happy to embrace change.

Over the next few weeks and months, we studied and worked on the mechanics of throwing a stone. When you play an up-weight shot (a hit rather than a draw), your left foot, the sliding one, should come back in behind the stone. Prior to the operation, mine crashed in, which would undoubtedly have contributed to the hip damage. So, the objective was to get the foot into position without that violent move. It felt a bit counter-intuitive to put more weight on my left leg in the pre-delivery position given that was where I had a weakness in my body, but it needed to be that way. Muscle memory fought against it but by the time the Stockholm Ladies came round at the start of October, there was no physical reason to stop me making my comeback and, more often than not, I was sliding Dave's way.

By then a new Team Muirhead had started the season without a Muirhead.

It made sense to have a team of five rather than a four for this season. Lauren and Vicki were staying, and we picked up Jen Dodds and Vicky Wright from Hannah Fleming's team. I was glad that we still had Glenn as our team coach. He had more still to give us and, with an imminent retirement from his day job in Canada, the plan was for him to get even more involved than he had been in the build-up to PyeongChang.

The Europeans came round too quickly for me to have realistic ambitions to win. I had barely managed any competitive curling and had never felt less equipped to wear the crown of defending champion. But conversely, I had never experienced a deeper sense of perspective and patience. This was the fifth version of Team Muirhead, but my physical challenges had taken the urgency out of this latest reset.

The Eve of 2016 or 2017 might have been a bit blasé about being awarded an honorary degree by the University of Stirling, but that was a humbling day not long before we flew out to Estonia for the Euros. I knew it was different from the farming qualifications Glen and Thomas had studied for, but formal education hadn't suited me. It was never going to happen. The university, which had been such a big part of my life since I became involved with British Curling, didn't throw honorary degrees about to everyone. It really touched me and made me appreciate I hadn't done too badly after all. Even if I never won another medal, I should be proud of myself if others have decided that I am worthy of their pride in the way the likes of Andy and Judy Murray were.

I didn't get another medal in Tallinn. The run of eight straight at the Europeans was over. In fact, we didn't even make the play-offs. We had the hammer in the extra end of our final round-robin game against Switzerland, but I left my last stone short, and we were knocked out early. But I didn't lose that new-found perspective. We had lost three single-point games, it was only the fourth tournament of my comeback and at least we had qualified Scotland for the worlds in the spring.

THIRTY-SEVEN

PLAYING FOR THE OTHER SIDE

There are certain competitions which put a smile on your face when you think about them. And it's not just the ones you win. The Continental Cup very much falls into that category. It is curling's answer to the Ryder Cup and Solheim Cup, albeit it has never got into a proper annual or biennial rhythm since the first one in 2001 and it has never been held outside North America. The home team has been Team Canada or Team North America and the away one has been Team Europe or Team World.

Apart from the time I got stung by a wasp, I loved team golf. And it brought out the best in me. I would be more envious of the golfers, watching the Ryder Cup or the Solheim Cup, than I would be watching an Open. I peaked at the Celebrity Cup at Celtic Manor in 2017 when the likes of Gareth Bale, Denise van Outen and Bradley Walsh were great company for a few days (I think Gareth was the only one who didn't drink the place dry). The competitive/social pendulum definitely swung towards the latter in Wales when it was an achievement in itself to drag yourself to the first tee given the amount of drink Mike Tindall and some of the rugby players were getting us to put away.

I'm told that the Continental Cup was every bit as bad (good) when it started out – so much so, that by the time I was selected for my first one in 2012, the organisers had introduced a booze ban. The hangovers had seriously impacted the quality of the competition, let's just say. Don't get me wrong, though, we still had some brilliant nights out when sleep was an afterthought, and it was a case of heading straight from the party to the ice. One year when it was in Vegas, a few of us went to a Calvin Harris concert on the last day of the trip. There's a farmer from Forfar – Durno, he gets called – who comes to loads of big curling events. I don't know how, but he got us into the VIP area at this gig, so it was a late one and a great time was had by all.

Back at the hotel, I started packing for home and realised I had lost my passport at the concert. I retraced my steps, as you do, phoned everywhere and everyone I could think of who might be able to help, all to no avail. Eventually, I got a call from Caesars Palace, where the concert had been, to give me the best news ever. Some kind soul had handed my passport in at reception. It had been found at the cash-in desk. I had run out of money for a taxi, had cashed in some chips that were at the bottom of my handbag and left the passport there.

Only people who have lost a passport abroad know what that relief feels like when it turns up! I had already started to plan my round-trip to Los Angeles to get a temporary one sorted.

Passport stress aside, there was no such thing as an unenjoyable Continental Cup. At the start of 2019, as a new Team Muirhead within the big Team World, a trip to Vegas was just what we needed. We were already feeling as if a corner had been turned in the new year. Beating a few big names in the Canadian Open on our way to the semi-finals boosted confidence – as did scoring a seven in the first end against Chelsea Carey. It was the first time

I had done that since the record-breaking end against America in Sochi.

There was certainly no booze ban this time and the Team World pre-tournament party in the Palms Hotel penthouse apartment Floyd Mayweather used to stay in when he was there was the perfect way to start the team bonding. And it turned out to be a perfect few days of competition for me. I was unbeaten and it fell to me to recover from a precarious position to get us over the line in the last end of the last game by drawing with Rachel Homan in a skins game. That shot was the most pressurised one I had faced since PyeongChang and there was a real sense of satisfaction – a relief – to punch out Rachel's counting stone. You never saw any curlers, or spectators, cross the line, as is sometimes the case when a European team is competing away from home in the Ryder Cup, but as much as Canadians like to think they're different from Americans, their hatred of losing is every bit as intense. There was plenty of sledging going on that day, that's for sure. A packed and partisan arena on live TV – the occasion had a real edge.

I was disappointed that a successful early year trip didn't put some momentum behind us for the regular season. My own form continued to be patchy and unpredictable. And, for once, the week when I was normally guaranteed to be good, turned out to be a real low point.

I had been Scottish champion seven times and would have strongly fancied my chances of it being eight had we not been denied the opportunity to compete one year. That only four women's teams entered in 2019 was really depressing for curling in our country when I thought back to the 12 who made up the Gold League when I was coming out of the juniors, as well as all the strong rinks in the Silver League beneath it. But Sophie Jackson's team were strong that week and they thoroughly deserved to win in Perth.

You can't argue when you lose to the same opposition twice in the round robin and then the final. I missed a shot in the eighth end which turned out to be decisive. I knew that I was still well below my best. That was bad enough, but we then got caught up in a controversy that had nothing to do with us. Team Jackson had been told before the Scottish that, if they won, they wouldn't be able to compete at the World University Games and the World Championships because they were so close together. They chose the University Games. Therefore, after the final, it was announced that we would be going to the worlds. Next thing we knew, there was an appeal lodged by Team Jackson and the decision was reversed.

We had zero input into the original call and zero input once the appeal process kicked in. There was a lot of gossiping behind our backs about what we had said and done – all of it rubbish. We had been dragged into a saga that had nothing to do with us. I had never benefitted from a free pass to anything in my career and didn't want one now. They had earned their spot, let them go.

The fact that Team Jackson finished 10th in the worlds and didn't pick up a medal at the University Games backed up why the coaches feared the schedule would be too much for them. It was neither here nor there as far as I was concerned, however. I had my own game and my own career to worry about and I was presented with a fascinating opportunity.

Our poor results in the Grand Slams meant we hadn't qualified for the end-of-season Champions Cup and my competition diary was frustratingly barren. Anna Hasselborg had been selected to represent Sweden at the World Mixed Doubles Championship and that event clashed with the Grand Slam finale. One of their team got in touch to ask if I would sub for Anna. It was a total no-brainer from my point of view on so many different levels.

I needed the ice time but, most of all, I needed the confidence boost that being the first name who came into their heads instantly gave me. We all want to feel valued. The best team in the world and the recently crowned Olympic champions putting their faith in me was the biggest curling compliment I had been given in a long time.

When I told British Curling about the offer, their first reaction was along the lines of: 'Why would you want to play for your biggest rivals?' My take on it was: 'Why on earth would I not want to?' There were no bigger shoes to fill than Anna's, but I was adamant that this would develop me as a curler and, more importantly, build up my self-esteem. I would also get to learn more about them from the inside. There really was no downside.

It turned out to be one of my most enjoyable weeks as a curler. The girls were so welcoming and there was a real buzz at the tournament about how this would go. #hasselhead was trending in Canada. We won our first game 7-1 and I had a 100 per cent shot percentage. That hadn't happened for a very long time. After beating Jennifer Jones, we made it through to the semi-final and should have gone all the way really. We lost a three in the last end to Kerri Einarson. There was one game we averaged 98 per cent as a team, which is as close to perfection as you can realistically get.

I had needed this. The girls had trusted me, taught me a few Swedish swear words, and I had made new friends and reminded myself that I was still a top curler. The biggest takeaway was the fact that when you put all the off-ice stuff to one side, top level curling hadn't changed as much as others would want you to believe. It still came down to good shot-making. This was the benchmark for me and Team Muirhead. We needed to aspire to be the very best again.

I had a few days to kill so I took the opportunity to drive to Swift Current and catch up with Kelly before flying to America for a charity event in Minneapolis. Lupus Spiel USA was one of the largest pro-ams for curling in the world and people had the chance to bid to play with professional skips like Chelsea Carey, Kevin Martin and me. Somebody paid $15,000 to curl in my team, which was the highest bid for the event. That was another nice, wee morale top-up.

Back with my own team for the season-ending competition, I was re-energised. I was also determined to see Vicki off on a high. Now Vicki Chalmers, not Adams, after getting married in the summer, she had sat myself and Vicky Wright down in Stirling to tell us she would be retiring. Then, at the airport, when we were about to fly out to Russia for her last tournament, she broke the news that she was pregnant. I was gutted Vicki was calling it a day but delighted for her and, after making more memories in Moscow on the tourist trail, we won the Arctic Cup in Siberia. Going all the way back to the juniors, Vicki and I had enjoyed so many successes. Most importantly, she had been a true pal through all the highs and lows. There was no way this would be a lost team-mate who would turn into a lost friend.

THIRTY-EIGHT

FINDING A CURLING GEEK

For seven years I had felt in control of the make-up of my team. There was always consultation with the people in charge at British Curling, and nothing major would get signed off without their approval, but when it came to players and coaches being brought in and being cut, as captain and skip, the buck stopped with me. Those days were over. I wasn't making the big decisions any more. If I had been, Glenn Howard wouldn't have been let go that summer. Three years wasn't long enough to get the full benefit from working alongside somebody as knowledgeable about our sport as Glenn. But British Curling wanted Stirling-based coaches, not remote ones, on the elite programme. It was the first time I wasn't given any input. Nancy Smith was their appointment for us.

We all made a conscious effort to commit to our team-building before the season began. There was a Land Rover experience, dinner in Edinburgh, golf, gigs, lots of fun days and nights. And we were back down to a four, with Vicki's departure making it a straightforward decision to promote Vicky Wright. Vicky would play lead, and Lauren would move up the order to third.

The omens weren't great at the start of our first trip of the season to Canada. After arriving in Ontario, we slept in three different beds in three nights. Our first B&B had a mouse problem, then it was on to the house of a friend of Nancy's which was lovely but too small for a team of five and finally a Holiday Inn hotel. A bit of pre-tournament chaos was worth it when we won the Oakville Classic, though. We needed good results to climb back up the world rankings and get into the Grand Slams. Picking up from where we left off in the Siberia Cup at the end of the previous season, this was another step in the right direction.

So were the European Championships in Helsingborg.

I had been no more than 50 per cent of the pre-surgery curler when I was a few weeks into my comeback at the Euros the year before, but 12 months on, I would put it at about 80 per cent. Scheduling of games was a more significant factor for me post-operation. Mornings meant early starts to get the muscles around my hip working, which presented a bigger problem than playing twice in one day. So, I was happy to only have a couple of 5am alarm calls in the round robin. More tired with less pain was preferable to less tired and more pain, if that makes sense.

We only had a couple of losses as well – Sweden and Russia. The Sweden game had a bit of drama in the sixth end when I fell face down on to the ice after tripping over one of their stones in the house. Unfortunately for me, that was the live TV game on Eurosport. We actually scored two in that end, but Anna ran away with things after that. Our semi-final against the Swiss, the reigning world champions, was incredibly cagey and risk-free, with six blanked ends and a final score of 3-2 to us.

The final was just as tense, but with a bit more scope to be bold. It was exactly as elite level curling should be – two teams at the top of their game and a final shot with real jeopardy. To Anna's credit, with us one up and lying shot, she produced with the pressure on. It hurt and it felt like one that had got away, but you have to tip your hat. This was peak Anna. They finished the calendar year by picking up the last Grand Slam and were undeniably the world's number one rink going into 2020.

We had to make sure we were Scotland's number one again.

A mid-season coaching change helped keep us on the right path. It hadn't taken me long to arrive at the conclusion that Nancy wasn't going to be the person this team needed but we had given it a few months. Glenn was always going to be a hard act to follow, and I knew that the only way we would advance was via tactical and technical gains. Nancy was a motherly, arm round the shoulder figure. I had known her from the juniors when she turned a blind eye to my poor excuse for being sick on the day of a game up north. She was great in that role, helping a young, up-and-coming curler navigate her way into the world of women's curling. She was a very organised team coach but I was a very organised team leader by that point. I was perfectly capable of making sure nobody missed a flight, and everybody remembered their brush pads. We were looking for – and got ourselves – a curling geek.

Kristian Lindström had been a member of Niklas Edin's successful Swedish team, but he wasn't a renowned coach by any stretch of the imagination. He had dipped his toe in the water with Spain but that was about it. I was confident he would immerse himself in the job of being our team coach, though. If there was curling being played anywhere in the world, Kristian would stay up until four in the morning to watch it. The next day he would be bursting to tell you about a shot he had seen in some obscure game. He was an encyclopaedia of statistics – most of them useful, some of them not. In opposition analysis, he could drill down into the sort of detail about shots played by any curler that would blow your mind.

My attention span in team meetings was notoriously short.

It goes back to my schooldays, never completing a novel from cover to cover and struggling to finish an exam paper. A movie would have to be very good for me to stick with it to the end, which made all my flights to and from Canada a real grind. It also meant that if you were going to hold my interest when it came to preparing for a game or a post-mortem on a game, 45 minutes would be my absolute limit before I drifted off. I wanted hard facts, and I wanted them delivered succinctly.

Kristian could also drill down into the nuances of shot-making. From the very beginning after he was hired by British Curling, our body position in relation to the brush, whether it was tight or wide, was a big focus. And, for Jen and Lauren in the middle order, power shots became an increasingly effective weapon as a result of Kristian's theory on how best to control up-weight stones. He was friendly without being your friend – healthily detached and straight to the point. His appointment was a gamble, but he opened our minds from day one and Nigel Holl and Dave Murdoch gave the change their seal of approval as, unlike Glenn, Kristian was happy to move to Scotland.

Winning our first tournament with him, the Perth Masters, was important. It validated things with British Curling. None of us were lacking motivation when we returned to my home ice for the next big event, the Scottish Championships. Losing three out of three to Sophie Jackson 12 months before, and all the other stuff that had gone with it, stung. It turned out we didn't end up playing Team Jackson in the final. Maggie Wilson's rink were our opponents, and we beat them convincingly.

My eighth Scottish title was as sweet as my first. Even though your horizons broaden as your career progresses, you never lose the taste for being the best in your country. And I hadn't won it for three years or since my operation. I didn't know it then, but it would be my last national women's crown. Without injury or scheduling clashes, I could have hit double figures, but a record eight is something to cherish. And even though I wasn't thinking at the time this would be my final Scottish triumph, it was worthy of a proper celebration.

We were sponsored by the Fairmont Hotel in St Andrews. The final was on the Saturday and I had arranged to pick Vicky up in Stirling on the Sunday morning. She had started the party early with a big night. Apparently, Vicky and my old flatmate Greg, by now her fiancé, had decided to attempt the famous *Dirty Dancing* lift. Unsurprisingly, a drunk Greg was no Patrick Swayze and she whacked her head on the floor. En route to St Andrews with Vicky, who was still worse for wear, I managed to get six penalty points added to my driving licence by not spotting the speed limit had dropped to 30 miles per hour on one of the back roads.

For Vicky, what she thought was a hangover, turned out to be *Dirty Dancing*-induced concussion.

For different reasons, neither of us would have cause to look back on that day with great affection, but we would soon have cause to be glad we seized the opportunity to celebrate as a team in a lovely hotel.

The world was about to change, and nobody would be taking run-of-the-mill get-togethers with friends or work colleagues for granted.

THIRTY-NINE

PIGGY IN THE MIDDLE

I'm not really a big one for reminiscing. Life moves too quickly and there are always new goals to strive for. But the Vancouver Olympics curling arena was so close to our practice venue for the 2020 World Championships that it would have been wrong not to pop in and have a look around. The old place hadn't changed that much. It was set up for ice hockey (no shock there) but they hadn't taken down some of the 2010 branding. All the good and bad memories came flooding back. Those walls could still talk of teenage dreams and broken brooms.

Where had 10 years gone?

After basking in a bit of nostalgia we were off to Prince George, British Columbia, feeling good about our prospects of contending for a world medal. That sense of anticipation had been a long time coming. This was the start of the points-gathering qualification process for the next Games in Beijing and I was in a good place, mentally and physically, to attack it.

Like everybody else on the planet, the words pandemic and coronavirus were in my vocabulary, but I had little to no appreciation of what Covid-19 really meant. Before we left, Mum had said: 'I think this thing could be quite serious.' But it didn't really register. I wrote my newspaper column just before getting on our flight from Vancouver. I talked about the new format for the event, a draw that had given us a game against Canada's Kerri Einarson in the opening game and whom I expected to be our biggest rivals. Over 500 words were dispatched to the sports desk. Only nine of them referred to a news story developing in China that was still remarkably low key.

'Thankfully, the coronavirus isn't going to affect our championships.'

Famous last words.

By the time we had checked into our hotel in Prince George and found ourselves a place to eat, everything had gone from nought to one hundred. On the TV screens in the sports bar, we could see events being cancelled one by one and it didn't take long before news reached us that the curling World Championships was the next domino to fall.

The message from the competition organisers was short and to the point – it's off, get home quickly. Mum and Dad had just arrived at Edinburgh Airport's long stay car park when I called them, but other families were less fortunate and were either already in Canada or on a flight. We were the last team to leave the tournament hotel and had to stay a night in Vancouver. There was no air of panic in that city. We even walked about the Granville Island Market, where it was as busy and buzzy as any other day I had spent there down the years. But by the time we were on our flight home, I felt awful. I will never know if I had picked up the virus at that packed street market but, in retrospect, I certainly had the symptoms. There was no such thing as a test back then. It was just a case of suffering for nine hours on a plane. We all went our separate ways once we touched down in Edinburgh, unable to say anything more concrete than 'see you when I see you'.

Back to our houses and into lockdown.

I don't think anybody could say they were prepared for many of the things we took for granted in life being taken away from us for a few months. If I had known how long lockdown was going to last, I would have gone to stay with Mum and Dad. As most single people would no doubt agree, the toughest part of it was the loneliness. I do like my own company and to not be dependent on anybody, but being forced into it is very different from choosing when you want to retreat to your own space.

I was envious of Vicky Wright. As a trained nurse, she had a wonderful purpose and went back to work in one of the wards at Forth Valley Hospital. I was so proud of her. I didn't have a cause anywhere near as worthwhile as that, but I needed to find a routine. That would be my way of dealing with the monotony.

My garage had been converted into a gym the previous summer and I had the time to grab some extra kit from Stirling University before the guidance of only essential contact turned into a full lockdown. So, my daily routine would be to get up at seven in the morning, have breakfast and then train between eight and 10. I would walk the same loop around King's Park, which would take about 45 minutes (I normally hate walking for the sake of it unless there's a golf ball at the end of it). That would see me through to lunch. Then it would be a bit of time spent in the garden if the weather was nice, start cooking dinner at five, eat at six, snack at half-seven, in bed by half-eight. And repeat.

Some media interviews helped break things up, a few Zoom calls and a Lego sheep. Yes, a Lego sheep. About 6,000 pieces. File that under 'things you would only do during a lockdown'. I was lucky to have a good bunch of neighbours in my street and a couple of times I got the bagpipes out when it was time to clap for carers on our doorsteps. Days were ticked off the calendar, my 30th birthday among them. Lots of cards and calls but no company, no cake and no champagne. That was a bit depressing, particularly knowing that if I had chosen to spend lockdown at Mum and Dad's it was lambing season, so there would have been plenty going on at the farm.

The positive aspect of Covid, and being forced to stay away from the ice, was I could dedicate proper time and energy to my hip rehab. There was an urgency to it after the operation, with the European Championships the big goal. That meant splitting hours between gym and curling work. Now, however, I couldn't get on the ice so there was a single focus. I filmed all my training and sent it to our fitness coaches. Strengthening the muscles around the bad hip was the purpose and I wasn't putting it through the closed position of a slide while doing that. Not being in a cold environment helped as well. My joints certainly felt the benefit of that.

The prospect of something approaching normality appearing on the horizon should have been the ideal psychological pick-me-up when British Curling made their announcement about the next season's teams.

It was reassuring that we were left alone as a four. But the men's side of the programme was far tougher for them. And the decision-making put me in a horrible position. Neither of my brothers had been reselected.

Both had been Olympians two years earlier and wanted to continue with a life that balanced farming and sport, but British Curling were fixed on an all-or-nothing approach. It was a debate that had been bubbling away for a while and one I could genuinely see both sides of. Glen and Thomas had found a successful balance. And it wasn't as if they were alone. Jennifer Jones, the most successful female curler of my generation and one of the greatest of all time, was a lawyer as well as an Olympic and world champion.

My main emotions were of a sister, though. Glen was 31, which was still short of the peak age for a curler, while Thomas was only 25. It probably hit Thomas harder because he had been involved at the top of the sport all the way through juniors. And he was years short of his prime.

It meant so much to me to be able to share their Olympic journey and compete alongside them for Scotland at European Championships. To think that it was now almost certain that I wouldn't be able to do that again was hard to get my head around.

Both were (are) such skilled curlers. Niklas Edin once told me that Thomas was among the most talented curlers he had ever seen, which is quite the compliment coming from a true great of our sport.

I was stuck in the middle, and I hated it. I knew fine well what my brothers and Dad thought about the situation. For a long time after, if curling came up as a topic when we were all together as a family, I would either sit in silence at the kitchen table, try and change the subject or leave the room. It will forever be a subject to avoid. I don't know if it was fully appreciated – within my family or the curling family – how tough it was for me to be the piggy in the middle.

Glen and Thomas chose to farm and wanted to protect that career. Back when I was driving up and down the A9 in my Corsa, living off next to nothing, I was committed to the life of a full-time curler. I took the gamble of not having a Plan B. All three of us had choices. For years, curling had been travelling towards becoming an all-in sport at elite level. It felt as if it had arrived at that destination.

FORTY

BUBBLE GLUM

The National Curling Academy in Stirling is part of The Peak, a big sports centre which is always busy, no matter the time of day. So, going into the NCA through a back door while the main building remained closed to the public was a reminder of how privileged professional athletes in Scotland were to be able to return to their work in August, about five months after the Covid lockdown had started.

Mask wearing, social distancing, form filling and temperature checking didn't feel like an inconvenience in the grand scheme of things. British Curling ticked all the boxes. Stringent health and safety regulations meant they had to invest in the air handling plant so that the air was 100 per cent fresh, rather than recirculated. Practice was shorter and we were only allowed ice time in pairs rather than a full team. Then, when we were able to compete, it was very much a watered-down version of what we were used to in the opening half of a season. No European Championships to aim for and no travel for us to compete abroad, or for others to compete against us in Scotland.

Everything was at the NCA.

The September Shoot-out was the first in-house competition of the season, and we didn't win it. There were another four teams on the programme and the strongest of them was Team Aitken, who beat us 8-4 in the final. There would have been serious concerns within our group – and serious pressure from outside it – if we hadn't won the November Classic. Thankfully, we did. It meant there wouldn't be a big debate or controversy over selection for the World Championships at the end of April 2021. It didn't necessarily follow that we would be a confident team going into them, mind you.

I had never experienced such doubt about where my form, my team's form and the form of my opponents would be. There were so many unknowns. You would hear lots of rumours about which countries were benefitting most from only being able to practise and compete in their own country.

We would only find out how the cards had fallen once all the top teams got into the Calgary bubble. Two Grand Slam events had been tagged on at the front of the worlds, all in that one place, with us the ninth-ranked of 12 teams.

In the first of them, the Champions' Cup, a record of two wins and two defeats in our group and then a 7-4 loss to Japan's Satsuki Fujisawa in a tiebreaker to get into the quarter-finals wasn't cause for utter panic, but it didn't fill me with belief that we were in a good place. Jen, Vicky and I all had very low shot percentages in that last loss. Mine was just 61 per cent. Then, in the second slam, the Players' Championship, we won just one game out of five.

With Bruce Mouat's team making history by becoming the first Scottish men's rink to win back-to-back slams, there were certainly no excuses about the Stirling environment over the previous few months. We would have to find the answers to our poor performances from within. Results weren't helping, obviously, but I certainly wasn't enjoying the bubble experience. Prior to our first tournament we had to quarantine in a holding hotel for five days. That was every bit as strict as it sounds. You weren't allowed to leave your room.

It was hell.

I had brought a 15kg dumb-bell and exercise bands in my suitcase and we would do team Zoom strength and conditioning sessions in our rooms every morning, but they passed far too quickly. Answering the door to pick up a tray for breakfast, lunch and dinner was the highlight of the day and the Calgary answer to my Lego lockdown sheep was doing some painting by numbers.

The bubble hotel we moved into after those first five days was better than the quarantine one but not by much. I managed to get an exercise bike in my room this time, which was a bonus, and every day we were allotted a slot for a 15-minute walk outside, like prisoners in a yard. Seeing Starbucks across the road and not being allowed to go was torture. At least we were allowed to meet with each other for meals in one of our rooms. Eating, playing and travelling in a minibus to the arena were the only times we were together as a four. We had PCR tests every morning, with all the stress and fear they bring, and it was a case of mask off when a game started and mask back on once it was finished.

In the most unnatural environment any of the curlers had ever known, success and failure at these World Championships would be determined as much by an ability to cope with the bubble claustrophobia as judging draw weight. Also, the fact that a year without qualification points for the 2022 Olympics meant the pressure on these worlds was greater than at any other I had known. The arithmetic was simple – top six got your country to Beijing. Anything below and it was into the last chance saloon of the Olympic qualifying tournament. I had felt good about our chances before Covid changed the landscape. A year and a bit later, hope and uncertainty had replaced expectation and conviction.

We started well, winning our first three games.

The last of those was against Germany, who had to compete without one of their players as a result of a positive Covid test. A couple of defeats were balanced out by a couple of victories and, sitting on a 5-2 record, we were looking pretty good for making the play-offs and very good for the chief goal of the top six. The competition flipped on our game against Canada's Kerri Einarson. We were 3-2 in front with the hammer, playing the eighth end, and lost a big steal of three, which we weren't able to recover from. It was downhill after that.

We lost four of our remaining five.

The Denmark defeat was a particularly bad one. I got really frustrated with myself in that game. There were echoes of the Beijing World Championships. Even the win in the middle of that run of five was a miserable experience. We were playing Estonia, who had only managed a single victory and would end up bottom of the round robin. It was a game we should have taken care of on autopilot, but we managed to find a way of making it far too tight for comfort.

It was 4-4 after six ends. The game was on the end sheet and our coaches, Kristian and Dave, were sitting on the bench next to it. I made a tactical call – to play a trickier shot than the obvious one. The message from the coaches was: 'Why did you do that?' I erupted and shouted back: 'Look, I don't know what I'm doing, I'm trying my fucking best.' With only players, coaches, officials and some cardboard cut-out spectators in the arena, you didn't need to be sitting close to hear me lose my temper. I had never shouted or sworn at a coach before. Ever. Frustration was overwhelming me, and Kristian and Dave had taken the brunt of it after pushing the wrong button. I apologised after the game, and they were fine. But the situation as a whole was anything but fine.

Even though we had scraped over the line against Estonia, by the time we were back on the ice for our last game against

China, we knew that even a win wouldn't be enough to get us into the knockouts or to the Olympics. It was another loss, and we couldn't get out of the bubble, and on to the plane home, quickly enough. It had been a grim slog in Calgary from start to finish and at the conclusion of it had come the biggest – and most costly – failure of my career.

We were ranked fourth going into the tournament and my shot percentage as skip actually ended up fourth. But there were no silver linings to this cloud. Eighth was my worst worlds placing – at the worst possible time. I would probably go so far as to say it was the first time I had truly failed at European, world or Olympic level.

Unfortunately, we weren't allowed to leave this wretched bubble until after the medal games, when the factory conveyor belt ushered the women out and the men in. The ordeal was dragged out to the bitter end.

What was in store on my return was far, far worse.

FORTY-ONE

WHEN SILENCE IS NOT GOLDEN

It had all got very serious, very quickly.

Within three days, British Curling had gone from their women's team sitting comfortably in the Beijing-bound positions at the World Championships to collapsing through the trapdoor into an event none of us had ever been to before. I couldn't have even told you where the Olympic qualification event was going to be held or when. There was an air of panic. What did all this mean?

While people above us and around us were contemplating all the big picture stuff, for the people in the middle, the curlers, their worlds were shrinking. After leaving Edinburgh Airport, days turned into weeks – alone with my thoughts and fears-type weeks. It's a difficult one to explain and make sense of. On one hand I didn't want anybody to get in touch, but on the other hand, the fact that my phone wasn't ringing or pinging like it usually would wasn't what I wanted either.

I was finding out the hard way that it's far more important for an athlete to have people checking in with them when they're at their lowest ebb than it is when they've just had a medal hung around their neck. I had suffered from loneliness and isolation before, but this was much, much worse. I wasn't angry. I was upset. I was going over everything I had done for curling in this country and arriving at the conclusion that it had all meant nothing. The prospect of a worst-case scenario, that hadn't happened yet, was enough to erase all the achievements that had. One day blurred into another, sometimes without even opening the curtains. I didn't leave the house. Eventually, I had no option but to. A few weeks after Beijing, there was a debrief into what went wrong at the worlds.

The gist of the group bit in a meeting room at the NCA was: 'You were shit, you were shit, you were shit, oh, and you were shit.' When it came to the individual one for me, it was pretty much more of the same. I couldn't stop the tears from falling but I wasn't going to open up on my deepest emotions. Not in this environment. Showing that type of weakness wasn't how it was supposed to be.

You can't hide them from your mum, though.

She knew the last thing I would have wanted would be for my curling bosses to learn I was broken. But enough was enough. And, of course, she was right. I think Mum phoned a few people and then came the call on my way to the driving range from a British Curling doctor who, either by accident or design, pushed the right buttons and opened the emotional floodgates.

I had never been this open, not even close. I told him that I didn't want to be here, and I meant every word. Did it make me feel better? In that moment, yes. It was a release and a relief. But nothing was solved or sorted. I was already on anti-depressants from the last time I had needed help, and they were upped to the strongest ones I could get prescribed. The medication did what it was supposed to, and it felt like people close to me were on a constant loop of phoning to ask where I was or coming to the house to check on me. But there was no sudden spike of feeling better. None of the issues that were at the root of my anxiety and depression had been fixed.

Naturally, I gave serious thought to giving up curling and giving up on the idea of going to another Olympics – I wouldn't say giving up on the idea of a gold medal because that felt so wildly unrealistic that it wasn't even entering my mind. It's hard to say what the main factor was that wouldn't let me do it, that wouldn't let me walk away. Earning money was one. 'What on earth will you do for a job?' might not be the most romantic of reasons to continue along the path most familiar, but it's a powerful one. If I stop curling, my source of income is gone. There was no second career to fall back on. Not wanting to quit on the back of my biggest failure was another. I was still a proud athlete who knew, deep down, that if I was right and my team was right, I would get to the Olympics again and be competitive. But probably the most significant element was how close the Games were.

If Beijing had been four or three years away, there would have been no chance I would have kept going. Maybe not even two or one. But, by the time we were due to return to practise, the countdown period was only seven months. That's a short race and, even in my fragile state, felt doable.

Those were the pillars of my decision to remain open to the possibility of keeping going. However, there was one fundamental obstacle that needed to be overcome. I didn't want to set foot back on the ice. The prospect filled me with dread. It was as far removed from the little girl waiting for her dad's game to finish so she could have a shot herself that you could possibly imagine. So, after letting British Curling know that I hadn't shut the door to the concept of staying on the programme, the reality of how that would happen soon became an issue. I was included on a group email that explained they wanted to have nine players in a women's squad for the season and asked if we could all meet at Stirling Rugby Club to learn the nuts and bolts of how it would work.

That was enough to put me into panic mode.

There was no way I was ready to be around all these people – curlers and the staff. The other eight athletes went to the rugby club and then back on to the ice soon after but not me. I don't know what the girls would have been told, if anything, but they wouldn't have had a clue that I was in a bad place and on strong medication. The coaches came up with a sensible plan to let me dip my toe back in the water. I went into the building when nobody else was there, around five in the afternoon. I just chucked stones for half an hour or so. Two days in the first week, three the next. I can't say that I got much from the experience, or that I was even thinking about the quality of the ice time, but I appreciated what it was – hopefully the start of a process.

The paranoia of worrying about what the other curlers would think if they found out was hard to shrug off. 'Why is she getting special treatment?' But it had come to the point that I would either have to commit to some group practice or quit. There was only so long they could keep the door open for me. Was I well enough to go back? No. Zara Lipsey, the psychologist I had been referred to, told me I would be signed off from work for six months if I was in an office job.

But I was willing to give it a go.

FORTY-TWO

A SQUAD AND A COLOUR

My sessions with Zara helped.

The next few months would be the most challenging of my life so I needed to have a plan that would give me a chance of navigating them. Not only was I emotionally brittle, I didn't even have a team. We were a squad of nine. We would be rotated so that the coaches could evaluate every different permutation and potential four in the run-up to the big events that mattered. Team Muirhead, which I had shaped and reshaped over the last 10 years, was no more.

I was in the same boat as the other eight girls – fighting for a place in the quartet who would earn selection for the European Championships, which would hopefully blend into the Olympic qualifiers and then, finally, the main thing, a fourth Olympic Games. The coping (hopefully, prospering) strategy was to take the stripping away of my control and authority as an opportunity. There was nothing else for it but to focus on myself. The dog-eat-dog nature of the squad system lent itself to tunnel vision and was actually ideal for my own circumstances. We're not talking about ignoring people, being abrasive or unfriendly – it was still a team sport and part of that is being a good team-mate – but it was quite cathartic to be able to focus solely on me when we were off the ice and not worry about anybody else's problems. There was no more 'Have we got enough brush pads for the week?' or 'I'll sort out the airport parking and the hire car.'

Two teams would go to the same tournaments. There were nine of us, so that meant on trips abroad, one person wouldn't be sharing. If it was possible, I would get the single room. British Curling were good about accommodating that. And, on the odd occasion I did end up sharing, I would hide my medication and take it without anyone seeing. In some ways, there were similarities to the pre-Vancouver squad but this time the numbers were bigger and the time frame shorter. And I was a completely different person. Back then I was soaking everything up, enjoying the freedom of being a wide-eyed teenager away from home and out of school, spending time with curlers I had looked up to. There wasn't the time to build the same camaraderie, nor the inclination on my part.

It was curling's answer to the Hunger Games.

We were all fighting for the same thing. Even the coaches weren't assured of being in charge of an Olympic team. British Curling was the talk of the sport. Why did the women not qualify? Is that the end of Team Muirhead? How is this squad thing actually working? We were the only major curling nation going down this route and it had been a pivot nearly three and a half years into a four-year cycle. Curling logic and curling history would suggest it had no chance of working and that it was a desperate gamble.

British Curling fully committed to it. They didn't compromise and allow themselves to consciously or subconsciously start to settle on a preferred line-up after a few weeks. The nine of us were Jen, Vicky, Lauren and I from our old team, and Gina Aitken, Hailey Duff, Rebecca Morrison, Sophie Sinclair and

Mili Smith. When the press release came out in July to confirm it all, they even felt the need to say they had listed the players in alphabetical order to make sure there was absolutely no suggestion of favouritism or names pencilled in. The chopping and changing was relentless. Every conceivable combination was tried in practice and competition. The only constant was the teams. Rather than using the surnames of the skips, as curling tradition would normally demand, it was colours. You were either blue or red. A few permutations clearly didn't work but, in the main, it was very hard to spot patterns or to second-guess.

Our first tournament was at the beginning of September. A Euro Super Series concept had been devised and the NCA was chosen as the host venue for the start of it. Rebecca Morrison skipped the red team, and I skipped the blue. It was a strong international field, with the best curlers from Sweden and Switzerland travelling to Stirling. The coaches would have been happy with the outcome. Rebecca's team won the tournament, while we won all our games through to the semi-final and only lost that one on the last stone. I would rather it had been the other way around, obviously, but it was a good way to get going.

We all got our eyes opened to the benefits of competing at home after our first foreign trip the following week. It was just as well we were a squad of nine because Jen didn't make it to St Petersburg. She was a victim of the never-ending paperwork to get into Russia, as was one of the two coaches due to travel, Kristian. In the St Petersburg Classic, we (red this time) finished third and the team skipped by Gina Aitken second. It was further validation of the squad system but there was no margin for error individually. Standards were high and two skips had finished ahead of me in two events.

There were three tournaments left – to be played in the space of four weeks – ahead of European Championship selection. The pressure would snowball from one to the next. Coaches and selectors would be looking at individual percentages and dynamics between team members but, for my own confidence as much as anything, I needed a win. Ticking that off in Basel was perfect timing and getting the better of Team Tirinzoni, the reigning world champions, in the semi-final marked it out as a significant achievement.

For the first time ever the line-up was Muirhead, Wright, Dodds and Duff. I would be rewriting history to say I was thinking at the time: 'This is it. This will be the Olympic four.' But that weekend in Switzerland turned out to be one of the most important in all our lives.

It had been a long time since I had lifted a trophy. Even then, though, British Curling stuck rigidly to the process.

We were back out to Switzerland, with another different line-up, this time getting as far as the semi-finals in the Basel Masters. Getting knocked out in the quarter-final of the Autumn Gold Classic (by the eventual winner, Tabitha Peterson from America) was statistically the worst result of my five tournaments, but it was the best I had felt about my own game and my chances of being picked for the Europeans. We beat some strong teams through the week – Jennifer Jones and Tracy Fleury among them. We were team blue, and it felt like there was now some clear blue water between the curlers likely to earn selection and those likely to miss out.

For the first time, you could read something into the blue/red split.

The Basel-winning four were reunited and Mili Smith was added to make it a five. That was all the incentive we needed to make sure we didn't muck things up because it felt like a European Championship team in waiting. That selection was confirmed. We weren't team blue or team red any more, we were Team Muirhead.

FORTY-THREE

INSIDE THE SPEED SKATING CURTAIN

You never play without pressure. But there is a sliding scale. And I had curled for long enough to realise I was as far along the pressure-free end of that sliding scale as you can possibly get for the 2021 European Championships. It wasn't that I didn't care, that I wasn't highly motivated, or that I wasn't acutely aware that if things didn't go well, this team would be broken up and another one would be given a shot at qualifying Britain for the Olympics. But I knew that sporting failure wasn't the worst thing that could happen to me.

I had reached what I hoped was my rock bottom and, maybe for the first time, curling didn't seem the most important thing in my life. I should have felt burdened, but I didn't. You can't choose to compete at top level sport while being at peace with whatever the outcome will be. We would all do it all the time if it was that easy. But it is empowering when it does happen. I wasn't scared of losing or making mistakes. I couldn't have told you the last time that had been the case.

We had already gelled as a group of five and the emotional strain of chopping and changing line-ups, while not knowing what the bosses were thinking, meant that when we did get into a team that was slightly settled, we thrived on that.

Hailey being part of it was a big factor. She was the left-field pick. Of the nine, Hailey was the only one who hadn't been part of the top two teams the season before. There was a refreshing, youthful naivety to her that reminded me of the way I had embraced the pre-Vancouver squad environment. It rubbed off on all of us. This was her first major tournament.

In the Lillehammer round robin there were lots of wins and most of them by a big margin. For our seven victories, nobody got closer to us than three points. The sole defeat was to Italy in the middle of the week when we went into the interval 6-1 down. Even then though, we nearly dug ourselves out of the hole.

We started our semi-final against Germany's Daniela Jentsch poorly and were 3-1 down at the halfway point. But the calmness that stood the group in good stead earlier in the week didn't desert us when we needed it most and we went through the gears in the last five ends to win 7-4.

Anna Hasselborg was waiting in the final, looking to make it three straight Europeans. As in the semi, we weren't fast starters. I made a mistake in the first end, and they stole one. Then there was another error in the second, which stopped us taking a two. By the ninth end we had got ourselves some control at 5-2, but Anna was always likely to make us work hard for the title, got her double and reduced our lead to just one for the 10th. They did their best to keep as many stones in play as possible and we did our best to clear them, before it was left for me to hit and stay for a two.

Gold.

I had delivered. I had led the girls in a way that brought the best out of them and me. I had the best individual shot percentage out of all the skips in Norway. With Bruce Mouat's team also beating Sweden in their final, this was history for Scotland, the first time there had been a double gold. It was also the first time not a drop of alcohol passed my lips at the banquet. The medication I was on was too strong for that. I had a plausible excuse of staying teetotal until after the Olympics, so no big questions were asked when I was the first to head back to the hotel for an early night, slipping away while the party was just getting started.

If there were whispers, so be it. For once, it was quite liberating to not worry or care about what people thought of me.

Poor Mili would have expected to wake up with a hangover, but she got a whole lot worse after testing positive for Covid. She had to stay in isolation in Norway for a week and it was a timely reminder to all of us how precarious the situation still was. I was supposed to be going to a sponsor's event at The Curling Club in London before returning to Edinburgh, but I knocked that on the head after getting Mili's news. I had been fortunate not to pick up Covid off Mili and going into the middle of London would be pushing my luck. The venue actually got closed down that night, so it was another decision I had got right.

After my previous two European wins, I had been able to savour them all the way through to Christmas. Not this year. It was a case of big job done, on to an even bigger one. There were just two weeks between winning my third European gold and embarking on my first Olympic qualifying event – in the Netherlands of all places. I had spent more hours than I would care to add up at Schiphol Airport, running about to make (or miss) connecting flights to here, there and everywhere. But I had never curled there. It was a strange choice of location for such an important event.

When we arrived at the competition hotel, we were met with lateral flow tests. Vicky was sitting next to me as we did them and I soon saw panic in her face. She was positive. She said she felt fine but that wouldn't make any difference. Vicky had worked in a hospital ward at the peak of the pandemic and didn't catch it. Now, here she was, a couple of days out from a competition that could get her to her first Olympics, staring at those dreaded purple lines in disbelief. We all got sent to our rooms and the next step for Vicky was to take a PCR test. By this point, she wasn't the only one panicking. Who would replace her? Would the chemistry between us that had worked so well in Lillehammer be lost? As British Curling were in the process of flying out Gina Aitken – she got as far as Heathrow, I think – we were heading to the Leeuwarden arena for official practice, having been waved off by Vicky, confined to her bedroom up on the 10th floor of the hotel. Then, after a few slides, Vicky arrived. The PCR results were back, and it had been a false positive. She had done her Joe Wicks fitness session in her room and was good to go! The sliding doors scenario of no Vicky didn't bear thinking about. Vicky was such a key cog in our wheel.

The Covid jeopardy was a permanent cloud that hung above you. Any other time, it would have been loss of form, injury, maybe illness, that carried the potential of ending an Olympic dream. Now, Covid was higher up the threat list than all of them combined. You thought about it constantly – that was two positive tests in our team in the space of a few weeks, albeit the second one turned out to be false. Opening a door, eating, drinking, talking – all the innocuous and mundane parts of life had the potential to bring everything crashing down.

I had navigated my career blissfully unaware of the nuts and bolts of an Olympic qualification event. It had never been on my radar. There would be no gold, silver or bronze medals handed out at the conclusion of this tournament, but the primary goal was still to finish in the top three. The top of the nine nations at the end of the round robin would be finished with their week's work there and then and be able to book their flights to China.

Second and third would play each other, the winner getting the second ticket to Beijing. And then the loser of that game would have one last bite at the cherry against the fourth-placed team.

Our mindset was: 'Let's keep this simple, finish first and go home.'

Even though the likes of Sweden and Canada had already qualified, the standard would be high. We were only ranked third highest of the nine teams. The silver and bronze medallists from the last Olympics (South Korea and Japan) were there. Then there was Germany, who won bronze at the Europeans and gave us a good game in the semi-final. Italy beat us in Lillehammer, and all the other nations had enjoyed some good results recently.

The key difference for us, compared to a few weeks before, was we now knew that we could produce as a team under big pressure rather than just hope that would be the case. One of my biggest worries was the condition of the ice. The Netherlands had never hosted a major international curling event before. It quickly became apparent that, although it wasn't the fault of the ice-makers, the size of the building made their work next to impossible. It was a speed skating arena, and we were in the middle of the track, with a big curtain the backdrop and the relentless scraping of skates on ice the soundtrack.

Narrowly beating the Czech Republic on the first morning got us up and running, but losing to Turkey on day two was a real shock to the system. Yes, you find a bit of unfair curling snobbery attached to defeats to non-traditional, warm weather nations, but we should always be beating Turkey. And we certainly shouldn't be losing 7-3. This was now serious.

We had the top two nations next and, as the German skip Daniela Jentsch said to me, we were curling on a potato field, the worst conditions I had encountered since the handles were falling off the stones in that Beijing hovel.

South Korea were a team I struggled against and this wasn't the best time to try and buck the trend. We suffered a heavy morning defeat. And then we endured the longest day of our lives as we had to fill a few hours before playing Japan, the only unbeaten team, in the evening. I took some time to myself. Another loss and we could forget about finishing top – just getting into the first four would be under real threat. I knew I needed to raise my game and start well.

I did both.

We strung a few shots together and managed the ice better with our game plan and execution to take a three-shot lead after three ends. We thought we had the fourth end locked up as well. Fujisawa Satsuki is a lovely girl. All the Japanese players are. They're such a happy bunch, annoyingly so in the middle of this match because Satsuki pulled off an unbelievably lucky shot that she wasn't even going for, which got them an undeserved two. They all burst out laughing. When someone flukes against you, you expect them to put their hand up and look sheepish. I was fighting hard to tell myself: 'That's just how they are.'

Thankfully, it proved to be a passing irritation.

An 8-5 win with an end to spare felt like a turning point and it was. We beat Germany by three, Estonia by seven and Latvia by four. Going into our last game of the round robin against Italy there was good news and bad news. The bad – finishing top and being spared more curling was out of our control. The good – if we were level with either Japan or South Korea we would beat them on curling's version of the penalty shoot-out, the draw shot challenge.

Before every game, one player from each team plays an in-turn draw and another plays an out-turn draw. Both get measured and the closest average distance to the button between the two players gets the hammer for that game and then, if two teams finish on the same win-loss record, the average draw shot distance determines who places highest.

All the players make two of each draw over the course of the round robin. Being able to get a stone to the heart of the circles is a fundamental part of curling so it's certainly a fair way to separate tied teams. Kristian had drilled into us how important the draw shot was before a game. At the beginning and end of every practice session, he would make sure we all practised it.

I wasn't paying attention to who was topping the table at the start or middle of the week, but by the time we faced Latvia, I certainly was. Going into the last game, we were at 20-plus centimetres, while Japan and South Korea were about 10 centimetres more. Considering the ice conditions, that wasn't bad at all on our part. Like us, South Korea had lost two games so we knew that if we beat Italy, they couldn't finish ahead of us, while Japan's opponents were Turkey, who had been the shock team of the tournament, as we had found out to our cost. Our game couldn't have gone any better – 8-1 and handshakes after six ends. Between ends, I had kept an eye on Japan against Turkey and, as we were finishing, Satsuki was one ahead.

None of us wanted to hang about the arena.

We had done our bit, were curling well now and feeling good about whatever came next, if that was to be another game or even another two games. We went back to the hotel and I couldn't even bring myself to watch it on my phone. While I lay on the bed in my room, the other four girls were far braver and huddled round a tablet to see Dilşat Yildiz hold her nerve and clinch victory for Turkey and end months of anguish, doubt and stress.

So, this was what relief felt like. No medal, nothing to boast about, job done, get the flight brought forward and go home. I drank the least amount of champagne out of the five of us but cried the biggest quantity of tears.

Failure inside the speed skating curtain would almost certainly have ended my career in circumstances I couldn't ever have imagined. Now though, I was a curler unshackled, and we were a team performing to a high standard who had the advantage of being tested in white-hot temperature less than two months before an Olympics.

We had sidestepped calamity and set up the possibility of what had long seemed to be unthinkable glory.

FORTY-FOUR

THE COVID GAMES

Omicron rather than Olympics was the buzzword around most dinner tables across the country on Christmas Day. The latest Covid-19 variant was on the rise and the stress levels were high in Blair Atholl. I could have stayed in Stirling, but everybody was under strict instructions to do their tests before heading to Mum and Dad's house for our family get-together.

I started Christmas morning by going for a run with Katie Robertson, Glen's future wife. Katie, an international hockey player, had set herself the task of completing a 5k for charity every day in December. I would have run anyway. Training at Christmas had become part of my routine since the build-up to Sochi a decade earlier. In the grand scheme of things, it wasn't a big deal – I was as fit as any curler. Probably fitter. It was a psychological exercise as much as anything. All athletes know the story of Seb Coe training on Christmas Day in the build-up to the 1980 Moscow Olympics because he feared his big rival, Steve Ovett, would be doing likewise.

On Boxing Day, I went out for another run and was sitting in the kitchen when Thomas came through, spluttering a bit.

'Did you do your Covid test?'

With a typical little brother to big sister reply, back came the answer: 'Of course I did. I even sent you a picture.'

'Well go and do another one.'

He did.

And this time it wasn't negative.

'I swear I did one the other day.'

Of course, he did. I knew that. But the look on his face was a mixture of horror and dread. He took another test. Positive again. Thomas went straight home, and I went straight back to Stirling, the first time I had abandoned a family Christmas on Boxing Day. He isolated for a week, or whatever the protocols stipulated at the time, and phoned at least once a day to check I hadn't caught it.

The chances were rapidly increasing that I would, and the dread was rising. Mum, Dad, Katie, Glen. One by one, like dominoes falling, they tested positive. Without telling British Curling, I booked a PCR test. Somehow, I was the only one from the Blair Atholl Christmas who hadn't contracted the virus.

For the three previous Olympics, there had been turn of the year stress of varying degrees about my form and prospects. This time, there was barely a thought about the curling. Merely getting to Beijing Covid-free was an all-consuming concern. Arriving at curling's holding camp, a lodge at Crieff Hydro Hotel, was quite comforting. If nothing else, we were all in it together now. You knew you were sharing your space with people who had the same hopes, nerves, fears and levels of vigilance.

Kitting out, previously such an amazing day when you can reflect on the achievement of becoming an Olympian, was inevitably more functional this time. The other girls who had never been to an Olympics before didn't have anything to compare it to, thankfully, but for me, it was a stark contrast to the trips to Heathrow or Adidas headquarters, being treated like royalty, that I had experienced. We got in the minibus along the road to a sports centre in Dundee, had a gym session and got all our gear after that. British Curling did their very best to make a fuss of us – for other sports, athletes just got their kit sent to them. They also did their very best to make the holding camp as special as it could be. We had a private chef and the food was amazing. There was a Burns Night put on for us. I would have brought my pipes if I had known. And on another evening, we all got to watch a video of messages from our families.

In terms of actual curling prep, it could well have been my best holding camp. The routine was perfect. We would get up at six, have breakfast before seven, head to Stirling for ice practice and then put in some strength and conditioning work.

Jen and the men's skip, Bruce Mouat, had left early because they were Britain's mixed doubles partnership and the rest of us flew out to Beijing via Helsinki two days into February. A philanthropist I met at a charity event in Canada had sent me a message asking if there was anything he could do to help us for these Olympics. Thanks to his generosity, we got upgraded. It makes such a big difference on a long-haul flight – more leg room being the main thing, but metal cutlery and a cup made of china are nice too. Having to wear a mask apart from when you were eating your meals wasn't quite so nice – even Ray's generosity couldn't help us on that front.

That discomfort was nothing compared to what was waiting for us at the airport after we landed.

A PCR test was no surprise, but this was the worst one that had ever been inflicted on me (and there had been a lot). It was verging on an assault. People were coming out of the room in tears and with bleeding noses. Mercifully, our daily PCRs at the Olympic village were more tolerable. The testing room was on our way to the food hall, so a Covid test became part of our pre-breakfast routine.

Even though it wasn't as brutal physically, it was still mentally draining. Every time you went in, you knew that the wrong result would end your Olympics there and then. It wasn't exaggerated scare stories and nightmares. I saw it happen twice. The ambulance arrived, out of it came guys in hazmat suits and then they left with the poor athlete who had to put one on as well. It was bad enough that these poor souls were robbed of their chance of competing, possibly medalling, at the Olympics. But word got around the village that they endured squalid conditions in the Covid hostels.

Mind you, the food they were getting couldn't have been much worse than the slop we were being served up.

The GB staff who were first in Beijing told us it was inedible at the start. Jen and Bruce said it was better by the time they arrived but if this was 'better' then I dread to think what it had been like before. The vegetables were reliably mushy, the chicken either green or brown and it was pure guesswork what some of the other discoloured meats were. Protein sources were few and far between. I'm not a picky eater but if you found something that was passable to eat, you stuck with it day after day. About halfway through the Games one of us discovered that the Halal chilli was OK so that became a popular dish with the team. I had brought my own porridge (a good tip from Jen) and I consumed so many boiled eggs (because they were still in their shell). The coffee was disgusting and the machine kept breaking. In summary, for food, it was my worst Olympics by a country mile.

An Olympic village isn't a natural environment at the best of times, but this one was even further removed from that because of the Covid aspect. Even if you don't like the food, sitting down for a meal should be a social, relaxing break to take your mind off your competition but it was anything but in Beijing. Individual plastic booths made meals more functional than enjoyable.

Team GB didn't enforce a hard and fast rule that we couldn't use the gym in the village (which we weren't allowed to leave) but they advised against it. I took the risk. Strength and conditioning sessions were such a big part of keeping my mind healthy. I had a Zoom meeting with Zara before flying out and we were in regular contact during the Games. That helped as well. To state the obvious, so did taking the medication I was still reliant upon.

The Calgary bubble at the 2021 worlds had been such a dispiriting slog – during and after – but it did benefit me in so much as it provided a 'nothing can be as bad as that' benchmark. I was mentally prepared for the long days before the curling started. I also had something to look forward to, which would be the nicest of distractions. Skier Dave Ryding and I were chosen as the Team GB flag-bearers for the opening ceremony. It was a wonderful honour to lead my fellow athletes during the parade of nations – really humbling to have been chosen. And the media duties that went with it helped fill some time, as did writing a speech. Dave and I both made short ones, and they seemed to be received well.

My main leadership focus, though, was looking out for the other four girls in our curling group.

And my first big test on that front came before a stone had even been thrown.

FORTY-FIVE

UNDER THE RADAR

Jen and Bruce missed out on a medal in the mixed doubles. They were the reigning world champions and had been favourites to take gold. In fact, they were probably Team GB's biggest hope. After five ends of an eight-end semi-final against Norway they were 4-2 up, but Jen made a mistake with her last shot in the sixth; their opponents edged in front with a three and stayed in front. Then, in the bronze medal play-off, they were beaten 9-3 by Sweden.

Almida Winquist de Val had a perfect shot percentage of 100 per cent.

Primarily, I was gutted for the two of them. I had been there, done that – tipped to win gold and ending up in the worst position of them all. Fourth.

From the selfish perspective of our team and our own medal prospects, I was worried.

I had always been worried about this moment.

It was the first Olympics Britain had entered a team for the mixed. I had hoped it would be me doubling up. I felt that Bobby

Lammie and I were just as strong a team as Jen and Bruce, but they beat us in the final of an event in Stirling when I had a shot to win and missed. That really stung. And it proved to be the crossroads moment for mixed selection because it meant they got selected for the worlds on the back of it, won gold and were the obvious picks for Beijing. I had no complaints. But doubling up was new territory. If they won, would Jen have the same drive and focus? Or would she be a freed-up curler who would perform better with a gold medal already banked? If they picked up silver or bronze, would it motivate her to get one or two steps higher on the podium?

Neither was the scenario she and we faced. Instead, after missing out on the medals, it was a case of would she be so devastated that she wouldn't be able to get back on track? Or would she be a fired-up curler, all the more determined to put things right?

My short-term dilemma after the bronze medal match was whether to leave Jen alone or not. I had messaged before the two big games and did the same in the wake of their loss to Sweden. As team captain, it was important that I let her know we were there for her. And, to Jen's credit, any fears that the crushing disappointment of the mixed would impact the start of our team round robin were unfounded. She just needed her own space for a bit, which I totally understood.

The day after, the two of us went for a walk through the village, talked about what had gone well and what hadn't and then she was like: 'Right, that's me back in the team now, close that book.'

It was all the reassurance I needed.

That afternoon Jen moved into our apartment, pillow in one hand, suitcase in the other and we were soon on the ice for our first official practice session. She couldn't have done a better job of flicking a switch.

Nobody was looking at us as gold medal favourites – neither the outside world nor our internal one. Media days back home had been predominantly focused on the men and the mixed. Apart from Jen, we would be practising in the NCA while the interviews were taking place nearby. It didn't faze me because I wasn't chasing the spotlight. In fact, it was nice to be under the radar for a change. Anna Hasselborg, Jennifer Jones and Silvana Tirinzoni were the big one, two, three. Between them they had the last two Olympic golds and the last World Championships title. And they were all in form. Most curling experts expected the medals to be divided up between Sweden, Canada and Switzerland, with it just being a matter of who won what colour.

Even though we had shifted the dial a bit by triumphing at the Europeans, were competition-ready on the back of the Olympic qualifiers and had a bit of an unknown factor created by the squad system, Britain were less fancied than in my previous three Games.

First up were the world champions, Switzerland.

I managed to fall over, while sliding backwards between shots. A sore bum and sore pride provided an apt metaphor for a game we let slip from our grasp. We were 4-2 up after seven ends. In the extra end, I had a very makeable draw for the win but didn't judge the weight well enough.

That had been in the morning, and this had the potential of being a very damaging day one, as we were back out in the arena for an evening game against Sweden. We couldn't have wished for this contest to have gone any better. We limited them to just two singles and leapt on Anna's mistakes in the fourth end to take a four. It was all over, 8-2, after eight ends. It was up there with my most emphatic victories over Team Hasselborg, and with my most important ones.

We had played well against the Swiss but didn't finish it off. Now we had played well against the favourites for gold and made sure there was no repeat.

It was a mid-afternoon, one-game day to follow – South Korea for us. Curling is no different from any other sport.

You get opponents who seem to suit you and those who don't. Styles? Bogey teams? Luck? A bit of all three? There was a theory doing the rounds at one stage of my career that if I wore my hair up rather than down, that meant I wasn't feeling good about my game! Trust me, I would have gladly succumbed to superstition and shaved my hair off if it meant beating South Korea at the Olympics because, whatever the reason or reasons, Kim Eun-jung and the rest of the Garlic Girls, who won silver in PyeongChang, had our number. And they knew it. Peter Gallant, a good Canadian curler, was their coach for a few years and he was never shy in reminding me that they had beaten us seven games in a row at one stage. It felt like 17.

It was a surprise to nobody that they beat us again.

We only had ourselves to blame. Kim made a foul in the eighth end when she didn't release her stone in time (I could feel her pain, of course, having been penalised for the same thing at a previous Olympics). So going from that, with her confidence affected and us a shot ahead, to letting them win in the ninth, was careless on our part. I over-curled my penultimate stone, they called their timeout to work out a game plan and, despite the fact I got my final stone into the house, it was wide open for a take-out. We conceded four.

The positive thought process of the last couple of months was being properly tested by this stage. When I told the media that it was the exact position we were in at the Olympic qualifiers – won one, lost two – I was speaking to myself as much as them. This was no time to let the glass become half-empty. Against the nine best nations in the world, two bad days in a row usually turns out to be fatal.

We needed all the positivity we could muster because we were eighth and our next opponents, America, were joint top and three from three. A 10-5 victory was just what we needed. The girls gave me an armchair ride.

And we followed it with another emphatic win by the same margin, this time against Denmark, to put us right back in the hunt for a top four place. It was a controlled performance again, forcing errors and capitalising on them, summed up by the game-winning steal of three in the penultimate end.

Facing Jennifer Jones next gave us the chance to solidify our own position and significantly undermine one of our main rivals. Like us, Canada had begun slowly but, ahead of our night game, they had beaten Russia heavily in the morning and I knew there was the potential of them building momentum.

In a contest of swapped singles and blanked ends, their three in the fifth was the move that mattered. 'Olympic Jen showed up today,' said their coach, Viktor Kjell, who had been in Thomas and the GB boys' corner at the last Games. I could understand Viktor's comment. When Jennifer is at the top of her game, you can see it in her body language. It was one high five after another. Jennifer was Canada's oldest female Olympian in any sport at 47 but you wouldn't have known it that night.

You can tie yourself up in knots, and get unhealthily consumed, by trying to predict how many wins you need to finish in the top four, but by this point we knew that six and three would be good enough. And that meant not dropping a game from here on in.

Going 6-1 up after three ends effectively put Japan to bed, barring a calamity. The calamity didn't come. That was saved for the game after.

China had only won twice but they were a team you could never underestimate. A small fortune had been invested in putting together their team of support staff in the hope of securing a medal as host nation. The Chinese girls were as diligent as any curlers on the scene, working hour after hour, day after day on textbook slides and deliveries and were technically very sound. They looked like a team who had googled 'how to curl' and had followed the instructions to the minutest detail.

Silly tactical decisions let them down on occasions but not this day. We suffered a devastating defeat.

Our destiny was out of our control, and it felt horrible.

Thankfully, though, it wasn't clutching at straws to hope that would change.

We had a day off before the final set of round-robin matches and after they were completed the wish list was clear – a win for us over Russia (or the Russian Olympic Committee, as it was known during the Olympics), Switzerland beating Japan and South Korea losing to Sweden.

With the possibility of a logjam at five wins and four losses, there wasn't any margin for error when it came to the draw shot challenge which, as in the qualifiers, would come into play to settle things.

It was much tighter than in the Netherlands. Jen and I were on pre-game draw duty and we both did well.

That was the first job done.

I produced two more inch-perfect draws to open the actual game, getting us into a lead that we never relinquished, with a four in the penultimate end sealing the deal. Russia had struggled throughout the tournament, only winning once. And, unlike China, they didn't find their best form against us.

I would defy any athlete to keep their mind purely on their own game in the circumstances we were thrust into. The team talk from Kristian and Dave was to concentrate on what we had to do, of course it was. But, if truth be told, I was almost as focused on what was happening on the other two thirds of the rink. When you're sharing the same ice as teams in the mix for the play-offs and hear the shouts and claps in a near-empty arena, it's unavoidable.

As we shook hands after beating Russia, Japan and South Korea were still playing their games. And it wasn't until we were in the post-match media area that their losses and our qualification were confirmed. Britain, Japan and Canada had five and four records. Our draw shot was just one centimetre better than Japan's and 10 centimetres better than Canada's. That meant we were third, Japan were fourth, and Canada were going home. None of us could claim to have been draw shot challenge specialists that week. Out of the 10 teams, we ranked eighth, ninth and 10th.

In big Canadian events, tiebreaker games were still used to decide play-off spots, but not at events managed by the World Curling Federation. Jennifer was in the traditionalist camp and was consistent in her opinion that the old way was the best so you couldn't accuse her of being hypocritical when she criticised the format after their exit. I'm sure I would have felt the same in her shoes, but it's not a case of one being fairer than the other. Whichever way you look at it, it comes down to executing good curling shots.

With a semi-final ahead of us, we would be needing a lot more of those.

FORTY-SIX

A GAME WITH A LIFE OF ITS OWN

It felt like a lifetime ago that we had beaten Sweden in the round robin. So much had happened since. They had only lost one game (doing us a favour by beating South Korea), while we had been on our emotional roller coaster. So, going into the semi-final, there was no psychological advantage to be taken from the previous game. They were a team who routinely produced when the stakes were high. I was expecting peak Anna.

But crucially, I also felt like her equal again. That belief in myself had eroded year after year since the last Olympics. Also, you can't overstate how reassuring it is when you look at all your team-mates and say: 'She's playing well. I can count on her today.'

It was the same with the coaches. They can't throw stones. Their function is to do as much as possible to bring out the best in the curlers. Showing they were pissed off, as they did in 2017 when our World Championships were unravelling, wasn't going to achieve that. I'm sure they would have spoken to each other about how they would work at these Games because it felt as if they had a better grasp of who would take the lead in different circumstances. I certainly had a clear picture of what I wanted from them. Dave was an experienced Olympian, knew me well and knew what to say before a game to get me in the right frame of mind, whether that was hyping me up or bringing me down. Kristian had less of an ego, which was just as well. At an Olympic Games, with a head coach on the scene, the team coach has a boss to defer to and if there's a time-out, he's not the one who comes on to the ice with advice.

Along with Mili, Kristian matched stones night after night, and he was the one I looked to for any tactical advantage I could get. Just as I had absolute faith that Glenn Howard's Canadian roots wouldn't compromise him in the slightest before we played his home country in a big game in PyeongChang, I knew Kristian's nationality wasn't a factor on this occasion. His girlfriend, who would become his wife, was Anna's alternate but I had no worries about any careless pre-game talk. In fact, Kristian being a Swedish speaker actually benefitted.

'They're nervous,' he told me ahead of the first end. 'I can tell by the way they're talking to each other.' Maybe he was right, maybe he was wrong, maybe he knew he was wrong. Whatever the truth, it helped my mindset.

As the higher-placed team in the round robin, they had the hammer. We didn't want to alter our game plan too much from what we had been doing to that stage, but we wanted to push them early to get the hammer flipped. They were the strongest front runners in the world and the best at scoring multiple points when they had the last stone. They were scoreboard bullies, who were extremely hard to peg back when they were in front because their up-weight, hitting game was so strong.

Forcing them to take a one was a big goal.

We went hard, in retrospect too hard, in our attempt to land an early psychological blow. It carried the risk of losing a big end. In my worst nightmares, though, I couldn't have envisaged that big end being a four. I had the chance to hit with my last stone and limit them to a three, but who accepts going three down in an Olympic semi-final against the best team in the world? I opted for a draw. Being short with it was the culmination of an end that had gone wrong from first stone to last. We had got our tactics wrong. We were far too aggressive. I knew my curling history and my percentages. Even if you strip away the identity of the opponents, it was almost unheard of to lose a four in the first end of a game of this magnitude and win. The chances of that happening were minuscule.

This was a time when leadership, my leadership, mattered.

I gathered the girls round me. They looked shell-shocked. No wonder. So was I. There was no point in coming away with stuff like: 'If ever there's a time to lose a big end, the first in a 10-end game is it.' That would be far too broad-brush. A short-term goal to keep us alive was required.

'Right, let's just get our two.'

We went one better. We got a three. I can't think of another occasion in a game when I've given a big fist pump after a second end. But it was warranted. It's probably the single end I'm most proud of in my whole career. Without patience, smart tactics, precise shot-making and emotional resilience, it wouldn't have been possible. I needed them all.

We were still behind by a point, still overwhelming underdogs but we had a chance again.

Forcing them to one in the third end and then taking singles ourselves in the fourth and fifth, truly made it 'game on'. For both teams, strategy was the casualty of chaos. Like so many great sporting encounters, this semi-final had taken on a life of its own.

Nobody would have predicted a ridiculously high-scoring game with not so much as a solitary blank end. It should have been cagey. This was a situation that suited me – thinking on my feet, reacting, painting freehand, not by numbers.

Talking is good in those circumstances. And we were talking a lot. Sweden, on the other hand, had gone from relaxed and in control to tetchy and bewildered. The best way of summing it up was their frustration at conceding a second end three was greater than our frustration at losing a first end four. And they hadn't shaken it off. By the ninth end, the fog around them hadn't lifted. We were outwitting them, more so than I could remember doing in a long time.

That ninth was another to be proud of.

Good skips leave things for their last shot. And good skips don't rush the conclusion. They have the patience to let an end build and back themselves to make all the preparation work of their team-mates and their own strategising pay off in one stone. That's the only time when lying shot matters. I was faced with a half-stone take-out, similar to the one I had (and failed with) to win bronze in PyeongChang. There was a realistic three for me if I caught the right amount of their stone, and a very tough four if I judged the weight to perfection to allow the back stone to cling to the scoring rings. It required equal parts pace and accuracy. The girls had done their bit to set it up but I didn't need them to do much sweeping for the final act of the end.

'Clean' is a reassuring shout if you're in the crowd or watching on TV. So is something like: 'Clean, yes, no, yes.' It might sound like indecision but it's code for: 'This is good, just please don't fall over and hit the stone.'

Securing that four was one of the most important shots I had delivered and one of the best. Not because of its technical difficulty – set it up in practice and it would be nothing special. Because of the circumstances. We were 11-8 up with one end to go. There had been a seven-shot swing. We had one foot in the final, my first Olympic final.

How to explain what followed?

A 180-degree change in mindset is a fair place to start.

This was a spectacular relapse. For the first time in the Games, I wasn't able to cling to a 'nothing to lose, everything to gain' mantra. There was now a lot to lose, and that fact proved impossible to block out. The Swedes had stolen our perspective, cast off their mental shackles and thrown them at us to put on.

The five rock rule in curling, which was implemented four years earlier, works in favour of dramatic end-of-game swings. Teams can't remove their opponents' stones from the free guard zone (in play but outside the rings) until five stones have been played. It has been a positive rule change for the sport, keeping more stones in play and putting the emphasis on shot-making rather than hitting, which is the real essence of curling. But, in this moment, I would quite happily have sacrificed my principles and the good of the game to be able to instruct my team to hit everything they saw and keep the house clear.

Individually, none of us played a good end.

I certainly made a few tactical blunders. My mind was frazzled. Clear thinking had deserted me. My last stone was the biggest blunder of them all. If I was watching this play out, I would have been shouting at my television: 'What the hell is she doing?' I'm sure my dad was. I should have played a shot with weight but decided to try and put a guard in place that would stop Anna having a chance for the three she needed to take it to an extra end or – heaven forbid – the four that would finish us off. The stone didn't curl enough. It was gut-churning stuff. A nightmare playing out in front of me. I had control, didn't use it, and now it was gone.

I felt physically sick.

A quick assessment of the lie of the land gave some relief – at least there was no route to a game-winning four. And the three wasn't straightforward. But this was Anna. Of course she made it.

The Swedish girls were every bit as animated as you would expect. They had come back from the dead. We had allowed them to come back from the dead. And they were filled with all the euphoria, adrenaline and confidence which comes with that. The psychology for them and us had see-sawed so dramatically over the course of this game and it fell to me to make sure there was one last, decisive swing of the pendulum left in it.

The bewilderment cleared and I had the presence of mind to think to myself and then say to the girls: 'Look, if we had been given the chance of an extra end with the hammer to beat Sweden and get to an Olympic final, we would have 100 per cent taken it.'

We would have taken it a year ago, a month ago, a week ago, an hour ago. Quietening the devil on the shoulder who was screaming, 'You wouldn't have taken it 10 minutes ago,' was the important bit. And we achieved it.

The 10th end was awful from start to finish, the 11th and last end was close to perfection. I was back in the zone, focusing on the small details, like timing the opposition stones. I might not have been calm but I did a good job of appearing that way. Anna played the shot I expected – and hoped – she would with her last stone. She tried to freeze against one of our stones on the edge of the eight-foot and make sure I had to draw inside it to win.

I had shown the presence of mind to play a draw with the first of my two stones to get a feel for what would be required with my second. I have never been so glad to not be needed. Anna didn't get her final stone into a scoring position. We had won. We were going to be playing for gold. I had an Olympic final to look forward to. The exhilaration was like nothing I had ever experienced. I had lived a career's worth of highs and lows in a couple of hours.

How many times do you see a game for the ages being followed up by an anti-climax, though?

A lot.

FORTY-SEVEN

AM I FIXED?

The semi-final was a night game so, with all the media commitments we had to fulfil, there wasn't any time to get carried away with what had just happened, even if we had been inclined to. By the time my head hit the pillow, exhaustion made sure I got a decent sleep.

From the moment we met up for breakfast, my job was clear – make this as normal a day as possible, filled with routine.

We had played at least once a day since the round robin started. There are occasions when you want to surf a wave and don't want to break your game rhythm. But I was glad we weren't going straight into a final. Breakfast was followed by a practice session. We bumped into the Swedish girls, who had a bronze medal play-off against Switzerland later that night, and the devastation of losing that titanic semi-final battle was still written all over their faces.

After lunch, we watched the men's gold medal game, which started at two o'clock, Chinese time. It was Britain against Sweden once more, but the polar opposite of the cricket score contest we had played out with Team Hasselborg. The curling was high quality but nervy and low risk. There was only one end that produced a score of more than a single and, to nobody's surprise in the arena, the game was decided by an extra end, with Team Edin securing the final point to win 5-4.

We were gutted for the Scottish boys. An Olympic silver medal is an Olympic silver medal – a magnificent achievement. But Bruce and his team weren't seeing it that way at this stage. Selfishly, we had to get ourselves back in our own small world, which meant a team meeting to firm up tactics for the final.

Switzerland had topped the table in the round robin, dropping just one game, while Japan, like us, had a record of five wins and four defeats. I expected Switzerland to win their semi. But the two Swiss shot-makers, Silvana Tirinzoni and Alina Pätz, dropped into the mid-70s for their individual percentages, which decided the game.

In pure curling terms, I would have chosen to face Team Fujisawa. I knew what I was going to get with them. They would almost always be a seven or eight out of 10 but Silvana and Alina, when they were at their best, had a higher ceiling and could hit nine or 10. Plus, we had beaten Japan three times in the space of a few months. Losing the bronze medal Olympic play-off to them four years earlier was ancient history. So much water had passed under my bridge since then.

But it was an Asian team in Asia. That meant a huge amount of media interest in the final. Even for a regular tour event, the Japanese press is on a different scale to any other nation, Canada included. I had been at Open Championships and seen what it was like for their star golfer, Hideki Matsuyama. The hype around this curling game was comparable. There was talk about putting the start time back for Japanese television. I was asked my opinion (I would rather it stayed the same because that was what we had been planning for) but I made sure I didn't get too involved. Control the controllables.

My nerves were fine. I was on the look-out for signs that the enormity of what was going to come the next morning was getting too much for any of the other girls, Hailey in particular, but there were none. We had negotiated a potentially tricky, and long, day well and hadn't got caught up in talk of Stone of Destiny part two and all that big picture stuff the British media would be writing and speaking about. A few texts were replied to on the burner phone we had been given for our stay in China. I had only given my number to a handful of people, so that didn't take long. Then I got another good night's sleep, after which I woke up confident and far less nervous than before the semi.

Controlled aggression would be the best description of our tactics.

There was no way we were going to let an Olympic final pass and have regrets about not being bold enough. But we also knew that Japan would be hoping we pushed too hard, too soon and they would have a chance to capitalise on our errors. We were basically going back to our pre-Sweden game plan.

Having the hammer certainly helped. The other three girls made it a routine first end and for my last shot I had a simple tap for a two. A very good start. Backing it up by restricting them to a single in the second meant that we were already the team shaping the direction of the game. They would have to chase and force. End by end it became increasingly clear that the two shot-makers in their rink – Satsuki on last stones and Chinami Yoshida at third – weren't at their best. And every time they made a mistake, we cashed in.

My mind never drifted. I didn't allow myself to think I was closing in on a gold medal. After each end I said: 'Right, it's 0-0, start again.'

I pulled off a very good draw to steal in the fifth and we didn't let them score again until the sixth. As the seventh end developed, it became apparent that this would be the game-defining one. They upped the risk-reward factor, realising that at 4-2 down, time wasn't on their side. With Vicky about to play her second stone (the third last for the team) I called our time-out. We had two scoring stones, but they had two of their own in the rings and a guard outside them. By the time Dave arrived to join the discussion, the girls had agreed with me that taking out the guard was the way to go. Dave gave the reassurance I was looking for. It would open up our route to the house and should keep us in control. Vicky did her job, then, with the first of my stones I took out two of the three Japanese stones.

They were lying one, but we had three yellows in the rings as I drew back my arm for the last stone of the end. My task was a raise shot (pushing one of my stones on to another) to knock their red out and leave us with a four. My 'yes, no' shouts to the sweepers were a sign all was well. It was on track. The connection with the first stone was perfect and everything fell into place from there. Like my short raise for the four against Sweden, the sight of stones clattering into each other to leave one colour dominating the house probably makes that type of shot look more difficult than it actually is, but they will be the two I'm remembered for above all the others.

We were 8-2 up and you could see by the reaction of everybody in Team GB kit that they thought it was game over. My face told a different story. I wasn't allowing myself to drift. Nothing was won yet. The first time I let myself think 'this is actually happening' was in the middle of the slide for my last stone of the match in the ninth end.

It was an open draw for a two after they had only managed one in the eighth. Out came the Japanese hands and then up went ours. We had won. And by the joint biggest margin ever in an Olympic final. Of all the scenarios that had gone through my head the night before, handshakes after the ninth end and a 10-3 scoreline wasn't one of them.

That's when the golden blur began.

Plenty of hugs, obviously. And plenty of media. Seeing Rhona in the mixed zone was an emotional moment for her – I'm sure the memories were flooding back from Salt Lake City. And it was the first time I let in the enormity of what I had achieved.

A career is full of stepping stones. Even the big victories were always part-viewed as a staging post to what I hoped would happen next. Winning an Olympic gold was different. It didn't mean I was retiring but this was a new sensation. Fulfilment. I had done it. I had got there.

Achieving *it* and getting *there* were overwhelming.

I was doing my very best to keep myself together. Thank goodness it didn't come into my mind that the hand which had delivered the gold medal-winning stone had a ring on one of its fingers which was made for my 30th birthday out of my two grannies' engagement rings. I had never worn it in competition before. Without family in Beijing to share this incredible moment with me, thinking about any of them, those back home or those no longer with me, would have turned me into a blubbering mess.

A wave of emotion was about to wash over me that was unavoidable, though.

The International Olympic Committee couldn't have chosen anybody better than Kate Caithness to present us with our medals. Kate, a fellow Scot, had been the president of the World Curling Federation for most of my career and we had known each other for even longer. You don't forget who was looking out for you when times were tough. I didn't have to go too far back to recall my darkest days. Kate was one of the people who got in touch after our disastrous Calgary World Championships. It meant a lot at the time and always will.

Probably for the first time since I returned to the National Curling Academy after everybody else had gone home, I let myself drift back to the ordeal that had led me to the top of this podium with a very heavy piece of metal around my neck. As the Union Jack was rising and I mumbled 'God Save the Queen', a thought went through my mind that I suspect not many other Olympians, if any, will have experienced.

'Does this mean I can stop taking my pills now? Am I fixed?'

I was proud of what I had done on the ice. I didn't stumble to an Olympic curling gold. There had been no shortcuts. This was a fourth time lucky fairy tale and, more recently, a story of sporting redemption. But I was even more proud of speaking up, asking for help, going back into an environment that had nearly broken me.

Above all, I just wanted to feel good about myself.

I did.

FORTY-EIGHT

THE BAUBLES OF BEIJING

With gold and silver medals in our hand luggage, the upgraded curlers had earned their extra leg room, the complimentary pyjamas and somebody tucking your sheets in for you. Oh, and the free drink. Vicky was the clear winner of that competition! So much so, that on the taxi journey from Heathrow to appear on the BBC's *The One Show*, she was out for the count. 'You'd better take most of the questions, Eve,' was the instruction from British Curling's PR official.

We got one night of five-star luxury in The Langham Hotel in London's West End before a full day of appearing on every TV and radio channel I had heard of – and a few I hadn't. I was ready to come home. Seeing Mum, Dad, Glen and Katie at Edinburgh Airport, along with loads of other familiar faces, was a lovely moment. That was to be expected, I suppose. The reception when I returned to Stirling certainly wasn't. My neighbours had changed the street name to Muirhead Avenue, put up loads of banners and balloons and were all outside to welcome me home. Even though I must have had about six hours' sleep in three days and was desperate for my own bed, it was a special gesture.

I met Thomas in Bridge of Allan for breakfast the next morning. It was the middle of lambing season so he couldn't get to the airport. Last time I had seen him, he had been sent packing by Dad from the family Christmas after his positive Covid test. Later that afternoon, it was my turn to be ill and it had nothing to do with Thomas or coronavirus.

My body had given up on me.

The ulcers and the tiredness were part of my post-competition routine, but never as bad as this. I was sick for two days. I couldn't have ventured further than my sofa even if I had wanted to.

I knew it would pass, though. I knew that this level of fame and attention would pass as well. There would be a big comedown at some point. My advice to the girls was to enjoy everything that came our way while it lasted. So many memories were made in the weeks and months that followed our return from China – whether it was in person or by learning about the kind gestures of others. They were our baubles of Beijing.

A photoshoot for *Hello* magazine.

The chippie I used to busk outside being painted gold.

'We are the Champions' getting played outside Buckingham Palace on the day of our win and then being invited there for a Tokyo and Beijing medal winners' reception.

Being treated like royalty on the middle Saturday of Wimbledon in the company of Max Whitlock, Adam Peaty, Tom Daley, Georgia Hall, Catriona Matthew and other world-class athletes.

Cycling against Olympic gold medal-winning rower, Helen Glover, in the Lee Valley Velodrome in London for Comic Relief.

Having a race named in our honour at Perth Racecourse.

Getting applauded on to the pitch at McDiarmid Park, the home of my local football team, St Johnstone, who I had watched as a young girl with Dad and Glen.

Being awarded the Freedom of the City of Perth.

Sitting for portrait artists on a TV programme and having my face painted on a mural on the side of a three-storey city centre building.

Getting OBE added to my name.

You can set life goals, sporting or otherwise, but nobody embarks on their career thinking that sort of recognition will come their way. The Olympic gold was the reason I was awarded the OBE, but because I hadn't yet had the chance to receive my MBE, I got two for one from Charles, then the Prince of Wales, at Windsor Castle, which he said was a first for him! They gave me the choice of waiting until the following year for my upgrade but I'm glad I doubled up. Everything about the day was perfect – the weather, the setting and going out for dinner with my family after. Uncle Rich and Aunts Sue and Ruth, from Mum's side of the family, joined us. All three had been a great support, from my aunts looking after me in the Kinross fields while Dad was lambing and Mum was still nursing, to Rich travelling out to all three Olympics and meeting me at Heathrow when I got back from my fourth and final one.

For Mum and Dad, seeing their wee girl standing in front of the future king was the moment that brought home what I had achieved and how I had achieved it. Sharing in their pride was worth even more than the two awards. Only the three of us had lived every twist and turn of the journey. More has been written and said about Dad, because of the sporting dynasty story. Mum can throw stones – the phrase 'if you can't beat them, join them' springs to mind – and always seemed to find a way to get to a big tournament, even when she had a job, a farm, a guest house, kids and goodness knows what else to juggle. But it was Mum being Mum away from curling which mattered most. Whether it was fundraising for kilts when the new pipe band was formed or helping set me up in a new home. Whether it was making sure there was always a roast dinner and a roaring fire when I got home from a curling trip or making a two-hour phone call to British Curling to open people's eyes to how far I had fallen. She was never anything less than totally invested in my life. No daughter could ask for more.

I met some fascinating people at Windsor that day. Sir David Attenborough was knighted for a second time. Incredible. My favourite had to be the brilliant actor, Toby Jones, who received an OBE, like me. He was hilarious. Toby and his mum were like a double act. We were all in hysterics when she was telling him to stop making jokes. It was like Ronnie Corbett and his mum in the old sitcom, *Sorry!* King Charles knows Highland Perthshire well, so he was on safe ground talking about my home area and he also wasn't too shabby on curling, reminiscing about the days when the sport was played on frozen ponds at Balmoral.

I would have loved to have seen the faces of my old English teachers as they settled down to watch *Countdown* on Channel 4 and saw that I was the guest in Dictionary Corner. I was even part of a bit of programme history – one of the contestants achieved a record score. Five episodes were filmed in one day. I'm sure there are some famous people who get invited on and actually come up with big words to impress the viewers on their own, but I wasn't one of them. Anything above six was being fed to me through an earpiece!

You need to know your limits, however.

The BBC wanted me to appear on *Celebrity Mastermind*. I had politely declined in 2018. Having initially given their second invitation a tentative 'OK', it didn't take long for me to see sense. A gold medal may have the power to change a few things, but finding a specialist subject that would lead to any other conclusion than me making a fool of myself in front of the nation wasn't among them. I wasn't allowed to pick curling and, even though I could play the bagpipes, I knew precious little about the history of the instrument. The same was true for golf and farming. There really was nothing. And that was before I contemplated my general knowledge! So, I told my management: 'You'll have to get me out of this.' Get me out of it they did, thankfully. Public humiliation was averted.

I hope that becoming an Olympic gold medal winner was as fulfilling for the other girls as it was for me. We were a five-person team, who became the perfect blend of characters and skill sets, as much by accident as design.

Vicky was the mothering personality of the group. Sometimes I wanted to say: 'Just focus on yourself because you can't worry about the rest of us.' Her calming influence was just what I needed in Beijing. The skip's job description is clear, but a third's is less so. I wanted to lean on somebody who was supportive rather than decisive or argumentative and I got that from Vicky in the heat of competition. She didn't harbour leadership ambitions or to even be a leader in this team. She was happy being the link between the front end of the group and me. Most importantly, Vicky was the best-performing player in her position during the Olympics. You can't ask for much more than that.

Jen would have got to a good level at whatever sport she chose. Her bench presses were more impressive than some of the guys, up at 80-plus kilos. She was probably the most physically powerful curler I played with. Jen came to us strong and got even stronger. There is an intimidation factor when you have someone who can sweep harder than everyone. Giving out a strong pre-match handshake doesn't do any harm either. I should know, because a few tried that on with me over the years.

I've got such admiration for Jen's bounce-back from the mixed doubles and the same goes for Hailey and the fact that a first Olympics – actually, a first year as an elite curler – didn't faze her at any point. She was driven to higher standards by being part of the team and was a great example of using your environment to improve. I saw my younger self in Hailey. If somebody went to the gym or put in extra practice on the ice, she felt she had to do that as well. That's how I was. That's how it should be. Hailey was laid-back (far more than me), verging on horizontal off the ice, but always striving to be better on it, which is a wonderful combination.

For whatever reason, Rhona's gold medal team have always been known as a four rather than a five. Margaret Morton seldom gets a mention. When a film was made, marking the 20th anniversary of Salt Lake City, there was talk of a fallout with Margaret, which is a real shame. I made sure that Mili would be included after Beijing. We all did. I can only imagine that being a fifth at an Olympics is a mental challenge. Sitting on the bench game after game can't be easy – thinking you could help when the team is struggling and yearning to be in the thick of it when the team is winning. Mili would have been desperate to get on the ice, but she knew her chores were away from the cameras and never approached them with anything less than full commitment.

I had forever been searching for that magical alchemy that produces greatness in a curling team, the intangibles that aren't an exact science. Maybe I was guilty of changing too often and too soon on occasions. I don't believe in fate. Not in a written in the stars type of way. I believe you have a better chance of success the more work you put in, whether that's over the course of a career, a season or a fortnight. We were the best team in Beijing, the best team in our semi-final and the best team in the final. And I had made sure I was the best curler I could be. Yes, that applied to China. But it was broader than that. From the moment, in my early twenties, the penny dropped that dedication would be just as important as raw talent, probably more so, I embraced that theory without compromise or complaint. It was at a cost to my body, my quality of life as others would view it, and my mental well-being. But it had paid off.

My individual story of pushing myself to the extremes, and sometimes beyond, fed into this collective triumph. But the fact that this team, of all my teams, turned out to be the golden one did defy a lot of the logic I had subscribed to. In some ways, character wise, I would have been better suited to a career as an individual athlete, but when you savour success of this magnitude, seeing your own emotions mirrored in others really did amplify the enjoyment. To know you will forever be inextricably associated with four other people you respect and like is to be cherished more than metal on a ribbon.

FORTY-NINE

IT'S OVER

All those trappings were spread out over a few months. But curling does get you back down to earth quickly better than any other sport. In the middle of the personal appearances and the palaces, there was competition. Just seven days after our Olympic final, all 10 curlers were present and correct at the Dewars Centre for the Scottish Mixed Doubles. Even for somebody like me, who was used to the sharp contrast between regular curling and Olympic curling, that long weekend felt surreal.

I would have loved it to have been promoted and showcased better. To only see the familiar faces, who would turn up at tournaments like this come wind, rain, or shine, was a bit deflating.

I really wanted to win, though. Missing out on the world mixed last time and, with it, the chance to double up at the Olympics, niggled. Bobby Lammie and I were highly motivated, and we played brilliantly. We didn't drop a game, beating Bruce and Jen 9-2 in a final that lasted just five ends. It earned us selection for the worlds in Geneva. Bobby was hard on himself after Beijing. He didn't play badly but he didn't produce his best form, certainly not in the final. He took a lot of responsibility for that loss on his shoulders. I knew how he felt. That was me four years earlier. The two of us were a very strong mixed combination. Bruce and Jen worked well because it was one front-end player and one back-end player, and it was the same for Bobby and me. He listened to me; that was the main thing!

Bobby was a sweeping machine all week at the worlds. I basically knew that as long as I didn't throw stones too heavy or too wide, nine times out of 10 I was going to make the shot because Bobby would do the rest.

There were 20 nations there, split into two groups. We won all nine of our round-robin games. It was as dominant as I've ever been in a tournament at world level. Canada were the only country to stay within four points of us in a game. We kept that going by thrashing Germany in the semi-final and then, in the final against Alina Pätz and Sven Michel of the host nation, we got the win and the title in the closest game of the competition, 9-7.

Another gold. And this was the last one I didn't have on my CV.

Not only was it a successful week, it was a really enjoyable one as well – a bit of a throwback to the old curling world. The World Seniors were taking place at the same time so there were lots of familiar faces about the place. Jackie was one of them. She got a bronze. We were at the same table as them for the closing banquet. A combination of the champagne bought for us in the hotel straight after our win, plenty of drink at the banquet and me having barely touched a drop for a year made it a big night and a big hangover. Our physio had put me to bed, but she couldn't do anything to make me feel any better on the flight home!

European champion, Olympic champion, World Mixed Doubles champion. I would have loved to have got the opportunity to make it a full set in one season, an unprecedented Grand Slam, but the Scottish Championships started the day after our gold medal match in Beijing. There were no Olympic qualification points at stake in that year's worlds so British Curling decided this was an opportunity to give someone else a chance.

Would we have won the World Championships? Probably not. We didn't do that well in the Canadian events post-Olympics and everything pointed to us being emotionally spent as a team. But my view on the fundamental principle that you earn your shot hadn't changed.

Retirement wasn't on my mind – not standing on the podium in Beijing, not in the weeks that followed, not at the end of the season and not even when there was time to take a deep breath and reflect. I had been around former athletes, spoken to them, heard regrets about calling it a day too soon, heard regrets about calling it a day too late. No two stories were the same, but the common thread was: 'You'll just know.'

Working for the BBC at the 150th Open Championship in St Andrews had the potential to make me think that life outside the ropes was now more appealing than life inside. But it didn't. If anything, it reminded me of all the addictive aspects to being in a pressure-filled sporting arena. That was what I knew, loved and lived for.

Two of my team had hung up their brooms by that point – one expected, one not.

It was an open secret in British Curling that Vicky would sign off, whatever the outcome in Beijing. Like Vicki, marriage and family were a stronger pull than four more years as a curler. Mili was a surprise, though. I didn't see that one coming. She was selected in British Curling's squad for the following season but decided to drop out at the last minute and study to become a primary school teacher.

That meant the five they named were Jen, Hailey, Beth Farmer, Fay Henderson and me.

I had spoken to Kristian quite regularly over the summer. Both of us thought him staying and me helping to coach, while continuing to be part of a five-person team, would work well. It would get my foot on the coaching ladder and, combined with increasing my mixed doubles schedule alongside Bobby, would make things fresh enough to keep me motivated. I had seen a lot of promise in Fay. She was 21, a skip with raw talent and I was keen to work with her as a mentor/team-mate. Kristian agreed with me that she had real potential.

Towards the end of July, when Kristian phoned as I was driving to the supermarket in Stirling, I just thought it would be to share his thoughts on our return to training, which was scheduled for the start of the following month. But he had other news. He was planning to quit British Curling and return home to Sweden. He didn't mention it at the time, but it turned out he was going to accept a job to coach Team Hasselborg. I could understand why they would head-hunt him and why he would move. Of all the possible triggers to end my curling career, this wouldn't have even made the shortlist. From being in a fairly settled place that I would keep going and give it at least another year, all of a sudden, I found myself with a pen and paper, writing down a list of pros and cons. One heading had far more underneath it than the other. The 'what's in this for me' balance had shifted.

I knew I wouldn't be consulted when it came to the appointment of Kristian's successor and that I would have to work at forging a relationship with whomever it was going to be. Building up a new team that would inevitably take a while to become competitive wasn't nearly as appealing without the dynamic at the top between Kristian and me that I had assumed would be in place.

All the negatives that had always been there were now screaming at me, without that one fundamental positive to drown them out.

I floated an idea with British Curling. Could I just do mixed doubles? It would have been the new challenge I needed and, who knows, might have led to a return to the team format at some point over the course of the four-year cycle. It was made abundantly clear by the bosses that was a non-starter. It was made clear to me that I could either do both or none.

I didn't rush into a decision but the probability of retirement, rather than just the possibility, didn't feel daunting. The exact opposite in fact. By the time there was one week to go before we were due to return to training, I was starting to feel apprehensive and scared about going back. Speaking to Mum and Dad gave me the affirmation I needed. If they had said things like 'don't be too hasty' or 'are you absolutely sure about this?' that might have put doubts in my mind and been enough to nudge me back into the curling comfort zone. But I could tell they wanted me to quit. They wanted the best for me and my emotional well-being and knew better than anyone that was no longer wrapped up in the life of a professional curler.

Nobody tried to talk me out of it, in fact. Family, friends, management – they knew it was the right call and that I wouldn't live to regret it.

My chat with Rowan and Becky of Red Sky was another one of those conversations that turned into tears. They asked me: 'Well, what are you going to do next?' I wasn't sure, but even that uncertainty didn't give me fear. I had had enough of curling, and I had been kidding myself for a couple of months that a bright enough flame was still burning. So, I made the call to British Curling. I was out. Everything was synchronised for the announcement. There was no going back.

Telling the other girls in the team wasn't easy, Fay and Beth in particular. I wanted them to know that my retirement was no reflection on them. If anything, the prospect of mentoring up-and-coming players had been the biggest pull left.

Everything else that happened in the months after made me feel so special and valued.

The public voting me third in the BBC's Sports Personality of the Year Awards, when I was on a shortlist with Jessica Gadirova, Beth Mead, Ben Stokes, Ronnie O'Sullivan and Jake Wightman, was the ultimate career bookend.

You get a different type of praise and appreciation when you retire, even compared to after winning an Olympic gold. None of us read our obituaries. This was as close as you can get. I can't rank them in order of which message meant most, but the skips I had battled with for so many years, like Anna and Alina, saying that I had driven them to higher standards got to the heart of what I had achieved as a curler. I had made my mark on the sport and helped push it forward in terms of my own accomplishments and those of others.

Fixating on medals doesn't give you a career that leaves you feeling fulfilled and regret-free. Knowing deep down that you pushed yourself as hard and as far as you could, dedicating your life to being the best competitor you were capable of being while trying to support others, does that.

Spending more time thinking about the big shots that weren't than were made is something all sports people will identify with. That doesn't mean I was left with any if onlys, however. I'm not saying everything happens for a reason but, for me, the ups and downs, all of them, led to a magical ending very few get to savour.

The curling part of my life had been boxed off, with a pretty bow immaculately tied on the top. On the ice, I had absorbed the blows and come back stronger.

Off it was a different story.

The missed shot that denied us a bronze in PyeongChang, the hotel room trauma, the Calgary bubble and its aftermath – they all made me weaker, more vulnerable and less content as a person.

I would be lying to pretend otherwise.

I needed life after curling to fix that, not a gold medal.

FIFTY

HAPPINESS

Curling doesn't leave you, not unless you want it to. I hadn't fallen out of love with the sport, just the institutional grind of being a player striving for the biggest prizes it had to offer. After removing myself as a competitive curler, I was happy to do a bit of coaching, a bit of commentating, start up my own academy and put my shoulder to the wheel to save my home ice rink from closure. I didn't even mind playing the odd game there.

Perth Super League might not hold quite the same appeal as it did when I was starting out, bickering with Glen about who played which position and barking at him if he over-swept. But when your dad speaks, you still listen. If he's a player short and I can't come up with a good enough excuse, I get roped in. Dad, one of my brothers, Stuart Stark and I against four local farmers. No warm-up to get the hip going, not much flexibility under half a dozen layers, a couple of practice slides, handshakes across the house and off you go. You play, you win (hopefully), you leave, and these days you're all still talking to each other.

I had no doubts that curling and I would find a new normal and get along just fine. I also knew, though, that curling, even Olympic gold medal-winning curling, hadn't brought me true happiness. That wasn't going to change.

Finding a life balance that works for you is probably the biggest challenge for any retired athlete. And, as with the big decision about when to call it quits, no two stories are the same. The loss of a cornerstone week is probably the one common theme that unites us. More often than not, mine was alarm, breakfast, training, lunch, physio, bed by eight. It was fixed, repetitive and, for me, therapeutic and reassuring. Then it stopped. Calendars and diaries got instantly emptier. Flexibility usurped order. Plenty of ex-athletes are quite happy to get a new order and groove in ways that don't require the sort of physical exertion that is essential to achievement in the sporting arena. But that's not how I'm built.

The flick of the switch in 2012 changed me – not just for the rest of my curling career but for life.

I had been a party animal, someone who could be relied upon to show up for a night out at the drop of a hat, and the definition of a social butterfly. Then, for the best part of a decade, I barely touched a drink, overhauled my diet, and turned down invites to the point of becoming antisocial. I had grown to hate going out. The struggle being around people who weren't family or close friends has followed me out of curling, and I can't see that changing.

If I've got an obsession, bordering on an addiction, it is pushing my body. This drive was an enormous factor in all the medals I won. I would like to think during the 10 years I became a European, world and Olympic champion, none of my peers dedicated more time and energy to honing their technique and strategically improving as a curler than I did. The number of extra solo ice sessions I booked so I could work things out for myself would suggest that may well have been the case. But I don't unequivocally know that. I do unequivocally know that nobody did more than me to be physically prepared.

Filming myself in the gym and sending the videos to Dave Leith was standard – whether I was just proud of a new mark I had set or needed his advice. If I missed a gym session, for whatever reason, I wouldn't be able to get it out of my head until I had completed an extra one to make up for the ground that I believed I had lost. Giving myself a rest day was a mental battle. It just didn't sit well. Again, ground had been lost, at least in my mind. I feel sorry for Vicki Chalmers, who spent more time as my room-mate on tour than anybody else. I suppose I must have helped her get ready for life as a mum with all the 5am alarm calls so I could be first into the hotel gym!

Deload weeks were torture. If a gym session didn't culminate in redlining exhaustion at the end of it, what was the point?

I worked incredibly hard for my medals. Somewhere between passion and compulsion, I pushed my body to its absolute limit, so I could earn my night's sleep, knowing that I hadn't left a stone unturned. Plenty of former athletes say that it was team camaraderie, competing, winning, even losing, that they found to be the deepest and hardest holes to fill – basically, the sporting aspects of competition.

I could cope without all of those, even the buzz of seeing the last stone track on target or standing at the top of a podium, but not without having physical goals.

I have hit the road on a bike – cycling 85 miles across parts of Highland Perthshire in the Etape Caledonia event.

I have hit the road on two feet. Many times.

Completing the London Marathon turned out to be one of the greatest challenges put in front of me. A few weeks before the race, I didn't think I would even make the starting line and was worried that I would let down all the people who had donated to the charity I was running to raise money for. A pain down the side of my right shin brought back the memories and tears of my pre-operation hip ordeal. I thought it was shin splints, but it turned out to be a nerve issue. Steve Cram putting a training schedule together for me was a real privilege and I needed a few six-hour round trips to Steve's physiotherapist in Newcastle, and plenty of sessions closer to home, to enable me to run. I allowed myself half a glass of wine the night before the race, when Steve and I went out for dinner for my birthday with Paula Radcliffe and Chris Evans. Then, with a pocketful of painkillers, I got myself to the finishing line, chuffed with a time of less than three and a half hours and relieved that the only fancy-dressed athlete to go past me was a man in a Big Ben costume.

Running for the sake of running has never been my thing, though. Combine it with gym work, though, and there's a sport that ticks all the boxes. HYROX has become a big part of my life. It's fitness racing. You run one kilometre and break it up by completing eight workout stations as quickly as you can. I won my first women's pro event in London and posted a fast enough time to qualify for the World Championships in Nice.

If anything, I'm fitter as a retired athlete than I was at the peak of my career. There won't be a curling comeback but, physically, I could slip straight back into that world if I chose to. More relevantly, I'm the Chef de Mission for Team GB at the 2026 Winter Olympics, which is a full-on job. Getting the best out of me in that role, and keeping irritability at bay, requires time in the gym to switch off.

Happiness isn't all about rowing machines, sled pulls, treadmills, bench presses, dead lifts and squats, however. It's not even about more golf and the clear-the-head time in the fresh air that affords. Happiness is also found in unextraordinary moments, like seeing the perfect colour and volume in your sourdough bread as it comes out of the oven. And it's also found when you share life (and sourdough bread) with someone who complements and brings out the best in you.

Previously, I was probably happiest as a person when I left school, found a vocation and was full of naivety and hope heading to the 2010 Olympics. As the sporting achievements broadly trended upwards, life contentment gradually went in the other direction. I wasn't afforded the pressure-free environment of a young, up-and-coming player for long. Before I was even 18, I was looked upon as someone who had arrived, and was established, rather than someone who needed to develop, grow and be left in the shadows to do that. That your sporting career, and all the good and bad stuff that goes with it, has chipped away at your happiness isn't something you properly grasp until you're out of it and consciously decide to reflect.

I would never use the word 'sacrifice'. Everything I did, I chose to do. Everything I didn't do, exactly the same. That meant saying 'no' a lot – to holidays, weekends away, nights out. And, in my case, it meant shutting down the idea of a relationship. It was a conscious decision and one I didn't, and don't, regret. The right person didn't come into my life when I was competing, which is probably just as well, because I wouldn't have entertained the idea of letting that right person in. No blurred lines, no distractions, no holding me back.

Deciding to be willing to let someone in and deciding to put my own happiness first was a big thing, which I hadn't truly done before. It wasn't about rediscovering the individual I used to be. It was about discovering the individual I wanted to be. That took some figuring out, some time and some taking down of barriers. I feel very fortunate to be happy now and to know that I'm happy. There's someone in my life to lean on who isn't a family member, someone who loves doing the same things as me, someone with whom I can be the playful, daft, immature Eve. My curling image was fair enough. In competition, I was all the things I looked – steely-eyed, impassive, demanding, driven, fiercely competitive, unyielding. An ice queen? I suppose that crown fitted.

But the ice queen has melted.

ACKNOWLEDGEMENTS

Writing this book has been a journey of its own. A time to look back, say thank you and remember everyone who has been part of my life in curling and beyond.

First and foremost, I want to say a heartfelt thank you to Eric Nicolson. Eric and I have worked together for many years and, as well as being a superb professional, he has become a great friend. It has been a wonderful experience writing this book with him. I'm incredibly grateful for the time, care, and dedication he poured into helping me share my story. Through many warm, honest and, at times, difficult conversations, Eric and I have traced the highs and lows of my journey, bringing to life the moments that really mattered. He's captured my voice and my memories with great sensitivity, and I hope the result is a story that not only entertains but also inspires. If anyone can take strength or encouragement from my experiences, that will mean everything to me.

To my parents, Gordon and Lin – thank you for teaching me the importance of hard work, staying humble, and never giving up. Dad, your curling journey gave me something to aim for, and Mum, your support kept me steady through all the ups and downs.

To my brothers Glen and Thomas, thank you for shaping who I am – from turning every moment into a competition to constantly pushing me to be better. And of course, the curling gossip and farm talk are still going strong (with Katie now holding her own in both!) some things never change. Katie, thank you for jumping right in and becoming such a fun and thoughtful part of the chaos, we're lucky to have you.

To my aunties Suzy and Ruth, and my uncle Richard. Thanks for always being there. Your support, the laughs, and just believing in me have really meant a lot. Those trips down to the south coast were the perfect break when I needed it – some of my favourite off-ice memories.

To all my teammates, you are at the heart of this story. Curling is a team sport and I'm so thankful for the friendships we shared during training, competition and through all the highs and lows. We shared the pressure, the grind and a lot of great moments along the way.

To British Curling, Scottish curling and Team GB, thank you for believing in me and giving me the chance to compete on the biggest stage in sport. I'll always be grateful for those opportunities.

To my coaches and support staff, thank you for your guidance, your honesty, and sometimes the tough lessons. You helped me grow into the athlete and the leader I became.

Dave Leith, thank you for being the man you are. You pushed me to be a better person and athlete through the pain and sweat (and maybe a few questionable life choices during those CrossFit sessions with you!).

Zara, you helped me get through the toughest time in my career, and without you, I'd have given up.

ACKNOWLEDGEMENTS

To the fans, especially those waving the Saltire and Union Jack around the world, your support meant more than I can put into words.

To curling itself, thank you for the challenges, the hard times and the amazing moments and memories. You gave me a life I could only dream of.

And finally, to you, the reader, thank you for picking up this book and wanting to hear the story behind the medals and the moments. I hope it inspires you to chase your own dreams, whatever they may be.

Eve Muirhead

Eve, when I first got to know you at the start of your curling journey, I had a feeling you would end up with a great career of sporting achievement to look back upon.

I'm sure I even said early on: "There will be a book in this!"

I've met a lot of athletes, in all manner of sports, during my time as a journalist but few, if any, have matched your mixture of talent, dedication, determination and resilience.

It was an honour that you put your faith in me to help tell your story.

Reflecting on all the medals and the moments was the easy bit, but the book is all the better for your willingness to open-up on the times of worry and despair.

There were a few tears over coffees at Friend of Mine in Bridge of Allan and Gloagburn in Tibbermore but I'd like to think we made the process as fun as we said it would be!

Mark, you armed me with the knowledge of the publishing world to get me started; Ed, you recommended Polaris as the perfect publisher; and Pete, you gave Eve and I valuable support throughout.

Mum and Dad, you fostered my passion for writing back in the day - and still do now. Ross and Millie might not choose to be writers but hopefully I can give them the same love and support for their careers as you have with mine.

And finally, Amanda, writing a book during a house move probably wasn't the best idea!

But before, during and after it, you were the rock for our family, as always. Eve dusting down the bagpipes for Millie's sponsored Highland Fling at Julie Young's Dance Studio, as we took a break from one of our chats, will always be the book's soundtrack in my mind!

Eric Nicolson

POLARIS
PUBLISHING